EDUCATION, POLITI⟮

Series Eu..u.s.
Henry A. Giroux, McMaster University
Susan Searls Giroux, McMaster University

Within the last three decades, education as a political, moral, and ideological practice has become central to rethinking not only the role of public and higher education, but also the emergence of pedagogical sites outside of the schools—which include but are not limited to the Internet, television, film, magazines, and the media of print culture. Education as both a form of schooling and public pedagogy reaches into every aspect of political, economic, and social life. What is particularly important in this highly interdisciplinary and politically nuanced view of education are a number of issues that now connect learning to social change, the operations of democratic public life, and the formation of critically engaged individual and social agents. At the center of this series will be questions regarding what young people, adults, academics, artists, and cultural workers need to know to be able to live in an inclusive and just democracy and what it would mean to develop institutional capacities to reintroduce politics and public commitment into everyday life. Books in this series aim to play a vital role in rethinking the entire project of the related themes of politics, democratic struggles, and critical education within the global public sphere.

SERIES EDITORS:

HENRY A. GIROUX holds the Global TV Network Chair in English and Cultural Studies at McMaster University in Canada. He is on the editorial and advisory boards of numerous national and international scholarly journals. Professor Giroux was selected as a Kappa Delta Pi Laureate in 1998 and was the recipient of a Getty Research Institute Visiting Scholar Award in 1999. He was the recipient of the Hooker Distinguished Professor Award for 2001. He received an Honorary Doctorate of Letters from Memorial University of Newfoundland in 2005. His most recent books include *Take Back Higher Education* (co-authored with Susan Searls Giroux, 2006); *America on the Edge* (2006); *Beyond the Spectacle of Terrorism* (2006), *Stormy Weather: Katrina and the Politics of Disposability* (2006), *The University in Chains: Confronting the Military-Industrial-Academic Complex* (2007), and *Against the Terror of Neoliberalism: Politics Beyond the Age of Greed* (2008).

SUSAN SEARLS GIROUX is Associate Professor of English and Cultural Studies at McMaster University. Her most recent books include *The Theory Toolbox* (co-authored with Jeff Nealon, 2004) and *Take Back Higher Education* (co-authored with Henry A. Giroux, 2006), and *Between Race and Reason: Violence, Intellectual Responsibility, and the University to Come* (2010). Professor Giroux is also the Managing Editor of *The Review of Education, Pedagogy, and Cultural Studies*.

Critical Pedagogy in Uncertain Times: Hope and Possibilities
Edited by Sheila L. Macrine

RITUALS AND STUDENT IDENTITY IN EDUCATION

RITUAL CRITIQUE FOR A NEW PEDAGOGY

Richard A. Quantz
with Terry O'Connor
and Peter Magolda

RITUALS AND STUDENT IDENTITY IN EDUCATION

Earlier versions of some parts of this book have appeared in the following journals as:

Quantz, R. A., & O'Connor, T. W. (1988). Writing critical ethnography. *Educational Theory, 38*(1), 95–109.

Quantz, R. A., & Magolda, P. M. (1997). Nonrational classroom performance: Ritual as aspect of action. *The Urban Review, 29*(4), 221–238.

Quantz, R. A. (1999). School ritual as performance: A reconstruction of Durkheim's and Turner's uses of ritual. *Educational Theory, 49*(4), 493–513.

Quantz, R. A. (2001). On seminars, ritual, and cowboys. *Teachers College Record, 103*(5), 896–922.

Quantz, R. A. (2003). The puzzlemasters: Performing the mundane, searching for intellect, and living in the belly of the corporation. *The Review of Education/Pedagogy/Cultural Studies, 25*, 115–157.

First published in 2011 by
PALGRAVE MACMILLAN®
in the United States—a division of St. Martin's Press LLC,
175 Fifth Avenue, New York, NY 10010.

Where this book is distributed in the UK, Europe and the rest of the world, this is by Palgrave Macmillan, a division of Macmillan Publishers Limited, registered in England, company number 785998, of Houndmills, Basingstoke, Hampshire RG21 6XS.

Palgrave Macmillan is the global academic imprint of the above companies and has companies and representatives throughout the world.

Palgrave® and Macmillan® are registered trademarks in the United States, the United Kingdom, Europe and other countries.

ISBN: 978–0–230–10115–9 (Hardcover)
ISBN: 978–0–230–10116–6 (Paperback)

Library of Congress Cataloging-in-Publication Data

Quantz, Richard A., 1947–
    Rituals and student identity in education : ritual critique for a new pedagogy / Richard A. Quantz with Terry O'Connor and Peter Magolda.
        p. cm.—(Education, politics, and public life)
        ISBN 978–0–230–10115–9 (alk. paper)—
        ISBN 978–0–230–10116–6 (alk. paper)
        1. Public schools—United States. 2. Education—Aims and objectives—United States. 3. Educational change—United States. 4. Academic rites and ceremonies—United States. I. O'Connor, Terry (Terry W.), d. 2009. II. Magolda, Peter Mark. III. Title.
LA217.2.Q36 2010
370.973—dc22   2010029927

A catalogue record of the book is available from the British Library.

Design by Newgen Imaging Systems (P) Ltd., Chennai, India.

First edition: February 2011

10 9 8 7 6 5 4 3 2 1

Printed in the United States of America.

To Betty, the best teacher I know.

To Allison, Elizabeth, and Rick, who, each in their own way, helped deepen my understanding and appreciation of the concepts of this book by sharing their lives with me.

To Terry whose friendship and continuous intellectual spirit made this work possible.

CONTENTS

PREFACE

Schooling is in crisis today. While such words have been written for at least a hundred years, I firmly believe that we are now in a critical moment. As with global warming, I can't help but wonder if we are nearing the "tipping point" in which there can be no turning back. The crisis we now address has been more than fifty years in the making. With its roots in the massive resistance to school integration of the 1950s and the precipitous abandonment of the public schools following their de-Protestantation in the 1960s and the political expedience of certain politicians to take advantage of an unpopular student movement of the late 1960s and early 1970s, the so-called reform movement has slowly but steadily pushed its agenda so successfully that there appears to be no cogent alternative. The present assumption that "accountability" equals "testing" and that "education" equals "measurable objectives" has occurred in a brief lifetime. American public schooling has all but abandoned its public obligations and replaced them with a "commonsense" of anti-intellectualism and antidemocracy. How has this happened? How has this so-called reform movement become so integral to commonsense that no real alternatives appear in the public conversation? That is the topic of this book. It is not a history of that movement, but an exploration of some of the mechanisms that have made it possible.

In the early 1980s I discovered the work of the Bakhtin Circle. M. M. Bakhtin, V. N. Volosinov, and P. N. Medvedev worked in Stalinist Russia to develop an alternative to the two competing European semiotics of the day: the "abstract objectivism" of Ferdinand de Saussure and the "individualistic subjectivism" of Wilhelm von Humboldt. In the 1980s, critical scholars were abandoning the essentialism of its early days and were being influenced by poststructuralism. In the Bakhtin Circle I found the possibilities of an alternative approach to the problems of critical theory: one that provided the benefits of poststructuralism without its pitfalls. Like Derrida, the Bakhtin Circle advocated a semiotics that rejected the signifier; but unlike Derrida, the Bakhtin Circle also abandoned the sign altogether. As a result, the lack of any stability in poststructuralism is replaced with the anchor of history. Whereas poststructuralism leads to inevitable postponement of meaning, the Bakhtin Circle leads us to understand meaning as always changing but also always located in the material politics of the moment. In the work of the Bakhtin Circle we find the integration of culture and structure that poststructuralism demands, but without abandoning the "modernist project" we understand as the utopian ideal of democracy.

Shortly after beginning to work with the Bakhtin Circle, I came to the conclusion that ritual was the best example of how the politics of meaning and the politics of the material became embodied in the individual and the community. This book represents my efforts to forge an alternative approach to the study of the social that abandons the modernist commitment to structure, fixedness, centeredness, essentialism, and science without abandoning its commitment to the hope of emancipation found in a radical democracy.

This book has been a quarter of a century in the making. It begins with a reconstruction of the concept of ritual moves to the development of a nonscientific empirical research approach then provides an evolution of the application of the method and ends with an exploration of how its lessons can be incorporated into a new pedagogy—a pedagogy that abandons the technical reasoning that dominates the field today and suggests an intellectual and moral approach to teaching. During these twenty-five years I've been frequently asked to publish my work into a single book, but until now that work had not been completed. It may have been a long time in the making, but sometimes intellectual work requires endurance and commitment as much as energy and desire. I hope that readers of this book will enjoy the journey and that it may stimulate alternatives strategies in the present war of position within which today's educators find themselves.

A WORD ON READING THIS TEXT

Chapters two and three are highly theoretical. Readers who find such abstract discussions off-putting can safely skip those two chapters and move to chapter four saving chapters two and three for last. Those, like me, who wish to understand and explore the theoretical underpinnings of empirical work before reading the work itself will find great value in the time necessary to read these two theoretical chapters.

Acknowledgments

How does one find a way to acknowledge all of the people in a twenty-five-year period who have helped in the journey that is this book? It is impossible. Several hundreds of students have struggled with the ideas found herein and their struggles, questions, rejections, and pushbacks have made this work that much stronger. Without them, this would have been a very different book. Then too, several dozens of colleagues both here at Miami, from my alma mater, at the University of Virginia, and across the country have read, commented, rejected, and otherwise bettered my thinking on the topics within these pages. There is no way to thank each of them individually. Please be assured that students and colleagues past and present whether named here or not are acknowledged in my heart.

First let me thank Vi Ernst for valuable research assistance at a critical time. I also wish to acknowledge my debt to the Department of Educational Leadership, Miami University, and The Department of the Sociology of Education, University of London, who provided material support that contributed to this book. While visiting the University of London and since, Tony Green has provided particularly apt critique. I also must thank Eric Bredo who provided critical feedback on early versions of some of these essays. Thanks go to the dozens of students and their teachers who permitted me and my co-author to observe and chronicle their lives. I hope they will feel that their trust has been kept.

Through the years several students have read and commented on aspects of the original essays of this book or have engaged me about some of my ideas in ways that have influenced my thinking or my writing of this work. They include Kamautu Ashanti, Moise Baptiste, Jennifer Bondy, James Campbell, Bryan Deever, C. P. Gause, Stephen Haymes, Quanyu Huang, Brent Johnson, Rob Karaba, Lauren Isaac, Frank Fitch, Winston Gittens, Marcia Moraes, Adisa Price, Alyia Rahman, Dan Reyes, Jay Roberts, Carl Robinson, Mike Romanowski, Susan Shramm-Pate, Moses Rumano, Llew Simmons, Kamara Sekeu, Dianne Smith, Kevin Talbert, Lori Varlotta, Amanda Luke Weatherwax, and Joe Wegwert. Surely, I have forgotten to mention

xii ACKNOWLEDGMENTS

several students whose influence is found in this book, but just as surely those mentioned here were critical to its completion.

I have been privileged to work with a terrific set of colleagues in the Department of Educational Leadership at Miami University. All have had an impact on me but special mention must be made of Kathleen Knight Abowitz, Denise Taliaferro Baszile, Nelda Cambron-McCabe, Dennis Carlson, Michael Dantley, Kate Rousmaniere, and Lisa Weems whose continuous intellectual engagement has kept me alert and careful. Their suggestions and critique make my work better. Also, mention must be made of João Paraskeva and Riyad Shahjahan whose very brief sojourns with us nevertheless left their mark on me and this book. Peter Magolda has a particular part in this book. He is not only the coauthor of one of the chapters, but his interest in ritual has mirrored mine and his exceptional research talents have continually amazed and influenced me.

There are two former colleagues and still friends who require special thanks. From his path-forging book *Schooling as a Ritual Performance*, Peter McLaren has unselfishly provided needed support throughout these years. Henry Giroux has a very special place in my evolving thought. Two minutes of conversation with Henry provides more exciting ideas than two days with anyone else. His influence can be found on every page.

A special word must be spoken of my closest friend, writing partner, colleague, and brother, Terry O'Connor, who was a part of every step of this process until the very last chapter. His friendship and intellectual curiosity and moral commitments made this work possible. This book is almost as much his as mine.

Finally, my deepest thanks must go to my family. Betty was there before the journey began and has cheerfully traveled along with me. Rick, Elizabeth, and Allison grew up with their father on a strange expedition and provided much needed correction from the world of youth to keep his coordinates properly oriented.

Introduction to the Nonrational in Education

Ritual in Schools

The air lies still across the coliseum. The murmurs and shuffling quiet as the black-robed figure of the Superintendent approaches the podium. Dr. Laffer pauses for effect. Her gaze moves from her right to her left taking in the packed audience of the families and friends of today's graduates. Then she looks downward at the graduates themselves. A small smile grows upon her face. Spread before her are 14 rows of peaceful and hopeful young adults beautifully arrayed in 14 blue and white columns in a natural symmetry that represents all that is good about American education. With calm voice Dr. Laffer addresses her audience, "Twelve years ago you began your schooling. It seems like an eternity to you, but to your parents it seems like yesterday. Whether an eternity or a mere moment, in that time, you have matured from small children to young adults. There have been many influences in your life from your parents to your siblings to your friends, but certainly some of those influences were found among your teachers and schoolmates. Part of who you are today grew in the education that you have pursued here. We are confident that your learning during these years is only the beginning of much more learning to come whether that future education is found in college or work." Dr. Laffer's address continues for only a few minutes more and then, to polite applause, she returns to her seat on the dais. While the president of the senior class begins to speak, Mr. Gadhand, president of the school board, leans over and whispers to Dr. Laffer, "When you look out at these fine young men and women—so proud and so pleased—you renew your faith in our future. You understand what all this hard work is about." Dr. Laffer nods her head, takes in the orderliness of the coliseum once more, and releases a deep sigh of satisfaction.

Far up in the visitors' seats a young woman observes the same venue, but she sees something dramatically different. Rising senior Sylvia Wright, here to watch her brother graduate, has trouble sitting still. She

*leans forward and then backward and various involuntary grunts let
her parents and sister, Annie, know that something is bothering her.
"What's the matter?" asks Annie.*

*At first, Sylvia doesn't acknowledge the question, but then she swings
her arm across her body in a dramatic gesture indicating the entire
floor where the graduates are gathered. Annie looks at the floor but her
puzzled face indicates that she had no idea what is upsetting her sister.
"Can't you see it?" Sylvia exclaims in exasperation. "Those rows of white
and blue!" Still no indication of understanding from Annie. "All the
boys are in blue robes and the girls are in white robes! White! For purity!
And the girls are carrying a rose!" the bitterness in her voice is barely
controlled. "Here we are. Gathered to celebrate the transition of young
people into adulthood and they are gendered! Marked by sex to take their
different places in society! Guilty as charged at the beginning!" Annie
just rolls her eyes and goes back to watching the commencement.*

Let me pause for a moment in the telling of this fictionalized rendition of a true story. I will return to the anecdote shortly, but before I
do that I'd like to shift voice and speak a bit about ritual. Here we have
witnessed a ritual common in American schools: The Commencement.
All ceremonies, like the one in the anecdote , have some common elements. First of all, notice that the whole ceremony is a performance,
a spectacle, meant to be observed. Also notice that different people
have different parts to play. Each is assigned a role and is expected to
perform that role in a particular manner and each is dressed specifically for that role—the students and the teachers and those on the dais
wear academic regalia, but no one in the audience is wearing a cap
and gown. In the case of this particular commencement, male and
female students wear different colors and the females carry a single
rose. Anyone walking in would only take a few seconds to recognize it as a graduation ceremony. It has a very clear form shared with
countless graduations around America now and in the past. Imagine a
high school graduation that does not have students and faculty wearing gowns or that groups the students with their parents allowing
them to sit wherever they desire or begins with a rock band and has
the students dance in. Make any of those changes and you may find
some takers, but you will also get a lot of resistance. In ritual, form is
central.

The ceremony described here also utilizes symbols. There is a reason the girls are in white and the boys in blue. When the superintendent officially declares them graduated, the students reach up and

move their tassel from the left of their mortarboard to the right. The colors of the gown and the position of the tassel on the mortarboard symbolize something. Without symbols, there is no ritual.

Ceremonies such as these are a common experience in schools. They are important and scholarly examination of such ceremonies provides insights into schooling. But while this book will address large ceremonies such as graduation, it is much more interested in the small, everyday interaction rituals. It focuses upon the mostly invisible ritual aspects of everyday school patterns and mostly ignores the ceremony that everyone recognizes as ritual. One rule of ritual is that the more we recognize it as a ritual, the less likely it is to affect us; while the less we realize we are participating in a ritual, the more likely it is that its effects will be realized. Still, the common ceremony is a good place to begin the exploration of ritual in schools for it will allow us to isolate some specific elements of ritual that can be used to examine and critique aspects of schooling.

Though ritual has been used as an analytic category since the beginning of social theory, educational scholars have not made much use of it. Perhaps some common misunderstandings have been responsible for this lack. Most people equate ritual with ceremonies such as the graduation exercise that weaves through this introduction. These ceremonies are recognized as having something important about them, but their limited existence in American schooling makes them inherently peripheral. After all, how important is the ritual impact of graduation or pep rallies or morning exercises given the sheer lack of time devoted to such ceremonies in comparison to the time spent engaged in other school activities? Even if these ceremonies are not empty of meaning (and most probably they are), do they really have much impact on a student's success or failure to learn? As this introduction will show, ceremonies can actually reveal much about the daily practices of schooling; but, as mentioned, the book as a whole will make the point that these ceremonies are much less important than the everyday, small rituals that organize daily life in a school.

Perhaps the failure to take advantage of ritual to analyze schooling results from a second misunderstanding: Most people seem to think that ritual refers to actions empty of meaning. Mention ritual and many people think of the softball player who always touches the brow of her cap before taking her batting stance or the morning ritual of a cup of coffee and a doughnut or, perhaps, the lack of effect that the morning pledge of allegiance to the flag seems to have on most

American students. Certainly some rituals can be empty of meaning, but I hope that by the end of this introduction, it will have become clear that many rituals overflow with meaning and have important social impact.

While some rituals are empty of meaning, this book will argue that the real work of schooling takes place in the small actions that are rarely even recognized as ritual. Think of the hundreds of interaction rituals that the typical student and teacher participate in during a single school day. There are the transition rituals such as shaking hands when greeting, waving a hand when parting, or the teacher's "okay class, settle down." There are the identity rituals such as the costuming of our body before we take the ritual stage at school, or the way we wear our hair, or the accessories we put on, or the way we move our body when we walk or dance or refuse to dance; or the tonal qualities of our voice, the grammar chosen, the slang injected, the music we listen to, and the jokes we tell. Then there are the rituals of solidarity we perform with others to show we are of the same identity group. Besides displaying the identity markers described in the last sentence, we purposively make eye contact in a particular way, or shake hands in a particular way, or perform a ritualized call-and-response greeting. Think too of the rituals of deference that students are expected to show their teachers (i.e., their "superiors"): the lowering of the eyes when being spoken to or, when being disciplined, the meeting of the eyes in an unchallenging manner, and the closed-in, unaggressive posture taken, the crispness in the voice when speaking the sacred words, "yes ma'am, sorry ma'am." Perhaps the quickest way for a student to be expelled in school is to fail to show ritual deference to one in authority. On getting caught pushing around a smaller kid the bullying student who quickly performs the proper rituals of deference to the teacher—ritually acknowledging the teacher's authority and ritually expressing regret—may just get away with no more than a warning. Do as little as accidentally let a paper slide onto the floor of the corridor between classes and fail to show ritual deference to the teacher who tells you to pick it up and you are written-up for detention; continue to fail to show deference to the legitimacy of the punishment and you'll find yourself in the principal's office; fail to perform proper deference to the principal and you will find yourself suspended and out of school. And just as students are expected to perform proper rituals of deference to their teachers, teachers are expected to perform rituals of deference to their administrators. Just as the students' quickest ticket out of the school is failure to show ritual deference, so too the teacher who

day to day rituals

fails to show ritual deference to the administrator may find himself or herself transferred to another school. Of course, while the student must show ritual deference to the teacher and the teacher to the administrator, we can only say that the administrator ought to be performing rituals of respect to the teachers and the teachers ought to be performing rituals of respect to students. Unfortunately, in America's large high schools, rituals of respect are few and far between.

Then there are the interaction patterns of the classroom that, when properly understood, reveal important ritual aspects. I'm thinking of things such as whether or not the teacher sits behind her desk or on it or even has a desk. Or whether the desks are set up in rows, in a semicircle facing the teacher, or in a circle facing each other, or in little islands. I'm speaking of whether or not the classroom proceeds with the teacher as the conductor orchestrating every student's move or whether the students have some control over the proceeding. How about the role of the textbook? Does it stand as the final authority or only the beginning of the search? Does the student speak directly to other students or only to each other through the instructor? Who talks? Whose head is closer to the ceiling? In fact, if we think about it, I think we will agree that it is the ritual performance of a teacher that is the most important indicator used by administrators when evaluating teachers. Does a teacher perform as a teacher is expected to perform in the school? Try to organize students' desks in a circle and have a democratically organized classroom in a school in which teachers are expected to perform as the sole authority in the classroom and see how the evaluation comes out. Or, reverse it. Try to put your desks in rows and maintain a classroom interaction pattern that ritually reinforces the teacher as the single and final authority in the room in a school in which democratic classrooms are expected.

Perhaps the biggest obstacle to recognizing the importance of ritual results from a larger problem: The assumption that the most important part of schooling is located in the rational intentions inscribed in the curriculum and pedagogy. Never has rationality been stressed more than under the "No Child Left Behind" policies that emphasize explicit outcomes, precise measures, and "research-based instruction." The assumption that humans act rationally is one of the earliest and most fundamental flaws of much of education policy.

While an ordinary term with a commonplace meaning in everyday lexicon, "rational" is also a special term in the distinctive discourse of socioeconomics. Originally it was used to describe the assumed behavior of autonomous individuals in marketplace exchange. The classic liberal economics (e.g., of Adam Smith) assumed that autonomous individuals acted in a rational manner by basing their actions solely on what was in their own economic interest. To this day the field of economics assumes this kind of rationality in the action of individuals. The classical social theorists (such as Marx, Durkheim, and Weber) challenged the economic description of human action by showing how factors other than those so-called rational ones entered into what appeared to be solely economically rational action. These other factors are often referred to as "nonrational." In fact, it can be argued that the very invention of social theory arose in the nineteenth and early twentieth centuries to challenge the assumption that humans act rationally. Of course, the differences among distinct social theories are wide and significant, but it might be instructional to focus for a moment on one thing that most of these theories have in common—the nonrationality of human action. While many may think that only contemporary postmodern/poststructuralist theories privilege nonrational action, in truth, nonrationality has been a part of social theory from its origins. Classical social theory is often presented as a conversation with three voices—that of Marx, Durkheim, and Weber. Of the three, only Durkheim provided a theory that accepted the modern focus on rationality as potentially desirable—but even Durkheim recognized that rationality had to take into consideration the nonrational.

Durkheim, modernization, and rationality. Durkheim (1964/1893) was less concerned with the causes of modernism itself and focused more on how to overcome the disruptions resulting from the specialization that accompanied the advancement of technology and the dislocations and anomie that were created by modernization. He argued that such cultural disturbances could be overcome by the careful harnessing of public institutions to the construction of an organic and functional solidarity. While Durkheim accepted modernization as a progressive and largely positive force, he also understood that the complex division of labor produced by modernization was destructive of social integration. For this reason, Durkheim focused much of his work on the processes of solidarity that, he argued, resulted from the ritualization of social life (see Durkheim, 1964/1893, 1965/1912, 1973/1925). Since modernization emphasizes rationalism, ritual becomes less significant and anomie grows. His solution was to turn schools into a kind of secular church to reinscribe ritual action into the populace and build an organic solidarity (Durkheim, 1973/1925). While Durkheim accepted the rationalization of the economy as positive, he clearly recognized the role of the nonrational in building community (1965/1912). In fact, Durkheim is one of the primary theorists of ritual solidarity.

Marx, capital relations, and rationality. On the other hand, Marx rejects not only the desirability of rationalization in economic relations, but also its very existence (Marx, 2007/1961). For Marx, production, rather than exchange, is the fundamental explanatory of economic action and production is organized by political, not just economic, structures. What appears to be rational economic exchange is built upon reified economic structures. In other words, people act *as if* the economy is a natural state when it is really a socially and politically constructed entity. If people were to actually act *rationally*, they would overturn the economic and political order.

Marx explained the transition from traditional to modern societies by a shift in the mode of production from land to capital (Marx & Engels, 1984). As a result of the shift, the culture also shifted from that of the aristocracy who controlled land (the mode of production in feudal times) to the bourgeoisie who controlled capital (the mode of production in modern times). Capitalist societies reify social relations by assuming social relations to be natural. Also, through the process of commodification, objects and workers come to be esteemed for their exchange-value rather than their use-value. As objects of means, workers and the products of their labor are to be rationally manipulated to achieve maximum profit. To combat the disruptions of modern times, Marx argued for a class revolution to turn the means of production over to the workers and, therefore, eliminate the disruptions that a class-based, capitalist society created and usher in a workers' culture that would de-commodify and de-rationalize both the worker and the products of their work.

Weber, rationalization, and nonrationality. While Marx and Durkheim both challenged the assumption that social action can be fully explained through rational choice, Weber made this challenge the center of his work. For liberal economists, such as Adam Smith (2003/1776), rational action was a given, but for Weber it was something to be explained. In Weber's theory, what we might call "rationalism" (the commitment to technical, means-ends reasoning) becomes the central cultural organizer of modernity. Weber (1978) argued that modernization was the inevitable result of the "rationalization" of society created by the advancement in such technologies as communications, transportation, and bookkeeping. For Weber, the epitome of rationalization is found in bureaucracy and its means-ends reasoning.

This technical reasoning characteristic of modern societies seemed to Weber to be replacing the value-based reasoning that characterized traditional societies and their organizations. Weber was fairly pessimistic about the ability of society to overcome the dislocations created by this technical reasoning, but he did have some hope that value-rationality might survive through the ongoing and continuous struggle over resources of power among various associational groups. For Weber, history was an open trajectory that resulted from such struggles.

For Marx, capitalism was the problem and the elimination of capitalism the solution. For Weber, the rationalization of society epitomized by bureaucracy created the dehumanization of the modern world. Weber does not actually propose a solution, but he does suggest the hope that struggle among various forms of power would continue to provide room for other than instrumental values. In their own ways, both Marx and Weber were foes of the growth of instrumental reasoning into human affairs.

For Durkheim, modernization was not itself a problem; only the responses of the institutions to modernization were a problem. The solution, therefore, was to change the institutions to meet the needs of the new times. That is, to rationalize them, to harness them to achieve the integration necessary for a well-functioning society. The dominant educational discourse may occasionally borrow terms from the Marxist or Weberian traditions (especially in the misappropriation of bureaucracy from Weber), but, for the most part, it accepts the theory and project of the Durkheimian tradition. That some seem to benefit more from this situation than others, when acknowledged, may be understood to be troublesome but is assumed to be unavoidable.

The most basic claim of this book is that the real work of schools occurs in the nonrational aspects of human action I call ritual. I will explicitly define ritual as *that aspect of action that is a formalized, symbolic performance* and suggest that while most teachers and administrators focus their attention on the rational aspects of action such as goals and outcomes, the real importance of education actually occurs in those nonrational areas that we rarely think about or plan. If there is a "new pedagogy," it will be in organizing and considering the nonrational aspects of schooling.

* * *

Rob pauses for a moment listening to the cracks and pings as the car begins to cool down. He takes in a deep breath of the fresh spring air from the open window and reflects on what has led him to this point. He pictures the first day of school that past fall when walking down the hallway with Sylvia they ran into the principal. "Hello, Dr. Williams," said Sylvia as she walked right up to him. "Requiring boys to wear blue robes and girls to wear white robes at commencement is illegal. It violates Title IX. Therefore, if that practice continues, I want you to know now that I will not be willing to wear a white robe. Don't you think that we can start the new millennium off with a practice that does not restrict males and females to traditional stereotyped roles?"

Dr. Williams looked only temporarily taken aback and then he put his head back and had a good laugh. Rob can't remember Dr. Williams's exact words but does remember the patronizing attitude in that laugh and in the body language. Clearly Dr. Williams had not taken Sylvia's comment seriously.

"What was that all about?" Rob asked as the two continued walking down the hall. His question opened up a floodgate of outrage as Sylvia explained the problem of having such an obvious symbol of gender inequality as part of their ritual transition to adulthood.

Through the school year Sylvia never missed an opportunity to let Dr. Williams know of her concern and Dr. Williams always appeared genial and unoffended by these comments though he also never really seemed to take them seriously. That is until a month ago when Rob accompanied Sylvia to a meeting in Dr. William's office. While still maintaining a quiet and gentle tone to his voice, Dr. Williams explained to Sylvia that it was time for her to get over her problem with the colors of the gowns. He explained to her that if she didn't want to wear a white gown then she didn't have to attend commencement or she could sit in the audience, but she would not be allowed to march in with her class unless she was wearing a white gown. As Sylvia pressed her point that the practice violated Title IX, Rob was dismayed to hear Dr. Williams deepening and more edged voice explain what might happen if Sylvia continued to insist on wearing a different color than white. Among the possible consequences was expulsion from school and, therefore, not being allowed to graduate until the following December after making up the lost credits. And even arrest and being charged with a crime. Rob was startled by the harshness of the punishment. "Just for not wearing the right color gown?" he had asked himself. Up until that point he had been supportive of his friend's position, but had not himself been willing to do much more then try to persuade his friends, teachers, and parents that Sylvia had a good point. Why should we mark the ceremony that symbolizes our transition to adulthood with such obvious gendered distinctions? For the next couple of weeks Rob had struggled with what to do. Sylvia had made it clear

*that she was not backing down. She was willing to risk her diploma and
her college scholarship and jail. What was he going to do?*

*Rob opens the car door and strides up to the front porch. Mr. Gadhand,
the president of the school board, answers the doorbell himself. Rob says, "I
wanted to make sure I gave this to you personally" and hands him a legal-
sized envelope containing a letter explaining his support for Sylvia and
her desire to eliminate the gender-biased practice of the two-colored gowns
at commencement. The letter also explains that he is going to publicly
express his support for this position by wearing a white gown at commencement. Rob's letter does more than just support Sylvia's position. It shifts the
legal debate in wearing a robe of white or blue from a Title IX issue to a
First-amendment issue.*

While ritual was one of the earliest concepts to be utilized in
social theory, only in recent years have scholars begun to use it to
analyze advanced industrial societies. Perhaps the first important
theoretical development of ritual in social theory can be found in
Durkheim's 1912 book *The Elementary Forms of the Religious Life:
A Study in Religious Sociology* (Durkheim, 1915). Drawing heavily
on the imprecise, and sometimes inaccurate, nineteenth-century
accounts of tribal peoples, Durkheim argued that religious behavior creates and represents the collective conscious of a community
(as if every community had a group mind). While few scholars
today are willing to accept the idea of a "collective conscious,"
many believe that Durkheim's claim that religious rites work to
create social solidarity was one of the most important insights in
all sociology. The realization that the very process of participation
in ritual helps to bind people together into a consensual group
has been used by many social analysts, none more than social
anthropologists who mined Durkheim's work again and again to
help explain the ritualistic foundation of much tribal life. While
these anthropologists have continuously refined Durkheim's particular concept, the relatively stable and consensual tribal societies (compared to the home societies of the anthropologists) led
anthropologists to take as a truism that rituals worked solely to
build solidarity and maintain the status quo. Not until the second
generation of social anthropologists began to compare their own
fieldwork with that of their mentors did anthropologists begin
to realize that tribal societies might not be as static as had been
assumed.

No anthropologist did more to challenge the assumptions of these
Durkheimians than Victor Turner. Turner, who began to write in

the 1950s and continued until his posthumously published book *The Anthropology of Performance* in 1988, argued that far from working to maintain the status quo, the concept of ritual should be reserved for those ceremonial actions that work to transform societies (Turner, 1988). Drawing more on the theoretical foundation of van Gennep's *Rites de Passage* (1960) than Durkheim's *The Elementary Forms of the Religious Life*, Turner revealed how ritual is used to open up as well as to give bounds to periods of uncertainty and instability. Turner's work has been an inspiration to many newer contemporary social analysts who are inclined to see the transformative possibilities in ritual instead of just its conservative limitations.

At the same time Turner appeared to be turning Durkheim on his head, Erving Goffman was breathing new life into Durkheim's initial insights by switching our focus from the study of tribal societies to the mundane use of ritual in the everyday life of modern industrial societies. By suggesting in his 1967 book *Interaction Ritual: Essays on Face-to-Face Behavior* that in nearly all social encounters we engage in little rituals of decorum that imply the sacredness of the individual, Goffman (1967) ensured that Durkheim's sense of ritual used to build solidarity would not be lost.

Quite recently, perhaps as a result of the influence of postmodern theories, there seems to be a revival of interest in ritual as a relevant concept in understanding contemporary society. Setting aside the pervasive American distrust of ritual as an empty, formal gesture, new scholars have begun to explore the ways in which ritual permeates the everyday world. For those of us interested in education, examining how ritual can work both to maintain solidarity and to promote transformation should help us understand a wide range of schooling phenomena, from the "absence of community" to the cultural politics of "spectacular" youth subcultures to the fundamental political aspects of contemporary schooling.

While ritual studies have not played a large part in educational research, it is not absent. Some scholars have given us a good place to begin our study of ritual in education. Much of that research has focused on the obvious rituals of schools, that kind of ritual that I refer to as "ceremony," of which the anecdote that runs through this chapter is a good example. Commencement exercises, along with morning exercises including the Pledge of Allegiance, assemblies, parents' events, pep rallies, and sporting events have all been examined as ritual. In chapter four, "Nonrational Classroom Performance: Ritual as Aspect of Action," Peter Magolda and I compare the morning ceremony of Harmon Elementary School with the interaction rituals of a college classroom in order to help clarify the importance of nonrational aspects of schooling. Here are some other observations about ceremony in schools.

Perhaps the classic statement about ceremonial rituals in schools can be found in Jacquetta Hill Burnett's 1960–61 ethnography of an American secondary school (Burnett, 1976). Burnett explored ceremonial rituals such as pep rallies, football games, sports banquets, dances that work as rites of intensification arising during stressful times to smooth the troubled interactions of students as they move through different statuses in their progression through the calendar year and the quadrennial high school career. Burnett was particularly interested in defending the use of rite and ceremony as a legitimate category of analysis in contemporary, urban institutions. By detailing the elements of these ceremonies, Burnett was able to show that even though the high school rites did not involve the supernatural or religion, that should not be taken to mean they were not rituals. The various ceremonies her ethnographic study addressed were, she argued, important elements in soothing status transitions allowing for the maintenance of culture and community.

Several other scholars have further developed the way ritual helps overcome moments of community stress through forging solidarity. For example, Mary Bushnell (1997) describes the process used by a private rural school to socialize parents into the school community. The introduction of new students and families into the private school certainly provides the possibility of rupture in the community and requires some mechanism to integrate the new students and their families into the extant school community. As a private school with strong desire for parent participation and support, "Oakleaf Country School" holds an annual potluck dinner at the beginning of the year. Bushnell's description and analysis reveals the way ritual can be used to construct a mythical ideal that the school staff and parents may use to help provide the hoped-for community even if the reality of the everyday often falls short. In a similar way, Patricia Scully and Jacqueline Howell (2008) give us a glimpse of an "I Love You Dinner" that a preschool classroom holds every year to promote community among teachers, students, and parents. In much the same way as Bushnell's private rural school, Scully and Howell's suburban child-care center creates a new tradition around the family ritual of a dinner that they assume will be familiar to the parents and their children. By bringing parents, teachers, and students together in this ritual event, both Bushnell's school and Scully and Howell's child-care center take advantage of the potential for ritual ceremonies to create solidarity at moments of transition.

Some studies focus on ritual's potential to create solidarity to over-come structural divisions and disparities that threaten to pull the com-munity apart. Nancy Lesko (1988) explores two ceremonies she found at a Catholic High School, which, she suggests, work to overcome divisions among students based largely on social class. She suggests that a mass and a pep rally are utilized by the school to "magically" overcome the clear divisions recognized as favoritism of some by the less privileged students. The mass utilized Christian love as a theme in a purposeful attempt to teach students their moral responsibility to treat others with care. Lesko also describes how a whole week of activities ending in a pep rally and the homecoming football game was designed to break down barriers amongst the student body and replace it with a common identity. Mary Henry (1993) describes ceremonial rituals found in a private Waldorf school and a Catholic school that work to naturalize common meanings hence creating mechanisms of control resulting in the creation of a kind of "extended family." Henry's descriptions and analysis reveal how two different schools with different belief systems and worldviews, both utilize ceremony to reinforce their own culture in order to promote the building of com-munity. Like Burnett, Lesko and Henry use ceremonial rituals as an analytic tool to describe the forging of community in schools.

One of the few to explore the fundamental political and ideologi-cal import of ceremony, Joseph Wegwert portrays the struggle over the Pledge of Allegiance at a privileged, suburban high school. For the administration the Pledge was seen as a ritual of solidarity. As Wegwert (2008) put it:

> In this context, instituting the daily, building wide recitation of the Pledge of Allegiance at CWHS offered the administration a ritual of *unity* embedded in tradition, supported by the current political context (post-9/11), and consistent with an ideologically conservative version of patriotism—one that emphasized a *unified* loyalty over *individual-ized* agency. (Pp. 46–47; emphasis in the original)

To the administration's credit, it recognized the right of students to not participate in this ritual. To the administration's discredit, it found reasons to justify the removal to the office of any student who refused to participate in the Pledge ritual. Rather than using the stu-dent resistance as an opportunity to learn civic engagement, student resistance was written off as immature and impolite (the latter being a serious social offense in Midwestern culture). In the face of the opin-ion of the administrators and most of the teachers, which Wegwert found created "discernable, socialized reticence [in students] to trust their own talents and those of their peers—a kind of institutional co-dependency," two students "exhibited compelling insights and powerful language, [which] provided well-considered challenges to the generalized assumptions held by many adults at CWHS about students' analytical capabilities" (p. 69). Wegwert reveals how the Pledge ritual, assumed and intended to be a ritual of unity became, instead, a "curriculum of intolerance" (pp. 70–73).

While much of the use of ritual in educational scholarship has focused on the more obvious ceremonial rituals, others have explored the micro-rituals that might be referred to as informal or interaction rituals that this book is primarily interested in. While these smaller, momentary interaction rituals occur at all levels of schooling, those interested in early childhood education have been particularly drawn to this level of analysis. This attraction may result from the practice of preschool and kindergarten teachers to so consciously utilize ritual in their classroom processes as children transition from home to school. Carmel Maloney (2000) makes a distinction between ceremony and interaction rituals by suggesting that ceremony is marked by invariant patterns that structure and sometime stifle classroom action whereas the interaction rituals are inherently variant and, as a result, lead to a more dynamic classroom environment and have the "potential to transmit deeper messages" (p. 146). Maloney also makes the claim that "in each of the classrooms the repetitive, deliberate, and stylized action was uncontested, accepted, and unquestioned by the teachers" (ibid.).

Brian McCadden (1997) explicitly studies the rituals in a kindergarten as a way to understand what it means to "be a student." Consciously utilizing a Genneppian and Turnerian approach to ritual, and echoing McLaren's *Schooling as a Ritual Performance* (1999/1986), McCadden's interest lies in kindergarten as a liminal space that exists as a child transitions from "child" to "student" where the conventionality of school becomes internalized in the individuals. In this way, McCadden reveals the way in which the institution uses its power to control and "reintegrate" the child's identity as a morally acceptable student.

Jette Kofoed (2008) also focused on smaller everyday rituals. In this case, however, instead of looking at teacher or school initiated rituals, Kofoed studied boys' selection of teams at recess that reveals how ritual not only works to construct solidarity, but also identity and status. The informal daily ritual of team selection "reiterates who the attractive boys are and who are the less attractive" (p. 422). Furthermore, by showing how one boy's position in the ritual changed over time, Kofoed claims to show how ritual not only works to reify status and community, but how it has the potential to transform it. By addressing this apparently innocuous and routine activity, Kofoed suggests that this daily ritual illustrates how pupilness is a daily enactment of social categories as well as the management of the components of the local hegemonic narrative. It illustrates how not only social categories such as gender, racialized ethnicity, and age intersect, but also how locally meaningful components such as pupilness and football qualifications become constituent parts.

While the research described in this chapter helps provide insights into the workings of the broader school culture, this book will focus more on the ritual patterns that might be found in classrooms that work to reproduce privilege and the status quo. Jacque Ensign (1997) also explores this potential of ritual analysis by describing how the ritualized patterns of mathematics classes in elementary schools separate them out from the other subjects. By pointing out the way in which quietness reinforces authority and preciseness defines discipline, mathematics classrooms turn the discipline of mathematics into a sacred process. Ensign claims that the more informal patterns of social studies and language arts classes invite students to connect through sharing (Ensign compares it to gift-giving, see Mauss, 1954), which, in turn, leads to stronger community. The sacredness of mathematics classes unfortunately, she concludes, leads to a disconnect between mathematics and the broader school community. In chapter six of this book, I will argue that in the high schools that I studied, there may be less of a distinction between mathematics and English than Ensign found, but my own study also found a clear distinction between the ritualized patterns of social studies and most other subjects.

In *It's All about Jesus!: Faith as an Oppositional Collegiate Subculture*, Peter Magolda and Kelsey Ebben Gross (2009) provide a look into the culture of an evangelical student organization at a university. Magolda and Ebben Gross, using the same definition of ritual that is used in this book (not surprisingly, since Magolda is the coauthor of the original article of which chapter three in this book is an updated version), present a classic ethnographic study that provides a frequently fascinating life of a conservative evangelical Christian organization on a public and secular university campus. Spending two years in fieldwork, Magolda and Ebben Gross utilize ritual as the primary analytic organizer of this student organizational culture. Each chapter is built around a different ritual such as rituals of faith, of recruitment, of difference, of outreach, and of transition. They also recognize the ritual aspects of their own scholarship in two chapters built around rituals of inquiry and of disclosure. *It's All about Jesus!* shows how ritual can be used in straight forward ethnography to reveal not only member beliefs, but their performances. Through their careful research and writing, we learn how one Christian student organization builds and strengthens an oppositional identity, in part, assisted by the secular university's refusal to bring honest engagement to the topic of religion into the formal curriculum. They reveal the unintended consequences of a curriculum that requires religious students to leave their religion behind when they enter the classroom and argue that professors need to find a way to integrate faith into their courses in an honest and respectful way.

But while Magolda and Ebben Gross use the same definition of ritual that I use in this book, their research methodology is considerably different. Where Magolda and Ebben Gross write an exemplary ethnography, I move away from the social science assumptions embedded in ethnography to develop and utilize a methodology I call ritual critique, which owes as much to the humanities as to the social sciences by recognizing that detailing and exploring ritual is as much about the reading of texts as it is about uncovering the patterns of lived culture. In this way, my book is much more in the tradition of Peter McLaren's canonical *Schooling as a Ritual Performance: Toward a Political Economy of Symbols and Gestures* (1999/1986) than to *It's All about Jesus!* despite my basic definitional agreement with Magolda and Ebben Gross.

Clearly the single most important work in education on ritual is Peter McLaren's *Schooling as a Ritual Performance*. First published in 1986 and now in its third edition, McLaren's book has introduced so many new ideas and possibilities for ritual in understanding schooling that the field has still not caught up. No one can write about ritual in education without referring to this book. McLaren's approach is scholarly, imaginative, detailed, exploratory, theoretical, concrete, packed, and exciting. Some find it exasperating and irritating, the rest of us are enthralled and inspired. The book you are about to read could not have been written without McLaren having given us *Schooling as a Ritual Performance*. In the next chapter I will investigate and expand ritual theory in some depth including that of McLaren; here I wish to lay out some of the important empirical findings of his book.

McLaren's ethnography challenges ritual studies in education by constructing ritual as multivocal and as a vehicle for ideological struggle. For too long scholars have recognized only the potentiality for ritual to bond people into community, sometimes almost automatically or by definition. McLaren shows us how ritual is both enacted and resisted. McLaren's sympathies are not hidden: He finds the routine of schooling deadening and hegemonic, used to naturalize a system of exploitation of working-class and ethnic minority youth that subverts their unorganized and inchoate attempts to resist. While typical ritual studies have focused on the ceremonies of schooling, McLaren addresses the basic ritual aspects found in the daily routines and ordinary practices. He shows how students move in and out of the "school state" transitioning through the "street-corner state"—a liminal place, betwixt and between (Turner, 1964), with both possibility and excitement where young people shed their student identities empty of worth and control and replace them with youth identities filled with worthiness and importance. For McLaren, student disruption is quite often ritual breach in a social drama (Turner, 1996/1957) where the school responds to student resistance with ritual intended to repair and to reinscribe the dominant order. Of course, in returning order to what the institutional authorities define as chaos, these rituals reintegrate by stripping the youth of worth and hope and working to reproduce the social order. In his study of a Catholic school serving a large population of working-class Azorean youth in Toronto, McLaren details the way in which "making Catholics" becomes entwined with "making capitalists" so that the revolutionary possibility of Christianity is tamed to the socioeconomic order. McLaren makes this clear in the introduction of the third edition, when he speaks of a

> Catholicism serving as a chronic defender of capital, as an ideological weapon of social and cultural indoctrination that consigned students to live in the abstract homogeneity of an empty sanctity, in the difference-crushing and privileging hierarchies that situated Azorean ethnicity within the explanatory categories for dysfunctionality. (P. xxxiii)

For many of us, this clear connection between the ritual deadening of hope becomes the central explanatory of both purpose and failure. It helps us see why many students from the margins reject what schools have to teach and why, so that it makes no difference whether the students reject the school's teachings or accept those teachings, either way the school fails them.

Unfortunately, even today, too many scholars who draw on ritual as an analytic concept fail to recognize the interplay between the cultural and the material relations that are realized in ritual. It remains an academic tool of analysis instead of an intellectual practice of critique. Typically ritual has followed the inclination of anthropologists who have located ritual solely in culture. But if we recognize that ritual is one place in which the symbolic aspects of culture become merged, quite literally, with the materiality of the human body (in a process McLaren refers to as enfleshment), we must begin to understand that it is in ritual that material politics becomes realized in cultural politics; that ideology gets turned into structure and structure into ideology. When we examine the rituals that schools impose on their students, we are not only observing attempts to forge community (which is generally a positive thing), but we are uncovering mechanisms of political enforcement to a status quo that advantages some to the disadvantage of others (which is always a negative thing). In other words, ritual is not merely a technique, a method for improving learning, it is an agonistic space of meaning-making that is worth struggling over—it is where the real work of schooling takes place and unless we are attuned to it, we will never be able to move toward the hope of a transformative education that many of us embrace.

For me, the brilliance of *Schooling as a Ritual Performance* shines in the way in which McLaren himself, through his rhetoric and storytelling, resists the ritual process of academic writing that deadens and empties more traditional ethnographies by bringing them under control of conventionality. McLaren's book is itself a form of ritual breach and creates a kind of academic liminal space that Turner might consider the liminoid—an aesthetic and contemporary space of artistic drama that opens up the possibility of the liminal for those willing to enter and accept its unruliness. For those who want to apply the rules of ethnography found in their graduate qualitative textbooks as a "rational" basis of determining trustworthiness, McLaren's approach will prove unsatisfactory. But for those who recognize that meaningful research can only be found in a rigor of a different type, a process of exploration and critical thought that challenges our basic assumptions, *Schooling as a Ritual Performance* will reward like no other book in education.

This book, the one you hold now and are about to read, has been tremendously inspired by McLaren's approach though it is conducted in a manner entirely my own. I can only hope that the violations of conventional research method found here, which I came to call ritual critique, can create half as much understanding of the way that contemporary schooling works to advance the material interests of a transnational corporate order as McLaren's *Schooling as a Ritual Performance* did in the 1980s and 1990s.

*   *   *

Dan Wright stands in Sylvia's doorway watching his daughter admire her blue graduation gown in the mirror. "You realize," he says, "that despite all of the support you may have received from your classmates, you will be the only person at this commencement wearing the wrong color."

"You're wrong," she responds without turning. "Rob will wear a white gown."

"No guy is going to be caught dead wearing a white gown!" Dan exclaims.

Sylvia simply turns and looks at her father. Slowly Dan's face begins to change. Understanding seeps into his eyes as he realizes what he has just said. For the first time since his daughter started this whole discussion nearly one year ago, he understands her point. He walks over and gives Sylvia a hug. Sylvia's phone rings, but she lets her answering machine get it.

"I thought you might like to know," says an unfamiliar voice, "that the school board just had an emergency meeting and they refused to change the requirement that boys wear blue and girls wear white, but they also voted not to punish or bother in any way students who wear the wrong color."

Less than 24 hours later, Dan Wright sits in the stands wearing a blue and white ribbon on the lapel of his jacket. To his right all the members of his family are wearing the ribbons which are being distributed outside by adults and underclassmen to show support for those seniors who choose to wear the wrong color gown.

Dan sits in almost the exact spot that he had last year when his son had graduated. From this distance the coliseum floor looks almost exactly the same. The same people on the dais, the same banners on the backdrop, the same music being played by the same high school orchestra wearing the same uniforms. There is one small difference, however. The carefully ordered blue and white columns of graduates are disrupted in a few places where a white or a blue gown is distinctly out of place.

As Sylvia showed her family, friends, and teachers, ritual is not innocent. It incorporates and reinforces power. When the rituals are established by the elite, their own power is deepened. Such hidden power needs a spotlight shined upon it. This is the potential of ritual critique: To find and illuminate the way in which material power is institutionalized into the nonrational practices of our schools and lead us to replace them with new practices designed to celebrate democracy and justice. This book is an attempt to reconceptualize ritual, provide an approach to ritual critique, and furnish some examples of how such critique can uncover the covert process that construct a distorted commonsense.

Chapters two and three develop a theory of ritual and of ritual critique. For those readers with an aversion to reading about theory, starting your reading with chapter four might be preferable. You can always return to chapters two and three after reading the rest of the book. For those readers particularly attracted to the elaboration and development of theory, chapters two and three are essential reading for they lay out the basic concept of ritual and the methodology of ritual critique developed in this book. Chapters four, five, and six are empirical examples of how ritual critique might work to reveal the ritual aspects of schooling. Chapter seven builds upon the rest of the book and suggests an alternative pedagogy, a "new pedagogy" that incorporates the nonrational realm of schools as central to its purpose and practice.

My hope is that by the end of this book, readers will begin to see that they have only been noticing half of what occurs in the classrooms and hallways of schools. I am convinced that as educators begin to focus their attention away from the illusions of rationalism schools may begin to fully engage their students and their teachers in a manner that makes critical and transformative education both interesting and possible. While I am not naïve at all about the forces lined up against such transformation, thirty years of teaching in the university classroom with practicing educators has also led me to maintain faith that when people begin to look at what happens in school more broadly in a manner that incorporates the nonrational, most readily commit to the desirability of transforming our public schools to work in the public interest by educating our students to take their place as active and critical participants in a practicing democratic community.

2

School Ritual as Performance

A Reconstruction of Durkheim's and Turner's Uses of Ritual

If man is a sapient animal, a toolmaking animal, a self-making animal, a symbol-using animal, he is, no less, a performing animal, *Homo performans*, not in the sense, perhaps, that a circus animal may be a performing animal, but in the sense that man is a self-performing animal—his performances are, in a way, *reflexive*, in performing he reveals himself to himself.

—Turner, 1988, p. 81

That people construct the social world is a commonplace assertion in the education literature today; *how* they construct the social, however, is less frequently addressed. To the extent that a social analyst does address the mechanisms used in social construction, the discussion is overwhelmingly in the realm of language; the focus is on what people say and what the researcher hears. Yet from the earliest work in theoretical sociology to the most recent postmodern influences in cultural studies, the influence of performance has been known. Durkheim's well-known 1912 study *The Elementary Forms of Religious Life* (1965) identified ritual performance as one key mechanism in the construction of the social. Since then, social analysts, particularly social anthropologists, have recognized ritual as an important social mechanism. And yet when it comes right down to it, with only a few notable exceptions (e.g., Lesko, 1988; Magolda & Gross, 2009; McLaren, 1999 little has actually been done to develop ritual into a key component of the social analysis of education. Educational ethnographers appear to prefer to *listen* to what their informants *say* rather than to *observe* what they *perform*. Ethnographers' evidence draws from their interviews with informants rather than the detailed visual and aural descriptions that one often finds in the classic ethnographies of tribal societies. In this way educational ethnographies are much like *Liturgical Renewal, 1963–1988: A Study of English Speaking Parishes in the United States*, a compilation of reports on liturgy in fifteen Roman Catholic parishes, which, according to Ronald Grimes (1990),

> assumes the primacy of auditory and visual sensoria and makes no systematic attempt to assess kinesthetic, gestural, and postural dimensions of liturgy. It attends primarily to the exegetical meanings of symbols (that is, what people say about those symbols), and it ignores their operational and positional meanings. (P. 50)

While there are many reasons why ethnographers have favored the static words of informants to close description of the processes of social performance, undoubtedly one of those reasons is that the wide literature on ritual has assumed that ritual is not a particularly important aspect of contemporary, complex societies. They assume that ritual performances are not as important in modern, bureaucratic, secular schools as they once were in communal, sacred tribal societies. This assumption is, I believe, simply not true and it is this assumption that this essay will primarily address by reviving a concept forged in structuralism (ritual) and redefining it as performative text therefore taking advantage of certain poststructural insights while, at the same time, maintaining much of the power of its forerunners.

DEFINING RITUAL

The field of ritology (the term sometimes used to describe the interdisciplinary field of ritual studies) has invested much effort attempting to answer precisely the question of what a ritual actually "is." Is it a social function as some (though not all) of the Durkheimians argue or is it a social process as the Turnerians suggest? Is it used to maintain the status quo (as some Durkheimians also seem to profess) or is it something that makes transformation possible (as Victor Turner appears to have maintained)? Must it be limited to sacred events (as assumed in traditional anthropology) or can it be applied to secular events (as developed by many contemporary theorists)? Must it be applied to ceremonial, special events such as weddings and commencements (as is typically the case) or can it be applied to micro, everyday events such as shaking hands and waving goodbye (as in Goffman's interaction ritual)?

Luckily, in this contemporary moment, the task of discovering precisely what constitutes ritual is no longer necessary. There is no longer a need to develop an analytically pure concept of ritual derived from empirical evidence. I do not mean by this that we do not want to construct a clear definition of ritual. We do. What I do mean is that when we construct our clear definition, we no longer assume that the concept of ritual has an ontological existence outside of our intellectual use. While congruent with our empirical understandings of the world, our concept is not merely a reflection of it. The long debate on what ritual is has made the assumption that ritual exists "in the world" and that our job as scholars is to describe it. I am saying that the way we signify the world is, at least partially, constitutive of that world. The call for empirical justification is misguided. For this reason we should reject arguments such as Goody's (1961) that claim "definitions of ritual and religion as 'symbolic' of social relations have the disadvantage, not only of being hampered by the ambiguities involved in the term symbolic, but of seeming to assert as a general principle precisely what requires to be demonstrated in each particular case" (p. 161). No amount of empirical evidence can settle the argument between whether ritual only applies to religious ceremonies or can be applied to secular ones or whether ritual is only to be applied to transformative ceremonies or only to those that maintain stasis. Empirical evidence cannot settle such arguments because they are arguments of concept, not fact. My interest is not in *discovering* what ritual actually might be *in the* world, but how we might *use* it to make sense *of our* world. In other words, my task is not to answer the question, "What is ritual?" but to answer, "What might I mean when I use the term 'ritual'?" While we want a clear definition of ritual, the test of the legitimacy of my concept of ritual is not in its empirical validity, but in its *interpretive usefulness*. In this I agree with Kertzer (1988) when he writes,

> In defining ritual, I am not, of course, trying to discover what ritual "really" is, for it is not an entity to be discovered. Rather, ritual is an analytical category that helps us deal with the chaos of human experience and put it into a coherent framework. There is thus no right or wrong definition of ritual, but only one that is more or less useful in helping us understand the world in which we live. (P. 8)

"Interpretive usefulness" seems to require a definition of ritual broad enough to accommodate the wide range of ways in which ritual might be recognized, yet distinct enough that not everything is understood to be a ritual (though, as will be seen, there may be a ritualistic *aspect* to all social action). With this in mind I have settled on the following: When I use the term "ritual," I will be referring to *that aspect of action that is formalized, symbolic performance*. Before elaborating this definition, I would like to contextualize it by discussing the long conversation that surrounds the definition of ritual.

Because much of the conversation surrounding the meaning of ritual may be understood as embedded in a larger modernist discourse, ritual has usually been discussed in terms that either extended one person's theoretical position or opposed another's as each social theorist attempted to search for the one true concept. My hope is to see these apparently conflicting views as various "takes" on a complex set of phenomena, each providing important insights while often allowing us to miss the insights of other views. The following exploration of a wide variety of theoretical and empirical studies of ritual should be seen as an attempt to construct a fly's eye view of ritual rather than as one more attempt to decide which of these positions is the correct one. In an attempt to provide a conceptual organization for disparate positions, I will discuss these concepts of ritual as either in the tradition of Durkheim or that of Turner. While such a division is obviously artificial since all theorists, even Turner, are to some extent influenced by Durkheim and anyone working in ritual since the 1950s is likely to owe something to Turner's work, nonetheless the division of concepts of ritual into two groups seems to describe some important differences between theorists, even if these differences are a little overdrawn in my description. As will be seen, I wish in this chapter to reduce rather than to reify any such differences that may already exist in the work of scholars utilizing ritual.

THE DURKHEIMIANS

In the work of Emile Durkheim and those who work in his tradition, three themes related to ritual regularly arise: Ritual has something to do with the sacred (though the meaning of "sacred" often radically differs from one theorist to another); in some way, ritual contributes to feelings of social solidarity; and ritual works to maintain the social order. These three themes are laid out in Durkheim's last major work, *The Elementary Forms of Religious Life* (1965/1912).

Durkheim claimed that one characteristic of all religions is their propensity to divide the world into the sacred and the profane. This division is, for Durkheim, one of attitude. Those objects toward which we maintain an attitude of "respect" belong to the sacred realm. Those objects toward which we feel no such sentiments belong to the profane realm. "We get the impression that we are in relations with two distinct sorts of reality and that a sharply drawn line of demarcation separates them from each other: on the one hand is the world of profane things, on the other, that of sacred things" (p. 243). This division between the sacred and the profane has frequently been confused with the difference between the religious and the secular. For Durkheim the point is not whether there is some metaphysical spirit or not, but whether there is an attitude of respect or not. In an extended example, Durkheim compares the respect that a king gets to the respect that a god gets. He points to the way in which people keep an appropriate distance from high personages, the way in which people only approach them with precautions, and the way in which the gestures and language used when interacting is different with kings than with ordinary mortals. "The sentiment felt on these occasions is so closely related to the religious sentiment that many peoples have confounded the two. In order to explain the consideration accorded to princes, nobles, and political chiefs, a sacred character has been attributed to them" (p. 244). In this example we not only see that sacred attitudes can be taken with secular personages, but that the taking of the sacred attitude is revealed in ritual performance: by the distance one keeps, the manner in which one approaches, and the special gestures reserved for the recipient of the respect.

Durkheim's focus on sacred attitude is influential in both Radcliffe-Brown's and Erving Goffman's uses of ritual. For Radcliffe-Brown (1952) "ritual attitude" becomes the key element of ritual because through ritual, symbols become marked and separated from other objects and treated with respect or with "ritual avoidance" (i.e., taboo). The mark of a sacred object is that it is the object of ritual attitude. Thus it is ritual performance that imbues symbols with their sacred power. Radcliffe-Brown's idea becomes fully developed in the work of Erving Goffman (1967). Drawing directly on Radcliffe-Brown's definition of ritual, Goffman argues that interactions of everyday life, such as deference and demeanor, are rituals because they take a ritual attitude toward others. Such "interaction rituals" can become more meaningful when we perceive them as establishing the symbolic sacredness of others through ordinary, everyday performances such as a hand shaking greeting or a wave goodbye. This sense that *ritual can be understood as a performance that reveals respect toward objects thus transforming them into sacred (though not necessarily religious) symbols* is one of the Durkheimian insights that may help us understand the importance of ritual in schools. This insight becomes particularly useful when expanded to include Radcliffe-Brown's ritual avoidance (Radcliffe-Brown, 1952) and Goffman's "interaction rituals" (Goffman, 1967). Such sacred attitude can clearly be seen in the way in which students are expected to address teachers and how both students and teachers are expected to address their principals.

One shouldn't be surprised that in a book on religious forms written in 1912 the rites of tribal societies played a central role. As the knowledge of distant cultures began to become better known in Europe, scholars attempted to incorporate these new findings into their explanations of social life. For Durkheim, whose central motivating social concern was the apparent breakdown of French civil society resulting from modernization, nascent knowledge of tribal rites surrounding totems provided him important insights into the construction of social solidarity. Durkheim came to believe that feelings of solidarity were cultivated as individuals came together and focused their attention on "totems," which are really no more than symbols of group identity. Since Durkheim, much effort has been focused on delineating the cognitive meanings of the symbols found in rituals in the hope of unlocking the true meaning of a particular culture. But what is frequently lost in these studies is Durkheim's recognition that the key to understanding ritual lies in the noncognitive effects of participation rather than in the cognitive meanings per se of the symbols around which rituals are performed. That is to say, it may be more important, or at least just as important, that we realize that participation in ritual helps create nonrational feelings of connectedness to other individuals and the group as a whole and feelings of commitment to specific symbols rather than attempt to rationally analyze the possible referents of those symbols.

Participants in ritual often experience awe or rapture, what Rappaport (1978) refers to as the "numinous." Rappaport is one of the few major ritual theorists who has focused on the nonrational aspects of ritual by reminding us that ritual not only *symbolizes* but it *embodies*. It connects the body to the symbols, the emotions to the mind. "This is to say that in its very form ritual does not merely symbolize but *embodies* social contract, and as such is the fundamental social act—that upon which society is founded" (p. 86). Through participation in ritual, we can not only become cognitively aware of identity, reality, and morality but identity, reality, and morality can actually become embodied in our person—a process McLaren (1999) refers to as "enfleshment." Through this embodiment or enfleshment, our emotional, physical being can become connected to our cognitive, symbolic world. Since, for Durkheim, the ultimate symbols of ritual are symbols of identity, social solidarity can be strengthened through the embodiment potential of ritual. McLaren (1999, pp. 86–94) shows brilliantly how ritual fills students' bodies as he describes the differences between students while in the "student state" and students in the "streetcorner state."

And Lesko (1988) gives excellent evidence of how the ritual of a pep rally can fill some students with the numinous spirit that Rappaport is concerned with.

The third Durkheimian theme relates to the manner in which ritual often appears to work to maintain the status quo. This theme has frequently been presented within a functionalist discourse, therefore overriding other less functionalist interpretations. Raymond Firth (1973) presents one of the more important structural-functionalist understandings of this theme: "What ritual performances do is to recall and present in symbol form the underlying order that is supposed to guide the members of the community, in their social activities" (p. 167). Basil Bernstein (1977) also understands ritual as a structure that serves the status quo.

> Here [in education], the symbolic function of ritual is to relate the individual through ritualistic acts to a social order, to heighten respect for that order, to revivify that order within the individual and, in particular, to deepen acceptance of the procedures which are used to maintain continuity, order and boundary and which control ambivalence towards the social order. (P. 54)

David Hansen (1989) has shown very nicely how the opening moments of classes can be seen as little ritual moments that reinforce the fundamental moral commitment to the idea that "classroom teaching and learning are worthy pursuits" (p. 263). Though different teachers may perform very different rituals—which include such things as reciting the Lord's Prayer, shutting the door as the bell rings, or reading the roll— the teachers and students appear to conspire to "revivify" the order.

Of course, one of the principal reasons Durkheim has suffered in contemporary social theory is because of the assumption that his functionalism cannot be separated from his more general theory, but there is no reason one cannot recognize the importance of the potential social effect of ritual (i.e., the strengthening of solidarity) without taking a functionalist approach. This task of separation has been made difficult by the overly rigid social systems theory that Parsons (1951) has laid over our understanding of Durkheim, but Randall Collins makes a persuasive argument that Durkheim's macro functionalist theory is not a necessary aspect of his more basic theoretical understandings. More strongly influenced by Goffman's use of Durkheim than of Parsons', Collins (1975) writes,

> The path forward from Durkheim, then, is not to accept his overall conception of societies, but to understand what he shows about the nature

of specific interactions. Particularly in his last work, *The Elementary Forms of the Religious Life*, Durkheim presented a powerful model of the ritual aspects of social behavior as the key to emotional solidarity and to our most fundamental conceptions of reality. (P. 43)

As Collins suggests, while it is probable that ritual often (perhaps even most often) works in the interest of the status quo, there is nothing inherent in Durkheim's basic understanding of ritual that makes such an assumption necessary. In fact, the ability of ritual to build social solidarity was understood by W. Lloyd Warner (1959) not as working to create one dominant social order, but as one important element of social conflict. For in the process of creating feelings of bonding toward those who are "us," ritual also helps create feelings of separateness from those who are "not us." When the teacher praises Mary for sitting still and chastises Jason for wiggling around, she may be creating solidarity with Mary but she is pushing Jason out and inducing him to form solidarity with other class outcasts. We need to remember that social conflict is not possible without social solidarity *within* the groups who are in conflict with each other. As Bernstein (1977) suggests, ritual works both to create solidarity and to create divisions by suggesting that in schools two major types of ritual dominate. "Consensual rituals" that work to "bind together all members of the school, staff and pupils as a moral community" such as school assemblies and football games and "differentiating rituals" that "mark off groups within the school from each other" such as which part of the playground is for boys' basketball only and which group of students wear their hair long (p. 55). As long as we live in a complex society where different individuals occupy different social positions, ritual is likely to be used as one aspect of social conflict.

THE TURNERIANS

Living in France in a period of apparent social confusion, Emile Durkheim was drawn to ritual as a social mechanism that might contribute to social cohesion. Working in post–World War II Britain and America, Victor Turner may have been drawn to ritual as a social mechanism with the potential to produce social transformation. Two themes remained remarkably consistent throughout Turner's four decades of work: society must be understood to be a dynamic entity in constant flux and ritual provides contradictory moments that reinforce structure while permitting the possibility of transformation.

Dynamic Society

When Turner works from the assumption that society is dynamic, he works squarely within the discourse associated with the Manchester school of social anthropology. The Manchester school (including such anthropologists as Max Gluckman and Sally Falk Moore) had long been influenced by the idea that society is dynamic and amorphous rather than static and clearly defined. Rather than thinking of society as a structure of girders upon which culture is applied, they thought of society as an indeterminate flux that people sometimes attempt to regularize through customs while at other times attempting to escape those very customs. In commenting on Sally Falk Moore's work, Victor Turner wrote,

> "Indeterminacy," for Moore, characterizes "the underlying quality of social life." . . . She argues that the ever-changing relationship between social life and its cultural representation can be better understood if we take fully into account the processual quality of both: maintaining form is a process, manipulating formal rules is a process, undermining prestigious structures of authority is a process, and societies and cultures are fields of interpenetrating processes . . . all are dependent on one another; their relationship is dialectical not polar. (From Turner's introduction to Moore & Myerhoff, 1975, pp. 6–7)

This idea that society is a struggle between forces of stability and change is fundamental to understanding the Turnerian world. As Moore and Myerhoff write, "Without communitas, man and society are incomplete; yet without structure, existence is impossible" (p. 35). McLaren (1999) shows this dialectic very nicely in the way in which students move through a school day shifting back and forth between the "student state" and the "streetcorner state." For McLaren this shift back and forth is a shift between the stability of the "student state" and the transformative possibilities found in the ludic qualities of the "streetcorner state." For McLaren, as for Turner, ritual is one of the key processes in this dialectic.

Ritual's Dual Role

After studying rituals of the African Ndembu, Turner turned to Van Gennep rather than to Durkheim for his theoretical inspiration. Van Gennep (1960) authored *Rites de Passage* in which he argued that rituals that mark the movement of a person from one social status to another follow a particular three-stage form that might be described as separation, margin (or *limen*), and aggregation. For example, rites that mark a young boy's movement from childhood to adulthood typically include elements that mark his "separation" from his old "childhood" status as well as his "aggregation" into his new "adult" status. In between these two stages is a stage of "betwixt and between" (Turner, 1964a) in which the individual has no status and is, therefore, *structurally* invisible. Turner was particularly drawn to this stage of "liminality" as one full of unrealized potential in which anything might be possible. He especially focused on the possibility of "communitas"—a spontaneous moment of human connectedness in which there are no statuses and, therefore, no hierarchy or inequality (a state reminiscent of Buber's "I-Thou" (Buber, 1955/1937) located between two statuses each of which is firmly positioned within the social order and, therefore, marked by hierarchy and inequality. Within the limen stage we find communitas, freedom, and anti-structure, within the two statuses we find societas, social obligation, and structure.

There is no doubt that in Turner's work liminality and communitas were understood as temporary reprieves from the felt oppressiveness of the regularized social order, but impossible as a permanent state. As enticing as communitas is, societas is necessary for long-term human existence and, as such, people are naturally attracted to both states. Turner (1977) wrote,

> From all this I infer that, for individuals and groups, social life is a type of dialectical process that involves successive experience of high and low, communitas and structure, homogeneity and differentiation, equality and inequality. The passage from lower to higher status is through a limbo of statuslessness. In such a process, the opposites, as it were, constitute one another and are mutually indispensable...In other words, each individual's life experience contains alternating exposure to structure and communitas, and to states and transitions. (P. 97)

To completely accept Turner's understanding of the dialectical relationship between structure and anti-structure found in the process of ritual requires one to also accept Turner's Anglo-American structural-functionalism. That is to say that if one is to accept Turner's understanding of ritual (as a process that includes a stage of liminality) one must also accept the idea that statuses are "structures" and the *rites de passage* serve a particular function (i.e., to transform the individual from one status to another). Within this framework it makes sense to talk of ritual as a process of "anti-structure" that is potentially freeing and to distinguish it from Durkheim's understanding of ritual as fundamentally structural and ultimately binding.

That ritual is dynamic rather than static is also brought out in Turner's recognition that symbols (the "smallest unit" of ritual; Turner, 1967) are "multivocal" or "polysemous." His recognition that a single symbol represents more than one cultural idea opens up the understanding that "the system of meaning" (Turner, 1964b, p. 50) created in ritual is not fixed and, therefore, able to change as internal and external demands change (p. 21). That different individuals and different times may emphasize one possible meaning of a symbol over others also creates the possibility that any particular ritual performance may be read in multiple ways. In this way ritual can help create a sense of unity within a group even when participants hold differing understandings of the meaning of the ritual.

> We can see how the same dominant symbol, which in one kind of ritual stands for one kind of social group, or for one principle of organisation, in another kind of ritual stands for another kind of group or principle, and in its aggregate of meanings stands for unity and continuity of the wider Ndembu society, embracing its contradictions. (P. 50)

In the same way, Lesko (1988) shows how Catholic school students divided by different class positions are brought together through a Mass built around the symbol of "love" even though students had some quite different understandings of the meaning of that Mass.

While in his early work Turner emphasized *rites de passage*, in his later work he turned to a different ritual performance: that of "social drama." In good Ganneppian fashion Turner (1974) defined social drama as a ritualized four-stage process of "disharmony" or conflict in which a violation of a social norm ("breach") was challenged, conflict around fundamental "root metaphors" or "paradigms" occurred ("crisis"), amends were enacted ("redressive action"), and normalcy returned ("reintegration") (pp. 38–41). During social drama, as in *rites de passage*, a moment of possibility exists, a time of potential transformation. Turner extends his meaning of liminality beyond that of the middle stage of a *rites de passage* "to refer to any condition outside or on the peripheries of everyday life" (p. 47). By shifting his focus to moments of social conflict and by extending his meaning of liminality, Turner could more easily make connections between the world of tribal societies and the worlds of the late-1960s and 1970s industrial societies. To accomplish this Turner expanded his use of liminality even further by creating the concept of the "liminoid" [moments of possibility in complex, industrial societies found in cultural practices such as literature, film, and drama in which one is "set aside not only from one's own social position but from all social positions and of formulating a potentially unlimited series of alternative social arrangements" (p. 14)]. This focus on liminality, the liminoid, communitas, social drama, and multivocality in the work of Turner has drawn many followers to see ritual more in terms of social transformation and to distance themselves from the Durkheimian sense that ritual is a mechanism of social maintenance.

THE FLY'S EYE

English-speaking social theorists tend to see Durkheim through the eye of Talcott Parsons who in turn seemed to situate Durkheim's structuralism into the Anglo-American structural-functionalism popular during the mid-twentieth century. But Durkheim can also be understood within the Continental discourse called "structuralism," which includes the linguist Saussure and found its epitome in the work of the anthropologist Lévi-Strauss. Whereas Anglo-American structural-functionalism focuses on the apparent fixity of institutional relations, Continental structuralism addresses the underlying mental frameworks or rules used to engage in social action. This different understanding of "structure" leaves room for a very different understanding of the relationship between Turner's and Durkheim's understandings of ritual than is often suggested by some of those influenced by Turner. Turner (1977) himself addressed this difference:

> By "structure" I mean, as before, "social structure," as used by the majority of British social anthropologists, that is as a more or less distinctive arrangement of specialized mutually dependent institutions and the institutional organization of positions and/or of actors which they imply. I am not referring to "structure" in the sense currently made popular by Lévi-Strauss, i.e., as concerned with logical categories and the form of the relations between them. *As a matter of fact, in the liminal phases of ritual, one often finds a simplification, even elimination, of social structure in the British sense and an amplification of structure in Lévi-Strauss's sense. We find social relationships simplified,* while myth and ritual are elaborated. (Emphasis added; pp. 166–167)

According to Turner himself, structure, as understood in Continental discourse, may actually be *strengthened* during the limen stage of *rites de passage*—a suggestion perhaps congruent with, rather than opposed to, Durkheim's argument that ritual works to strengthen rather than weaken social bonds since Durkheim's concept focuses on mental frameworks rather than institutional positions. To be sure, Turner did want to distance himself from Durkheim, but primarily in their differing emphases on human relations rather than on their differing emphases on social maintenance. Turner wrote, "Communitas is in this respect strikingly different from Durkheimian 'solidarity,' the force of which depends upon an in-group/out-group contrast" (p. 132). There are differences between Durkheim and Turner—one worked within Continental structuralism, while the other worked within Anglo-American structural-functionalism; one emphasized ritual as a mechanism of social stasis, while the other stressed its role in social transition; but the differences may not be as substantial as they appear at first glance. Turner's emphasis on ritual's part in social transition results from his very restrictive use of the term ritual. Turner (1964b) *arbitrarily* restricts ritual to transformative processes by assigning the term "ceremony" to all of those symbolic performances that look like ritual but are static or confirmatory in their effect:

> I may state here, partly as an aside, that I consider the term "ritual" to be more fittingly applied to forms of religious behavior associated with social transitions, while the term "ceremony" has a closer bearing on religious behavior associated with social states, where politico-legal institutions also have greater importance. Ritual is transformative, ceremony confirmatory. (P. 95)

For Turner there are two kinds of symbolic performance: One is confirmatory and called ceremony and the other is transformative and called ritual. But where is the advantage to this classification? Is it a useful categorization? I think not, because it creates the appearance of two distinct phenomena rather than one type of phenomenon with varying effects. If we assign the term ritual to the general case, than we can argue that ritual can be both confirmatory and transformative and still be consistent with Turner. Terry O'Connor has suggested that Turner's distinction may be inappropriate and misleading. O'Connor (personal communication, 1995) says, "Celebration may be the confirmatory rituals and liminal rites may be the transformative rituals." In fact, Turner's claim that liminal rites (*rites de passage* and social dramas) are transformative may be overstating the case. When we use the term "transformative" we usually imply the fundamental change in the way in which social life is organized. But Turner doesn't really claim that social life is fundamentally altered in *rites de passage*, only individuals' positions within it. And while society may be altered during social drama, these changes are quite minor and are more evolutionary than transformative when considering the society and culture as a whole. The effect of Turner's rituals is not so much to "transform" society as to make the "transition" of individuals and of social states possible. In fact, one can argue that *rites de passage* and social dramas not only do not transform the fundamental structure of society but they confirm it. In other words, Turner's liminal rites are both transitional and confirmatory *at the same time.* They are fundamentally multivocal. *Perhaps what is most important about Turner, then, is not so much his claim that ritual is transformative, but that social life is a dynamic process between social forces that attempt to impose determinacy and counterforces that open up indeterminacy.* In this way, Turner can be understood to be more in accordance with Durkheim than in opposition to him.

Those who have been influenced by Turner's sense of ritual maintain a flexible sense of ritual. They tend to see ritual as complex, multivocal, and having various effects at differing times. While ritual should always be understood to possess the potential for regularization, we should also recognize that ritual provides potential for more than just the enforcement of the status quo. Ritual, in the hands of Turnerians such as Barbara Myerhoff (1978, 1992), Ronald Grimes (1982, 1990), and, in education, Peter McLaren (1999), becomes a dynamic, inconclusive cultural process that often opens up as much possibility as it closes down chaos.

When we begin to realize that ritual is a complex, multivoiced, even contradictory, set of phenomena, we begin to realize its potential to affect social life. When we fall into the trap of accepting the Durkheimian and Turnerian concepts of ritual as bipolar opposites, we lose a potentially rich construction. If there were a way to understand ritual that allows us to build on both discourses, we would have a powerful concept for social analysis.

PERFORMANCE AND POSTMODERNISM

How do we conceptualize ritual so as to avoid the artificial opposition between the Durkheimian and Turnerian concepts of ritual? Turner, himself, points the way in his posthumously published essay, *The Anthropology of Performance,* in which he (1988) not only addresses performance per se, but also appeals directly to postmodernism as descriptive of his project. By pointing to the way he—and Goffman (1967) and Schechner (1990, 2006)—focus on processes such as performance, movement, staging, and plot, Turner (1988) equates postmodernism with the "processualization of space, its temporalization, as against the spatialization of process or time" (p. 76). In *The Anthropology of Performance,* Turner (1988) remarks on his constant struggle against modernist emphasis on such static things as structure, science, grammar, and *langue*. In its place he suggests the dynamics of performance that is filled with possibility, narrative, rhetoric, and *parole*.

> Postmodern theory would see in the very flaws, hesitations, personal factors, incomplete, elliptical, context-dependent, situational components of performance, clues to the very nature of human process itself...What was once considered "contaminated," "promiscuous," "impure" is becoming the focus of postmodern analytical attention (p. 77).

But despite Turner's important moves toward postmodernism, his theory is, understandably, hopelessly embedded in modernism. As has been shown earlier, Turner defines both ritual and social drama as processes embedded in a structured world. Ritual is understood to be centered on liminality, a concept that derives its very meaning from the interstices of structured relations. While Turner is interested in these interstices and in the possibilities unleashed through social drama, he still understands the fundamental state of social life as structured. It may be that Turner shifts our attention away from Durkheimian structures themselves to the dynamics of the anti-structure, but his is still only a partial view.

In fact, not only does Turner define ritual against structure, ultimately he defines ritual in terms of function: The only way to distinguish a ritual from a ceremony is to ascertain whether or not the performance functions to support or to dissolve structure. For Turner, ritual is always pointing toward the liminal. It is erasing roles, abolishing structure, it is play, imagination: A respite from quotidian life. On the other hand, ceremony reinforces structure. It is always pointing toward the inertial aspects of social life. So for Turner shaking hands when meeting another is ceremony since such an action typically celebrates the status quo structure: a mundane celebration of mutual connectedness. But why must we understand the handshake or the bow or the doffed hat as quotidian. Aren't these actions fundamentally performances? Aren't they actions taken primarily to be seen by others? To "appear to be" something? Certainly mundane acts of decorum are as much in the subjunctive as Ndembu puberty rites. When we shake hands, we create a little pocket of imagination as we perform *as if* we are friends and allies. It makes no difference whether we really are or are not friends or social equals. As Goffman (1967) has so clearly shown, these acts of decorum are little performances that publicly dramatize an imagined relationship (pp. 90–91). To believe that the status quo is *indicative* whereas the liminal moments of social drama are *subjunctive*, as Turner repeatedly proclaims, is to not only misunderstand the force through which the status quo remains in

.o misunderstand our reliance on rhetoric and power for
of a naturalized reality. Far from there being "a status
;tatus quo must continually be created and recreated by
the forces of the powerful within a society. And, equally important,
that reality is constantly being challenged by the less powerful. The
status quo is as much about imagination as it is about real power. As
Kertzer (1988) writes, "the hallmark of power is the construction of
reality" (p. 5). When we are structural-functionalists then the ludic,
the subjunctive is understood in relation to those socially enforced
structures, but when we no longer believe in those structures, then it
is *all* play. Lyotard realizes this in his focus on "language games," but
the playfulness of society extends way beyond language. It includes
all of the multitude of ways in which we construct little bubbles of
reality in our social encounters. While much of ordinary daily life
may be instrumental or indicative, much is equally performative and
subjunctive. This is, of course, not a new idea. Shakespeare ("All the
world's a stage…") and Goffman (1973/1959) are but two who have
recognized the ultimate dramatic form of social life. But such insights
are usually seen as metaphoric and, therefore, not the stuff of serious
social analysis. Its insights are regularly forgotten and its implications
have yet to be fully developed.

RITUAL AS FORMALIZED, SYMBOLIC PERFORMANCE

If we conceptualize *ritual as that aspect of action that is formalized,
symbolic performance*, then we are able to reap the benefits of the work
of both the Durkheimians and Turnerians without falling into the
traps of either. Let me further develop this understanding of ritual.

Performance

First, ritual can be seen as a performance—an action intended for
an audience (even if the audience is oneself[1]). The point of performance is that the action is not simply instrumental to achieving an
overt end, but is acted in a manner to be seen or heard and "read" by
others; therefore, it is also a text, a dramatic text. As Schechner has
stated it, "These situations—arguments, combats, rites of passage—
are inherently dramatic because participants not only do things, they
try *to show others what they are doing or have done*; actions take on a
'performed-for-an-audience' aspect" (quoted in Turner, 1988, p. 74;
emphasis in the original). The intended observation of the act is not
just a by-product of the act, it is an important *constitutive* element of

the ritual. The act gains meaning, not only from the consequences of the action, but in the manner in which the action is carried out. It can be performed well providing a convincing performance or it can be performed poorly raising doubts about the sincerity of the actor. Performed one way, the act of greeting another with a handshake can mean one thing; performed another way, its meaning can greatly change. Part of the reason recognizing ritual as a performance is important is because it allows us to recognize that much public action is a "show."

Since ritual is performed in front of an audience, the actors' bodies are as important to the meaning of the action as their words and frequently even more important. The body's movements, mien, and posture are central elements to a performance. Of course, this is the area that Goffman analyzed so brilliantly in his classic *Interaction Ritual* (1967). Goffman shows us how deference and demeanor are performances of respect toward individuals. But recognizing that performance is embodied action has more implications than merely public expression of honor; it also connects the body and the mind in a manner that helps fill the numinous with emotional impact that really successful ritual creates. Because ritual is *performed* its importance lies in much more than the cognitive associations one can make to its defining symbols. While the cognitive associations of symbols are important to ritual, by *physically acting out meaning in the world* one imbues that constructed meaning with a nonrational spirit of ontological existence that is far more persuasive for most people than any rational discursive argument.

By recognizing that the most mundane of social interactions are little ritual-inflating bubbles of reality, we can also begin to recognize that the actors in these ritual performances must carefully make-up and costume themselves for their parts. Clearly public sites, being the center of most ritual activity, require a careful consideration of the actors' "make-up and costume." Before heading to work or to school or to the restaurant or the nightclub, we must prepare ourselves for the possible unplanned ritual that occurs when we encounter others. We must carefully imbue our self, our identity, our claims to power into our wardrobe and our grooming so that if a chance ritual encounter should arise, we are in the best position to perform our roles in the manner we wish others to perceive us or in the manner we assume others expect of us. When getting dressed to go out to school, we are not simply getting dressed; we are costuming ourselves. Whether we are the teacher who is attempting to dress as "a professional," a teacher who is trying to dress in "solidarity with the

" or some combination of both, our dress aids us in perform-
identity.

Symbolic

Emphasizing the performative aspect of ritual is not to deny the importance of the symbolic. It is merely to shift our attention from the cognitive referents of symbols to the performative display of symbols. The
meaning of the term "symbol" in the academic literature may be even
more contested than that of "ritual," particularly between different
disciplines where some use the term in completely different, almost
opposite, manners. Here, I use the term symbol to imply a subset of
the larger category of signification (see MacCannell & MacCannell,
1982). Namely, *symbols represent things indirectly through association.*
Symbols "re-present" rather than name. Therefore when referring to
"symbolic performance," I am referring to performances that have,
in much the same manner as Bernstein (1977), "meaning over and
beyond the specific situational meanings" (p. 54). By restricting ritual
to symbolic performance, we create the possibility that any particular
set of behaviors may be ritual in one context and not ritual in another
depending on whether or not the act is symbolic. For example, the
Irish custom of enjoying a pint of stout at the local pub may be merely
a common way to relax in Dublin; while in Boston, it may become a
ritual of ethnic identity.

The stylized costumes and accessories that we wear; the stylized
way in which we talk, from our language to our dialect, to our accent,
to the stories we tell, even the stylized way in which we walk are all
potential symbols of group identity or of power resources or of moral
commitments. All of these things may "represent things indirectly."
They rarely name us or our ideologies, but they may, under certain circumstances, carry undeniable meaning to those who observe our performances of daily life. Typically ethnographers reserve the idea of the
symbol for the most obvious of symbols such as the rites of a Catholic
mass (see Lesko, 1988). Certainly these traditional and stylized symbols of our institutions are important to address, but my point here
is that these symbols are no more important than the button-down,
Oxford shirt and chinos or the black tee-shirt and Doc Martins or the
"inarticulate vocal gestures" of some "disaffected youth" (found in
such screen representations as Marlon Brando's "wild one" or James
Dean's "rebel").

When these symbols are displayed, for others to observe, then they
are being ritually displayed. Middle schools and high schools are

filled with individuals ritually displaying their group meml
their ideologies, their resistance, their connection to power groups,
their identities and they use these ritual displays in an active drama.
McLaren (1999) is quite brilliant in helping us understand the shifting modes between "street" and "school" states, but we should be
able to realize that while the cultural politics of ritual display may be
more spectacular in street mode, it hardly ends in school mode. Watch
any classroom and you will observe students and teachers engaged in
subtle ritual performances that focus our attention on the symbols
that each holds dear.

Formalized

In a broad definition, one might be tempted to include only these first
two aspects of ritual, being satisfied with the idea that ritual is any
symbolic performance. However, I believe that restricting the term
ritual to only those symbolic performances that can clearly be seen as
"formalized" adds one more important and helpful dimension. Here
the term formalized refers to the idea that a ritual has an expected
form: that witnesses to a ritual bring certain expectations as to the
appropriate and expected temporal and spatial organization of a ritual.
As Moore and Myerhoff (1975) put it:

> Myerhoff proposes conceptualizing collective ceremony in its formal
> aspect as a container, a vessel which holds something. It gives form to
> that which it contains. Ritual is in part a form, and a form which gives
> certain meanings to its contents. The work of ritual, then, is partly
> attributable to its morphological characteristics. Its medium is part of
> its message. It can contain almost anything, for any aspect of social
> life, any aspect of behavior or ideology, may lend itself to ritualiza-
> tion... (P. 8)

The form of rituals carries meaning as much as the symbols themselves and as much as that which is derived from performance. Even in
one-time rituals, form is important. For example, in the Graduation-
Siyum so wonderfully described in Myerhoff's study *Number Our Days*
(1978), the audience expected certain forms. As a result they argued
about the appropriateness of the activities that were performed in this
one-time-only ritual, some arguing that some procedures were in
poor taste or counter to the intent of the ritual, while others disagreeing. And in a wonderful example of appropriated ritual, McClellan
(1991) tells of a family in Madison, Wisconsin, that borrowed and
reconstructed the Scandinavian Santa Lucia's Day ritual to build both

expectation - in formalized there is an
expectation

family and neighborhood solidarity. Even though their version of St. Lucia's day is freely adapted and dramatically altered to fit the particular circumstances of a contemporary, middle-class American family in a small Midwestern city, certain forms of that traditional Scandinavian ritual are clearly visible and important in this new setting.

On the other hand, symbolic performance without a recognizable form seems to lack an important aspect of what we understand as ritual, even if it is an important aspect of social behavior in some other way. Consider this anecdote from Douglas Foley's ethnography (1990) of a Texas border town fraught with ethnic conflict.

> One of the most telling incidents occurred over the painting of toilet walls. The school board accused the director of the Head Start Program, a suspected Ciudadanos sympathizer, of turning the bathrooms into a political billboard. The director had organized parents and various volunteers to fix up and paint their building. They painted the bathroom walls in bright yellows, blues, and greens. The decor included a golden rising sun and a brilliant rainbow. Everyone from the parents to the children admired their colorful new building. When the school board heard about the new color schemes it quickly investigated. Several BGL members claimed the Head Start staff had painted an "Aztec sun," which was being used as political propaganda. The board ordered the bathrooms repainted a standard beige color. The director was informed that noncompliance would be considered an act of insubordination and defacing school property. After much teethgnashing, the walls were repainted beige. (Pp. 22–23)

Certainly the painting of the bathroom is understood as a symbolic performance, but it would be hard to understand this particular painting as a ritual in the same way that painting one's house at Christmas time is a seasonal ritual in many places in the Caribbean. In the case of the painted bathroom walls, it is neither the *form of the act* of painting that is important nor the *form of the act* of symbolic display, but only the symbolic meaning of the colors used and the object represented. On the other hand, Foley also shows us the importance of form when expected form is violated in a public ritual.

> On the particular occasion that I observed, the homecoming halftime ceremony took place as it always did, but with one major difference. The customary convertibles for the queen and her court were missing; consequently, the queen and her court, on this occasion all Mexicanas, had to walk to their crowning. This evoked numerous criticisms among Mexicano students and parents in attendance. Many felt it was a gringo plot to rob the Mexicanos of their chance to be leaders in

the community. The *Chicano Times*, a radical San Antonio newspaper, screamed out headlines that accused the school officials of blatant discrimination. The administrators and teachers in charge of organizing the event denied these charges, but were left embarrassed and without any acceptable defense. (P. 49)

In this case, due to the violation of form, a ritual of solidarity became one of divisiveness and unlike the painting of the bathroom, it is precisely the *form of the act* that is important to the meaning of the ritual.

By defining ritual as formalized, symbolic performance we have a concept that is flexible enough to recognize both the Durkheimians and the Turnerians, the sacred and the secular, the large gatherings of ceremony and the small everyday acts of social decorum. And yet it is specific enough to distinguish between the cleaning of my child's face to remove the remains of a peanut butter and jelly sandwich and the ceremonial wiping of her face with a facecloth before she goes out the door to school; or to treat as different, in some fundamental way, the explosion of anger in a teacher's exasperated attempt to bring order to a classroom by yelling for quiet and the methodical and stylized ritual performance of a teacher with head erect, eyes piercing, jaw set, and two feet planted at the front of the room staring down, one at a time, the miscreant students of a disorderly class.

Ritual as an Aspect of Action

There is one further understanding to explore. Typically ritual is defined in a manner to suggest that human acts can be categorized as either an example of ritual or not. That is, typical definitions suggest that we ought to be able to determine if any particular act is an example of ritual or not. This, however, would be an oversimplification of what happens, because many actions appear to be only partially ritualistic. As Middleton (1977) explains,

> Even the most technical behavior contains some touch of the ritual; and even the most religious act some aspect of the technical. This is a commonplace but we do not always remember it. So if we see these as aspects of behavior rather than as types of behavior we can expect to make greater sense of the social reality before us. (P. 73)

So any, perhaps even most, social acts may have an element of ritual within them. Perhaps it is more important to begin to recognize those aspects of a social act that are formalized, symbolic performances rather than attempting to label any particular act as ritual or non-ritual. Perhaps we should think of acts as fitting on a continuum of heavily ritualized to lightly ritualized action rather than looking for qualitatively different behaviors (ibid.). Doing so would require us to say that any particular act can be "ritualized" referring to *that aspect of an act that is formalized, symbolic, and performative.*

But if ritual is an aspect of most action, has its meaning become so broad as to violate my proclaimed interest in constructing a concept that is intellectually useful? Has the concept become so broad as to include everything and, therefore, nothing? Well it certainly does not include everything. Any aspect of social action that is instrumental, has no meaning beyond itself, *or* without expectant form would not be ritual under my definition. So when a teacher erases a chalkboard in order to write something on it, we might typically understand that as an instrumental, nonformalized act without further meaning. So clearly there are many actions that are not ritual. Of course, if every-day at the beginning of the class the instructor took the eraser and erased the board so as to start the class with a wiped chalkboard, we might understand such action as partially ritualistic. So that the deter-mination of whether or not an act has aspect of ritual depends a lot on the particulars of the context. What might be ritual in one situation may not be ritual in another.

But are these distinctions too minor to be intellectually useful? I think not, because the idea of ritual as the aspect of action that is for-malized, symbolic performance helps us distinguish between certain socially expressive aspects of cultural politics and other more mun-dane instrumental actions not particularly relevant to understanding the cultural politics of a situation. For example, when a high school teacher presents a lecture there are clearly certain ritual as well as non-ritual aspects that ought to be considered. Let us first look at some of the nonritual aspects. In many ways lecture can be seen as an instru-mental activity. One central purpose of lecture is to deliver up-to-date information not available in texts. Another is that it allows the instruc-tor to present his/her own contexts for the delivery of that informa-tion permitting her/him to connect the information more closely to the individual circumstances of the students in the class. Textbooks are written with the average student nationwide, not the specific stu-dents in a specific classroom. Now we may raise objections to lectur-ing aimed at precisely the instrumental aspects of lecturing. As an instrument for the delivery of information to a specific population of students is it effective? Are there better ways to deliver information? Perhaps we object to the idea that information can even be "delivered" arguing instead that information may need to be made "available" but that it requires students to go to it, not be delivered to them. Typically our professional arguments around pedagogy have focused on such instrumental issues surrounding efficacy. But most of us also know that the objections to lecture may be less about the instrumental effectiveness of lecture than about the ritual focus of the lecture.

While I believe that lecture certainly has important instrumental aspects, it also has ritual aspects. Certainly the lecturer is not only "delivering information" but "putting on a performance." In fact we know that the most popular lecturers are those who take the performance seriously and "put on a show." Lecture also has its expected forms. While there are variations permitted such as using a lectern or not or delivering while standing or sitting, there are other aspects that are less variable. When lecturing, the lecturer has control of the conversation. The lecturer is the one doing nearly all of the talking. The student's job is to listen carefully and (hopefully) critically and to take note of those things that are important. This very form (lecturer lecturing, student ingesting) is, of course, symbolic of a hierarchical relationship between teacher and student. It is as a symbol of hierarchy that lecture is found to be objectionable to many of us. We do not object to lecture because we think it is ineffective, but because we think it is too often effective in teaching the wrong thing—that students should be docile subordinates. By shifting our attention from the instrumental to the ritual aspects of lecturing we are able to see how politics enters into the classroom. While it is true that my definition of ritual is broad, it is not too broad to be useful. By focusing our attention on the ritual aspects of classrooms and other school activities we begin to see more clearly where the real work of schools occurs.

Conclusion

Durkheim's genius was in recognizing the connection between body and mind that is forged in ritual and through the focused emotional energy to create the bonds of solidarity. Unfortunately his structuralism led him to layer this insight with static, cognitive constructs imbued with external quiddity such as the "collective conscience." Turner's genius was to recognize that ritual is as much about the freedom that is released in the emotional and spiritual energy of many rituals as it is about the bonds that are forged; and, therefore, the recognition that ritual often leads to transformation rather than always reinforcing the status quo. But both of them (even when Turner portrays himself as accepting the "postmodern turn") are bounded by a social world embedded in structured social organization. Both are unable to recognize the fundamental creativity of everyday social life, of the playfulness or ludic quality of ordinary affairs, of the subjunctive mood (as Turner liked to refer to it) even in the grinding normalness of quotidian life. When we recognize the full implications of human action as typically including an aspect of performance, of drama, of play, we are able to move beyond Durkheim's bounded sense of ritual as always a tool of solidarity and conservatism as well as beyond Turner's limited construction of ritual drama. By recognizing the performative aspect of ritual action, we are able to build on Durkheim's nonrational, numinous effect of solidarity while, at the same time, employing Turner's nonrational, numinous reconstruction of cultural meaning. By leaving the fundamental assumptions of structuralism behind and embracing the full implications of ritual as performance, we are able to create a much more useful concept of ritual. And with this more useful concept of ritual, we will be able to better explore the everyday cultural politics of school life.

Thinking of ritual as being an aspect of much, perhaps even most, actions will help educational researchers shift their attention from the larger, more obvious, and, in my opinion, less important rituals such as pep rallies and the flag pledge, to the more mundane and more important ritualistic performances of ordinary school life. In the larger rituals, we may find the heavy hand of the power structure clumsily applied, but in the smaller, daily rituals we are likely to find the real stuff of cultural politics. It is there that we are able to see how power is skillfully applied and just as skillfully resisted. It is in the rituals of everyday life that the real school politics is performed and it is the performances themselves that we should be more clearly attuned to in our descriptions of school practices. What people say about the performances is important, but how they actually perform their identities and their politics is even more important.

3

FROM ETHNOGRAPHY TO
RITUAL CRITIQUE

THE EVOLUTION OF A METHOD

With Terry O'Connor

PART I: WRITING CRITICAL ETHNOGRAPHY—
DIALOGUE, MULTIVOICEDNESS, AND CARNIVAL
IN CULTURAL TEXTS

Don't let us forget that the causes of human actions are usually immeasurably more complex and varied than our subsequent explanations of them.

—Fyodor Dostoevsky, *The Idiot*, p. 469

The narrator in Dostoevsky's novel *The Idiot* shows an awareness of human cultures that ethnographers have all too often failed to appreciate. Traditionally, ethnographers have tended to describe complex, historical, social activities as homogeneous, rule-governed, ahistorical entities. This ethnographic tradition has reinforced a conception of culture as a single, unified set of patterns, passed down from generation to generation, that governs life within a community. Such a conception masks the dynamic and conflictual nature of culture in pluralistic societies and effectively reinforces the idea that education must be reproductive rather than transformative. While the more recent postcritical ethnographies (Clifford & Marcus, 1986; Noblit et al., 2004) have done much to correct this tendency, in the 1980s, when I first approached this topic, such ethnographic work was only just beginning to be considered. From my own position as critical theorist in education, the need to write ethnographies that reflected the emancipatory impulses found in marginalized cultures required a concept of culture that recognized the complex contradictions between the material existence in society and the narrative constructions cultures often create to explain away or to hide these material realities. The recognition and naming of such contradictions is the heart of the critical approach and provides the possibility for transformation.

While today ethnographers reject claims to objectivity and scientific neutrality, traditionally, ethnographers attempted to view society with an objective, scientific detachment that transformed disparate acts into a set of universal, homogeneous abstractions. Material goods, social institutions, and rituals have all been used to construct coherence and regularity. For example, Spradley and McCurdy (1972), by describing culture as "the knowledge people use to generate and interpret social behavior" (p. 8), portrayed culture as a unified, consensual system of abstractions located in the human mind. Since knowledge is an invisible artifact, Spradley and McCurdy turned the study of culture into the study of language, arguing that language provides a single, concrete, and immediate manifestation of thought; but their techniques searched for regularities and overlooked aberrations and infractions and showed little understanding of postmodern ideas of language as existing outside of mind. The result was the reduction of cultural life to a static system of categorical relationships that left untouched many critical factors involved in the construction of cultural exchanges. As Henry Glassie (1982), a folklorist equally concerned with finding the mental roots of cultural commonalities, pointed out, "The timeless portrait of a culture gives it shape but no direction. It gives people no intention or decision, no way to create their own destiny. [It] petrifies them in an inhuman state, thrall to the scholar's model of consistency" (p. 375). This error obscured the life of people whose thoughts conflict with the status quo, misrepresented the problem that those with little power have to shape the community's public symbols and institutions, and offered no mechanism for ideological and political transformation.

To overcome these shortcomings of traditional ethnography, anthropologist James Clifford (1983, pp. 118–146) suggested we examine Mikhail Bakhtin's concept of "heteroglossia," a Bakhtinian term that implies that culture and society, as well as individuals, are constituted by multiple voices.[1] The concept of heteroglossia recognizes the multiple dimensions of cultural life and is, therefore, an important corrective to static, unified conceptions of culture. It legitimates difference of opinion and restores the individual's voice in the creation of their cultural patterns. In this view, culture is seen not as a superorganic entity demanding obedience; rather, it is a world full of unique individuals, each expressing personal views within their cultural interactions. This point led Clifford and others to emphasize the central role of heteroglossia in collecting and analyzing social evidence.

But while Clifford recognized the complex, multivoiced character of society in Bakhtin's work, Bakhtin's emphasis on the historical and ideological nature of dialogue is lost in Clifford's concern for heteroglossia. While Clifford recognized the importance of history and ideology in the work of Edward Said (1973), he interpreted Bakhtin's ideas as essentially reducible to heteroglossic concerns. This one-sided emphasis could lead to a kind of liberal relativism where cultural differences are viewed as mutually exclusive, self-sufficient sets of patterns-in-mind and detached from material politics. This approach fails to engage adequately the forces of struggle among individuals and among groups and generally fails to conceptualize the emancipatory impulse of many marginalized cultures. On the other hand, a Bakhtinian concept of culture that includes not only heteroglossia, but also history and ideology, makes possible the clear depiction of nascent emancipatory struggle (e.g., see Crapanzano, 1985).

One of the reasons for Clifford's error is his reading of Bakhtin independently from the work of Volosinov and Medvedev. The three theorists were known to be working together in the attempt to create a semiotics more compatible with their understanding of Marxism. Unfortunately, they were writing in the period of Stalinist repression and such attempts to forge a theoretical alternative to the orthodoxy of the day required courage and careful construction of texts. One way to read the work of this group (the Bakhtin Circle) is to recognize that texts that appear under Bakhtin's own name and focused on literary analysis actually use these literary texts as a proxy for social life. Texts that appear under the name of Volosinov lay out a more direct theoretical challenge to Marxist orthodoxy but stay away from social or cultural concreteness. Read separately, they reduce the danger to their authors. Read together and in relation to each other, they lay out a radical philosophy that could not help but put all three in danger. As it was, Volosinov was arrested and sent to Siberia where his existence has been lost to history. My argument is that we can only understand the texts under Bakhtin's name by reading them in conjunction with those of Medvedev and, especially, of Volosinov. While I do not go as far as some to claim that the texts of Volosinov were actually authored by Bakhtin, I do accept that one must read the total opus of all three men to understand their theoretical semiotics.

One of the lessons we learn from reading the Bakhtin Circle is that culture is riddled through and through with power and ideology and, therefore, provides a terrain for struggle. The belief that culture can include resistance to social order while, at the same time, it operates as a power that dominates human lives became an important theme for early educational resistance theorists (see Aronowitz & Giroux, 1985; Connell, 1982; Giroux, 1983; McLaren, 1999/1986; Weis, 1985; Willis, 1981). This realization forces critical ethnographers to read cultural texts as multivoiced phenomena as well as to write multivoiced ethnographic texts. One way we can critically read and portray culture in its intricate web of diverse worlds is by employing the work of the Bakhtin Circle. This section of the chapter presents a discussion of how the Bakhtin Circle can help us read and write such multivoiced situations. The original version was published in 1988 and written with Terry O'Connor. It presents three major theoretical elements central to a Bakhtinian worldview (dialogue, multivoicedness, and carnival) to develop a dialectical and transformative reading of culture, and describes four familiar literary devices (time and space, characterization, ideology, ambivalence) that allow critical ethnographers to unpack and reconstruct the terrain of everyday life. In this manner Bakhtin's theoretical portrayal of culture may become a practical philosophy of action. Following an elaboration of how the Bakhtin Circle might improve our ethnographies in the first part of this chapter, in the second I expand on my progression from conducting ethnography to engaging in ritual critique.

By focusing on the Bakhtin Circle's ideas of dialogue, multivoicedness, and carnival, Terry O'Connor and I hoped to create a more satisfactory understanding of culture. The Bakhtin Circle's emphasis on multivoicedness and dialogue provided a basis for understanding and describing complex and contradictory cultural actions by placing culture in the flow of history. Bakhtin's interest in carnival makes possible our recognition that at least some cultural actions are regenerative democratic impulses. Dialogue, multivoicedness, and carnival are interrelated concepts that lie at the center of a Bakhtinian understanding of culture.

Dialogue

The Bakhtin Circle argued that the key conceptual tool for analysis is language or, more specifically, the utterance (Volosinov, 1976, 1986). Because the Bakhtinians anchored their work on the utterance, they emphasized that social context is essential to meaning. Whereas the "word" is abstract and removed from the speaker and listener, the "utterance" is concrete and can only be understood in the context of the specific speaker and listeners (Volosinov, 1976, p. 101). The Bakhtinian's insistence on tying meaning to the concrete situation forces us to deal with language as a social process instead of as an individual object. Since "meaning" can only be constructed in the concrete utterance, language only makes sense as a social concept. Descriptions that portray language as an individual act ignore the social medium in which language conveys meaning, thereby overlooking the heart of the process and preventing it from being a useful tool of cultural analysis.

In describing language as social, the Bakhtin Circle directs our attention to the communication process itself. They used the concept of dialogue to focus on the continuous flow of interaction and response among individuals. Verbal performance, whether oral or written, responds in some way to previous performances and, in turn, calls forth a response from others (Volosinov, 1986, pp. 95, 102). Language, as dialogue, is always in the process of becoming. "Individuals do not receive a ready-made language at all" (p. 81), Volosinov wrote, "rather, they enter upon the stream of verbal communication; indeed, only in this stream does their consciousness first begin to operate." Volosinov suggested that the individual first acquires language as a social activity and only then internalizes outward speech into inward speech. And since Volosinov also argues that individual thought is carried out in inward speech, individual consciousness arises from an ongoing process of social communication. The process of inner thought is not mechanical but a dynamic, internalized dialogue.

This dynamic conceptualization of the individual's relation to the social world provides a vital theoretical advance over the often stated portrayal of the individual as a passive instrument of a larger social structure. Instead it presumes that every individual has an active role in affecting the communication process and, hence, in continuing the ongoing reshaping of the culture. In short, human agency within the community is an essential consequence of this social dialogue.

For the Bakhtin Circle dialogic consciousness is not only social, it is historically and ideologically located within specific material and symbolic realms. Because individuals must construct their private thoughts and their public communication within the limit of language opportunities available at a given time and place, the individual human utterance is formed within historical constraints. Accordingly, Volosinov (1976) chose to call speech "behavioral ideology" (p. 91; 1986, p. 83). As part of a historically situated social dialogue, behavioral ideology represents the concrete manifestation of these limitations on the speech used by an individual (Volosinov, 1986, p. 70).

Volosinov developed his strongest analysis of behavioral ideology in his critique of Freud. In Freud, Volosinov (1976) found classic bourgeois philosophy at work: "A *sui generis* fear of history, an ambition to locate a world beyond the social and the historical, a search for this world precisely in the depths of the organic" (p. 14). In place of this classic liberal interpretation, Volosinov suggested that Freud's concept of the "unconscious" is no more than "unofficial conscious," those dialogic voices that are not recognized as legitimate by one's peers and, therefore, are not outwardly spoken (p. 85). Accordingly, Freudian psychoanalysis can be recast as a social dialogue located in a historical situation and ideologically bound where official and unofficial conscious struggle to direct the individual's public speech. The dialogic process, wherein the individual must enter into the flow of meaningful exchanges, represents the dynamic through which the individual is tied to historical and material conditions. In conversation one allows some and forbids some of the inward speech to become vocalized. Inward speech that becomes outwardly vocalized is probably that which is most compatible with the socially recognized ideology. The Bakhtinian concepts of official and unofficial conscious might be better conceived as "legitimated" and "nonlegitimated" voice. *In trying to understand human behavior, we must be cognizant that some voices are legitimated by the community and, therefore, vocalized, while other are nonlegitimated and, therefore, unspoken.*

With the Bakhtinian concept of dialogue the dualistic conceptualization of the individual and the society, whether Marxist or liberal, must be rejected. In its place, a dynamic concept of dialogue between inward and outward speech acts offers a way to understand the unification of human agency and culture, one that includes an understanding of the material representation of history and ideology. As a result, it can provide the theoretical groundwork from which ethnographers can study the opportunities and obstacles that affect the voices of the disempowered. But while the concept of dialogue helps explain the relationships between structure and agency, the Bakhtinian concept of multivoicedness helps show the complexity and contradictions that mark the lives of minority group members.

Multivoicedness

The Bakhtinians' contemporary L. S. Vygotsky understood clearly the need to conceive of a non-dualistic individual-society. For Vygotsky, like the Bakhtinians, the mechanism for this unification was found in language. Although we cannot be sure that the Bakhtin Circle and

Vygotsky knew of each other's work, they clearly had a similar vision regarding the social nature of the individual found in internal language. For Vygotsky inner speech was the mechanism whereby people become both more social and more individual. They become more social because their very thought is intimately tied to language. Yet the power of language makes possible the independence of the child, the potential extension of thought and activity through language. "Just as a mold gives shape to a substance," Vygotsky (1978) wrote, "words can shape an activity into a structure. However, that structure may be changed or reshaped when children learn to use language in ways that allow them to go beyond previous experiences when planning future action" (p. 28). The dialectic between thought and language was equated with the dialectic between the symbolic world and the material world and between the individual and the social. But emphasizing "inner" speech, Vygotsky converted this social process into a psychological concept. The Bakhtin Circle, on the other hand, maintained the sociological understanding by referring to "inward speech," "unofficial consciousnesses," and "voice," concepts related to social dialogue and historical conditions. Voice explicitly recalls the idea of utterance and, as a result, must always be located in dialogue, whether vocalized or inward. Consequently, while Vygotsky's concept of inner speech connects the individual and society, the Bakhtinian idea of nonlegitimated voice further locates consciousness in the social dialogue of the historical moment.

While this notion of dialogue unifies the traditional distinction between the individual and the social, the Bakhtinian use of the concept of multivoicedness *prohibits a* unified individual or a consensual society. This is so because a dialogue requires more than one voice and each voice has its own identity. Since individuals' inward speech is dialogical and social, individuals must be understood to speak with many voices. Official and unofficial consciousness are merely reflections of the multivoicedness of individuals' inward speech, of which some voices are legitimated and some are not. Likewise, language, as the concrete manifestation of historically situated culture, is impossible to perceive as something other than, in Bakhtin's words (1984), "an authentic dialogue of unmerged consciousnesses" (p. 221). Society must be understood as in continuous dialogue and, therefore, multivoiced and nonconsensual. This idea of autonomous, unmerged voices was called several things by Bakhtin, including heteroglossia, polyglot, polyphony, and multivocality, but multivoicedness seems to be a term that best captures the idea that any particular, concrete, historical dialogue is best described in terms of the multiple voices participating.

This multivoiced conceptualization of social moments was a direct challenge to both functionalists and those Marxists who portrayed social relations as monophonic ideological activities resulting from a predefined social structure. By contrast, the concept of dialogue as a multivoiced social activity explained how the ideas of the powerful gain and maintain legitimacy as well as how the disempowered can attempt to legitimate their ideas and beliefs to others. Through the concepts of dialogue and multivoicedness the Bakhtin Circle offered a framework for examining cultural continuity and change. Their ideas showed us that culture should be seen as a collection of historical events laden with a range of possibilities and shaped by the power resources of the individuals present. Thus, as the multiple voices within the individual and within the community struggle to control the direction of the acceptable dialogue, ideological expressions may be reinforced, reinterpreted, or rejected. An understanding of these processes is critical to radical ideological efforts to reformulate the terms of collective action.

A multivoiced ethnography, with its presentation of both dominant and other voices, should provide an approach that offers a more accurate rendition of the complex relations of cultural life. Moreover, by recognizing and recording the multiple voices occurring within communities, we should be able to analyze the specific factors that affect the formation in historical situations of legitimated collusions and subsequent social actions.

Carnival

Describing nonlegitimated voice within a community of powerfully maintained legitimated voices is made difficult by historical and ideological forces that affect expression in social dialogue. There are, nonetheless, points in community life that permit and even encourage expression of nonlegitimated voice. One such juncture is the carnivalesque. Similar to Turner's concept of the liminal and the liminoid, in *Rabelais and His World* (1984), Bakhtin suggests the twin concepts of the carnival (the carnival text, a medieval genre that represents the essence of popular culture in its freest, most democratic, most social form) and the carnivalesque (the modern remnant of the medieval carnival). The study of the medieval carnival can provide an example of one site where the nonlegitimated voice can find communal expression and establish the potential for legitimation and eventual collective action and suggest carnivalesque possibilities for our contemporary times.

Carnival is a public occasion marked by festivity, laughter, licentiousness, excess, and grotesqueness. Events such as New Orleans' Mardi Gras, Germany's Fasching, and Brazil's Carnival should not be confused with the carnival of medieval times. Rather they are examples of the carnivalesque that represent modern *remnants* of the medieval carnival. These modern versions possess some elements of their medieval forerunner while missing others. For our purpose, carnival should be understood as the "popular-festive life of the Middle Ages and the Renaissance; [where] all the peculiarities of this life have been preserved" (Bakhtin, 1984, p. 218). Medieval carnival with its belly-shaking laughter, its grotesque humor, its emphasis on feasting, defecating, disembowelment, coitus, and other body-related actions, its exaggeration, and its unwillingness to accept anything as sacred creates an arena where free expression of nonlegitimated voices can compete with the ideologies of the status quo. It contains the fundamental elements of popular critique as well as those of transformation and renewal. Bakhtin (1984) wrote,

> For the medieval parodist everything without exception was comic. Laughter was as universal as seriousness; it was directed at the whole world, at history, at all societies, at ideology. It was the world's second truth extended to everything and from which nothing is taken away. It was, as it were, the festive aspect of the whole world in all its elements, the second revelation of the world in play and laughter. (P. 84)

This second "revelation" is an occurrence that is often ignored by today's carnivalesque. True carnival life is not a debased, cynical, and negative derision of marginal groups as it has been distortedly conceived in modern times, but a rejuvenating, optimistic, and positive mockery aimed at everyone. When understood in its most universal sense, carnival offers a democratic, emancipatory, and transformative genre of social expression.

Vocalization

Carnival acts to release social tensions and to permit the formation of nascent counterhegemony. It accomplishes this through the laughter of the marketplace, the festivity of feasts, the material bodily principle, and images of death and rebirth. Combined, these features of carnival allow new expressions of freedom, recognize the dialectics of opposition, create the social bonds of human community, and celebrate the rejuvenation of human prospects. Such an arena contains the conditions necessary for the creation of class-consciousness, that is, the social legitimation of silenced voices. — carnival

voiced/non-voiced voice what is not acceptable
To show things are deemed acceptable

To those mired in the status quo, carnival's most noticeable feature is its shocking freedom, its license, its rejection of social norms, and its display of bizarre, grotesque images and behaviors couched in raucous, obscene laughter. To those within carnival, however, these actions mark the features of democratic possibility. Bakhtin (1984) explains, "Carnival celebrated temporary liberation from the prevailing truth and from the established order; it marked the suspension of all hierarchical rank, privileges, norms and prohibitions...It was hostile to all that was immortalized and completed" (p. 10). Medieval carnival represented a deliberate juncture from the normal social relationships, a meaningful reveling in the subversion of standard meaning. "For a short time life came out of its usual, legalized and consecrated furrows and entered the sphere of Utopian freedom" (p. 89).

This moment of freedom is revealed in the very laughter of the people, its liberating effects being the source of the humor. At a deep level, laughter releases people from fear of an inequitable, immutable society and, therefore, it deflates the seriousness of social relations, which depend on such assumptions. The feeling of escape created by laughter is a first step in the creation of alternative social expressions. As Bakhtin notes, "Complete liberty is possible only in the completely fearless world" (p. 47). Laughter, then, displaces the constraints of everyday definitions and allows the free expression of unofficial opinions. This, in itself, reveals carnival as an important psychosocial arena; however, its contribution to the formation of an alternative public consciousness is equally important.

Democracy in Opposition

Bakhtin's idea (1984) of medieval carnival presents a democratic setting not merely for some but for all. It incorporates all people, whether high-born or low, not discriminating among people in its mockery and laughter, but rather representing "the Utopian kingdom of absolute equality and freedom" (p. 264). By being drawn into the expression of the people's nonlegitimated culture, all hierarchy could be repudiated, all static definitions redefined, all truth ridiculed. Control over social symbols is restored to the power of individuals. In short, carnival established a realm where all had the right to legitimate expression of the unthinkable. As a result, this kind of social moment permits the restoration of democracy of expression and provides the potential for the formation of new, transformative conceptions capable of standing in opposition to the controlled structures of the official world.

For Bakhtin, this free, democratic setting promoted a capacity to create and sustain an alternative sociocultural framework. Carnival festivities, he wrote, "offered completely different, nonofficial, extra-ecclesiastical and extra-political aspects of the world, of man, and of human relations; they built a second world and a second life outside of officialdom, a world in which they lived during a given time of the year" (p. 6). This nonlegitimated community is more than an escape from "real" life. Bakhtin claimed that festive humor allows this social framework to challenge and symbolically overthrow the official order. In other words, carnival engages the serious world in direct, open opposition. As Bakhtin argued, "Festive folk laughter presents an element of victory not only over supernatural awe, over the sacred, over death; it also means the defeat of power, of earthly kings, of the earthly upper classes, of all that oppresses and restricts (p. 92).

Feasts provide an example of this oppositional potential. Official feasts of court or of "proper society" with their monolithic serious-ness and eternal and immutable truth supported the hierarchical and undemocratic status quo, while carnival feasts with their festive laugh-ter and temporary emancipation from the prevailing truth and estab-lished order claimed the exclusion of all hierarchical rank, privileges, norms, and prohibitions (p. 30). What is important about this parallel structure is not simply that a liberating setting and a democratic lev-eling allow the fool to become a king, but that the carnival laughter produces a subversive dialectical counterpoint. Writing about how the second world stands in opposition to the official state-defined world, Bakhtin said,

> Medieval laughter is directed at the same object as medieval serious-ness. Not only does laughter make no exception for the upper stratum, but indeed it is usually directed toward it. Furthermore, it is directed not at one part only, but at the whole. One might say that it builds its own world versus the official world, its own church versus the official church, its own state versus the official state. (P. 85)

This unofficial world of carnival is a world where all "first truths" are questioned and mocked, a world in which the dispossessed come to gain some control over the public definitions of interaction.

The laughter of the carnival feast is not just a personal strategy for coping with social order, but is a social strategy laden with the pos-sibility of transfer back to the social relations of the official world. "Through this victory, laughter clarified man's consciousness and gave him a new outlook on life," Bakhtin explained. "This truth was ephemeral; it was followed by the fears and expressions of everyday life, but from these brief moments another unofficial truth emerged, truth about the world and man which prepared the new Renaissance consciousness" (pp. 90–91). Carnival with all its grotesque images and bizarre humor is not a defeatist attitude accepting the inevitability of servitude, but rather a victorious celebration of the liberation of people over fear and oppression. The escape from the hopeless inevitability of the official world provides a second world where universal freedom and democracy permit the expression of unofficial voice. This victory of laughter over fear provides the key to carnival's potential as a site for open dialogue.

Social Solidarity
Victorious laughter alone is not enough to sustain a dialectic of opposition. The formation of social groups requires the establishment of bonds of solidarity. The process through which carnival encourages social solidarity begins with its drive to reduce, ideologically, all people to the same social level. This is evident in its use of the body. Carnival is not the abandonment of self to hedonistic egocentrism, as it is often portrayed, but a social affair acting as a continuous reminder that people find humanity in social communion rather than individual self-fulfillment. It is a celebration of people. Bakhtin (1984) recognized this in carnival's exaggerated interest in the human body.

> The material body is contained not in the biological individual, not in the bourgeois ego, but in people, a people who are continually growing and renewed...Manifestations of this [bodily] life refer not to the isolated biological individual, not to the private, egotistic economic man, but to the collective ancestral body of all the people. (P. 9)

In modern life the ribaldry of the medieval feast is seen as distasteful and degrading individual excess; however, feasting can be understood as a banquet for all the world because people, through their labor and struggle, have triumphed (p. 32). The bourgeois mentality conceives the human body as an individual isolated corpus and draws a protecting, impenetrable curtain between the individual and the world; but such thoughts do not apply to carnival where the body is not only penetrable, it is openly and graphically drawn into union with the world. In carnival's images the body is created by and in turn creates the external world. Eating and drinking, urinating and defecating, sexual intercourse and birth are all processes whereby the body is built, flushed, and renewed. Of course, it is precisely these raw, universal images that official culture rejects and fights to discredit and outlaw. In carnival, the emphasis on the material bodily principle inverts this official voice and displays officially private and vulnerable parts of life in order to break down the barrier between individuals in carnival laughter. By using these images to provoke laughter, carnival attempts to shock individuals into feelings of social community. "Medieval laughter," wrote Bakhtin, "is the social consciousness of all the people" (p. 92). Through festivity "the individual feels that he is an indissoluble part of the collectivity, a member of the people's mass body" (p. 255).

Because the symbols and actions of carnival shock individuals into a sense of solidarity, carnival promotes a social understanding of democratic freedom. It creates a primordial social ocean wherein nonlegitimated thoughts and feelings may join together in new expressions of social opinion. This potential realignment of the legitimated tensions of official social relations requires a transformative promise in addition to the vocalization and solidarity already discussed. Again, Bakhtin readily illustrates how this potential can be found in the swirl of carnival.

Transformative Promise

To understand how carnival, in promoting the generation of new forms of expression and solidarity, can serve as a potential site for renewal and transformation, it is necessary to understand the grotesque images of death and rebirth that are central to carnival festivities. Bakhtin (1984) pointed to the laughing, senile, and pregnant old women of Kerch to make this point. "It is pregnant death, a death that gives birth. There is nothing completed, nothing calm and stable in the bodies of these old hags. They combine a senile, decaying and deformed flesh with the flesh of new life, conceived but as yet unformed" (pp. 25–26). Bakhtin's point may be difficult for some of us to understand today since we are likely to read the medieval text within a modern (or postmodern) discourse. Some contemporary readers may have trouble grasping that this is a *positive* description bidding us to embrace the fullness of life in all its stages. Many modern readers may not be able to read this as anything but a negative depiction of women, but such a reading would be a mistake. It is in this image of pregnant and decaying "old hags" that hope for rebirth and democracy is found. Those who are only able to see this image as "grotesque" are trapped in the structures of a patriarchal bourgeois hegemony.

For Bakhtin, banquet images must be understood in terms of regeneration, in terms of life over death. "In this respect," he wrote, "it is equivalent to conception and birth. The victorious body receives the defeated world and is renewed" (p. 283). To the modern eye the black humor of medieval carnival seems to wallow in death, but that is because we tend to miss the link of death to birth that is an integral aspect of carnival. To defeat the unjust world is not enough, the social moment also contains an impetus requiring the death of the old to include the promise of rebirth. In other words, it is essential to understand that such social occasions contain strong relations between life, death, struggle, triumph, and regeneration. For revolution to succeed, the old must die and the new be built on its decayed flesh.

Bakhtin specifically notes that Rabelais wrote in a period of social reconstruction and that the spirit of Rabelais's work reflects the transformative nature of carnival (p. 403). In Rabelais, he explains,

> the old dying world gives birth to the new one. Death throes are combined with birth in one indissoluble whole. This process is represented in the images of the material bodily lower stratum; everything descends into earth and the bodily grave in order to die and to be reborn. This is why the downward movement pervades Rabelais' entire imagery from beginning to end. All these images throw down, debase, swallow, condemn, deny (topographically), kill, bury, send down to the underworld, abuse, curse; and at the same time they all conceive anew, fertilize, sow, rejuvenate, regenerate, praise and glorify. This general downward thrust, which kills and regenerates, unifies such different phenomena as blows, abuses, the underworld, and the act of devouring. (P. 435)

In carnival, Bakhtin shows us a genre capable of depicting the expression of nonlegitimated voices. Moreover, he illustrates how this expression provides for a democratic and emancipatory impulse for countercultures in the ideological dialogue of the community, one that can give birth to new social movements. Disempowered people, when forced to live within a stable, hierarchical system, often turn to the carnivalesque for rejuvenation. Surrounded by the "inevitability" of their lives, they may often seek the festivity of the bizarre and the freedom of the absurd in order to find an equitable world: a world in which all people, powerless or powerful, come to inhabit the same flow of life. Our tendency to label the grotesque and festive as delinquent, immature, or sadistic tells as much about our own immutable ties to our historical moment as it does about the true meaning of the acts. The grotesque and all the other carnivalesque behaviors must be understood as having the potential for emancipation and the kernels of transformation: they must be seen as the self-preserving actions of people seeking dignity.

While carnival holds much promise, we must always keep in mind that true carnival died with modernity. Carnival is a genre of the middle ages, not a social event likely to be found in the present. The point is not that carnival exists today, but that carnivalesque moments, which share some of the fundamental elements of carnival while lacking others, do arise. For those of us interested in the possibility of transformation, these carnivalesque moments should be understood to be imperfect examples of carnival and, therefore, flawed emancipatory moments. Like all cultural events, carnivalesque activities must be understood to be multivoiced, speaking partly to emancipation but also partly to oppression. Critical ethnographers should be as interested in revealing how carnivalesque moments differ from carnival as in showing how they are similar. They must reveal how the carnivalesque creates both possibility and reproduction at the same time.

In this way, carnival exposes the complexities inherent in community tensions and reveals the seeds of transformation located in the voices of the oppressed. It is one prominent point where multiple voices may find equality of expression in the public domain, where conditions for solidarity may be formed, and where mediated acceptance or resistance may be formulated by the oppressed. On the other hand, they are also moments in which the oppressed fail to complete the emancipatory impulses and to understand the democratic possibilities; these moments may even result in the participation of the oppressed in their own oppression. The carnivalesque activities of marginal people, the raucous laughter of many students, and the rowdy mockery of society's institutions by disenchanted youth (e.g., "punk") may all be understood as examples of nonlegitimated voice. The class clown, like the medieval clown, may in fact be the "herald of the second truth"; may in fact represent the expression of unofficial voice: however, we must understand this as an incomplete carnivalesque moment (Bakhtin, 1984, p. 95). While this extension of carnival deserves greater discussion, the argument here is for the need to recognize the profound importance of these interstitial social moments for scholars studying the problems of the disempowered. As multivoiced ethnographies emerge, particularistic analysis of these points may clarify the factors that restrict or promote the legitimation of the silenced voices.

Writing Ethnography of Marginalized Cultures

So far, part I of this chapter has explored some Bakhtinian themes that might help us read cultural texts; the second part will develop other Bakhtinian ideas that may help us write ethnographic texts. In researching and writing ethnography, one must describe the dynamic

marginalized cultures/
ethnography work

and conflictual nature of marginalized cultures, record the dialogues that bind the individual into a private world and a social community, and reveal the many voices struggling for expression. Realizing this, the ethnographer must not construct a single set of patterns from single-minded individuals, but must present a range of legitimated and nonlegitimated voices found in the community. This range may be focused by centering on those points in the community (like carnival) where the relationships among history, people, and ideas are revealed. In his analysis of fiction Bakhtin provided us with analytic concepts that can help accomplish this task. Accordingly, we shall explore his notions of time and space, characterization, ideology, and ambivalence for their value in creating critical ethnography and lead us to the possibility of ritual critique.

Time and Space

According to Bakhtin, Dostoevsky's principal literary technique was to make time stand still and reveal life by bringing contradictions into a common space. In this way, the multidimensional aspects of characters, social situations, or issues are revealed. "Dostoevsky," Bakhtin (1973) wrote,

> attempted to perceive the very stages themselves in *their simultaneity,* to *juxtapose* and *counterpose* them dramatically, and not stretch them out into an evolving sequence. For him, to get one's bearings on the world meant to conceive all its contents as simultaneous, and *to guess at their interrelationships in the cross-section of a single moment.* (P. 30; emphasis in the original)

Coexistence and interaction are the fundamental principles of dialogue and, consequently, of life. To illustrate this point, Dostoevsky suspended the flow of time in his stories and made possible the careful presentation of all the voices speaking at once. This strategy allowed the author to emphasize the relationship of ideas, people, and historical conditions. As a result, ideas can be viewed in context of competing ideologies, people can be seen in conflict with others, and material conditions can be drawn as historical moments. In writing up the results of our observations, we should also seek to present these contexts.

Like Dostoevsky, the ethnographer who wishes to represent the coexistence of multiple voices in the social arena must reexamine the framework of space and time within which they present their findings. Traditional methods generally attempt to distill ideas into a unified, abstract structure, to isolate individuals as objectified subjectivities, and to organize cultural patterns into atemporal systems. Bakhtin's theory of alternative space/time presentation provides the ethnographer with a way to avoid these biases. His ideas demand that the ethnographer replay the multiple voices that created the original scene. The presentation of informants' comments in such temporally situated, multiple-coexistent writing would, in a sense, parallel the presentation of disparate perspective found in cubist painting or polyphonic music. Bakhtin used the music metaphor in describing Dostoevsky's novels as polyphonic. Bakhtin's use (1973) of polyphony implies the weaving of autonomous, unmerged themes throughout a single composition. The polyphonic novel builds a single text out of the unmerged consciousness of the various characters. Each voice maintains an integrity even while contributing to the whole (p. 28). Accordingly, we can use Bakhtin's metaphor to call such cultural descriptions "polyphonic ethnography" and contrast it with the typical practice, "homophonic ethnography."

Polyphonic ethnographies could present the utterances of disempowered groups in dialogue both externally and internally. They would show people in dialogue amongst themselves as well as in dialogue with social elites. Also these dialogues should be isolated in time. Portraying a cultural scene as isolated in time does *not* mean to present culture as atemporal. To see a culture as isolated in time is to recognize that time is an essential element that contributes to the existing relationships. Thus while ethnographers must stop time to juxtapose elements spatially, they must also explain the historical moment in which these relationships exist. As we have pointed out, Bakhtin sees historical conditions as crucial to an understanding of dialogue. Unfortunately, when writing ethnographies of the disempowered groups, many ethnographers tend to ignore the historical conditions that help constitute the cultural dynamic. The traditional "ethnographic present" seems to make timeless that which, in reality, exists in time and makes the culture appear to be "outside of" rather than "isolated in" time. And while newer ethnographies have abandoned the use of the ever-present, they still typically avoid placing their cultural descriptions in material constraints. Bakhtin's work suggests that such ethnography fails to portray an accurate picture of the culture. Yet, when analysis and description of history are combined with the spatial juxtaposition, the utterances of the disempowered can be situated within the greater dialogue of the day. Subcultures thus are not isolated from the powerful, their culture is set into relation to the dominant cultures surrounding them; they are not portrayed as outside of time, but seen in relation to historical forces.

Characterization

Writers of polyphonic ethnographies must characterize their informants differently than traditional ethnographers. Again, Dostoevsky's literary techniques provide possibilities for this process.

Bakhtin (1973) described a Dostoevsky hero as a character who makes possible the presentation of a perspective.

> The hero interests Dostoevsky as a *particular point of view on the world and on oneself,* as the position enabling a person to interpret and evaluate his own self and his surrounding reality. What is important to Dostoevsky is not how his hero appears in the world but first and foremost how the world appears to his hero, and how the hero appears to himself. (P. 47; emphasis in the original)

This approach to the hero stands in contrast to those novelists who fill their characters with ideas and words that fit the story constructions rather than the character. Bakhtin was suspicious of these authors. Their characters do not remain true to themselves, but are prisoners of the author's discretion. He argued that Dostoevsky attempted to retain the integrity of each character's voices. A similar concern must be shared by the polyphonic ethnographer.

Dostoevsky's approach to this problem follows from the idea that dialogue is the person. "The author constructs the hero not out of words foreign to the hero," Bakhtin wrote, "not out of neutral definitions; he constructs not a character, nor a type, nor a temperament, in fact he constructs no objectified image of the hero at all, but rather the hero's *discourse* about himself and his world" (p. 53; emphasis in the original). Following such a principle, ethnography can be seen as essentially a process of uncovering and presenting the voices of historical characters. To avoid shaping these individuals into the image preconceived by the author, it is essential to illustrate their vision of the world and themselves through their dialogue. To understand and recreate the social dimensions of the community, characters need to be seen as important because of their discourse rather than because of our descriptions of them.

While Bakhtin was willing to allow characters to represent a particular point of view, he was not interested in artificially portraying individuals as unified voices. He reminded us that individuals are polyglot. Inner speech is constituted of many voices, some legitimated and others not. This contradiction is evident in Dostoevsky's frequent division of characters into more than one so that he could set up a dialogue between one voice and another, which, as Bakhtin wrote, ended up forcing a character to converse with his own double, with the devil, with his alter ego, with his own caricature (Ivan and the Devil, Ivan and Smerdyakov, Raskolnikov and Svidrigailov, and so forth). This characteristic explains the frequent occurrence of paired characters in Dostoevsky's work. One could say, in fact, that out of every contradiction within a single person Dostoevsky tries to create two persons, in order to dramatize the contradiction and develop it extensively (p. 28).

While novelists have the ability to divide these voices artificially, ethnographers do not. Of course, occasionally one's "double" actually does exist in real life, and ethnographers, rather than ignoring such "alter egos" as contradictory in those cases where they are found, must listen carefully for evidence of the multivoicedness that characterizes their informants' consciousnesses. Instead of pushing for some form of consistency and coherence, ethnographers must chart the contradictions and conflicts that mark their informants' lives.

When listening to the disempowered, we must listen closely to the multiple voices with which they speak. Accordingly, we should expect to hear the conflicts that have been set up within them. This is especially true for those ethnographers interested in discovering how the dominant cultures have penetrated the consciousness of the disempowered and given them a voice that leads them to participate in their own oppression. If we listen to individuals as if they were Dostoevsky heroes and accept them as contradictory polyglots, then we should, in our ethnographic portrayal of them, be more likely to treat them with integrity than as products of our own constructions.

Ideology

The presentation of dialogue is not simply an act of accurate reporting. As Volosinov showed, dialogue is an ideological process; consequently, polyphonic ethnographies are inherently concerned with ideology. The same is true of Dostoevsky novels. His stories are written around ideas. These ideas are presented only within the speech of the characters, thus the inward and outward dialogues become the embodiment of each book's ideas. Bakhtin (1973) explained,

> The ideas begin to live, that is, to take shape, to develop, to find and renew its verbal expression, to give birth to new ideas, only when it enters into genuine dialogic relationships with other ideas, with the ideas of *others*. Human thought becomes genuine thought, that is, an idea, only under conditions of living contact with another and alien thought, a thought embodied in someone else's voice, that is, in someone else's consciousness expressed in discourse. At that point of contact

between voice-consciousness the idea is born and lives. (P. 88; emphasis in the original)

Like novels, historical moments involve the working out of ideas. Polyphonic ethnographies, in their recording of dialogue, are engaged in examining the ideology of the culture at that point in time.

Volosinov's critique of Freud lays the groundwork for the exploration of ideology in minority cultures. His use of official and unofficial consciousness to replace Freud's conscious and unconscious makes possible the revelation of ideology through the internal dialogue of informants. Of course this also requires the ethnographer to establish a relationship with informants that enables him or her to hear their fears, fantasies, and dreams. It demands that the ethnographer have skill and patience enough to obtain his or her informants' confidences. This is not a matter of psychological analysis, but rather a concern to learn about the nonlegitimated voices of a people, the boundaries of the ideology of the time.

By searching for ideologies within the dialogue of individuals in a historical setting, the ethnographer must be willing to juxtapose outward vocalizations that comprise public acts. This treatment, however preferable to homophonic studies, may still overlook the underlying ideological tensions within the community, the forces leading to the unfolding of the ideas present and possible. To do this, one must compare outward speech to inward speech and look for the contradictions of the moment. Not only should the unvoiced speech of the disempowered help lay bare the hegemonic workings of the dominant ideologies, but it should also reveal the potential for ideological transformation.

outward speech / inward speech [handwritten marginal note]

Ambivalence

The ideological tension between inward and outward voice that supports the public culture means that the polyphonic writer must be especially sensitive to the many ambivalences contained in cultural expressions. Official symbols purport to be universal and noncontradictory; yet, rarely do individuals live within such monolithic arrangements. Their real lives are spent manipulating the undefined terms of cultural discourse to their advantage. Laws are both protecting and oppressing, institutions are both helpful and obstructive, the critical difference lies in the terms in which one negotiates this ambivalence.

Similarly, unofficial symbols carry their ideological potential in ambivalence. Bakhtin's analysis of Rabelais emphasized the ambivalence that is essential to carnival life. If the grotesque forms of carnival are not to be debased to mere mockery and trivialized to coarse humor (as happens so much with parody in the modern world), then it is essential that these symbols contain the latitude for individuals to negotiate the dialectical tensions of unofficial and official ideology. The world of carnival thus maintains double meanings in all its images; death is linked to birth, defecation with eating, urinating with drinking, war with celebration. In these unofficial moments, the individual must reconceive his or her full relation to social life. The ambivalence that permits the expression of fear of death and hope of rebirth, of misery in laughter and laughter in misery, of good in evil and evil in good provides a rich and complex site for the development of an ideological voice.

The polyphonic writer, then, must examine the ways in which individuals create and maintain ambivalence in their ideological communities. The researcher of disempowered cultures must learn to use these ambivalences to create alternative images and actions; that is, in carnival terms, to reflect the second truths of the nonlegitimated voices. Thus, our study of schools may reveal that the high status of the class clown, the ribaldry found in making a fool of the teacher, the decidedly festive atmosphere of school cafeterias serve as carnivalesque moments. These unofficial moments of social expression may illustrate how the grotesque humor of disempowered students may be fundamentally democratic, potentially emancipatory ideological actions taken within the ambivalences of the carnivalesque. Likewise, the odd sounds, the flippant jokes behind teachers' backs may serve as ideological challenges to the stifling seriousness of official school life. Certainly the sociability engendered by such festive acts suggests the utilization of these moments to counter the moments of individual risk of failure in official class activities. Approaching the ethnography of the disempowered people with the recognition of the ambivalences of social discourse, especially those promoted by the unofficial and the carnivalesque, may help us understand the ideological dynamics of the oppressed.

By implicating the researcher in the construction of the culture being described, this essay shares much with those ethnographers influenced by poststructural and postmodern theory. On the other hand, with its clear recognition of material history as equally implicated in the structuring of culture, the Bakhtin Circle keeps us firmly in the modernist project of critical theory. With Volosinov's insistence that all speech acts are no more than behavioral ideology, we are forced to explore and clarify the material history that fills cultural performances. As I explored both ethnography and ritual in light of the writing of the Bakhtin Circle I began to suspect that "ethnography" with its goal and claim to "describe culture" might not be a productive approach to researching ritual. After working with Peter Magolda on an exploration of a university class in science education (see chapter four), I began to research ritual in seminar-style undergraduate classes. The more I observed and reflected on this process, the more I felt that in order to take full advantage of the Bakhtinian insights I needed to move in a different direction than what we normally consider ethnography.

PART II: CONSIDERING RITUAL CRITIQUE

By the time I had completed my study of undergraduate seminar teaching, I had abandoned the idea of ethnography but not yet fully embraced the idea of critique. The result is a study that exists somewhere in between (see chapter five). But as I worked on my next study, which involved a full year of fieldwork in five high schools, I became much more confident in the direction my methodology had to move. I returned to the Bakhtin Circle for a few more concepts and the result is the method I refer to as "ritual critique." While ritual critique, as I have developed it, shares some vocabulary with and has much sympathy for approaches to research influenced by French poststructuralism, it is influenced much more by the Russian Bakhtin Circle (particularly the work of Bakhtin and Volosinov). Like consciously poststructural (or postmodern) approaches to research, ritual critique is skeptical of social scholarship that considers itself a "science" and that objectifies, distances, abstracts, and de-politicizes the research process. Unlike consciously poststructural approaches to research, however, ritual critique assumes a different understanding of semiotic construction. This different semiotics leads to a subtle, but not unimportant, difference in meaning making and, therefore, in methodology.

Many suggest that the work of Bakhtin is, in fact, postmodern. With its shift from the sign to the utterance as the smallest unit of meaning, the Bakhtinians share much with poststructuralists. However, the Bakhtinians never abandoned their commitment to a Marxist semiotics that recognized the centrality of material history in the structuring of social life. In this manner, the Bakhtin Circle provides us with a way to gain the advantage of poststructuralism and postmodernism without abandoning the modernist democratic project that many of us remain committed to. In the following paragraphs I provide some further reflections on some Bakhtinian concepts discussed earlier but developed in ways to clarify their importance to ritual critique, plus I present some Bakhtinian ideas not discussed earlier at all.

The most useful of the several Bakhtinian contributions to social and linguistic philosophy derive from what is often referred to as "dialogism" (a frequently misunderstood set of ideas often confused with mere "conversation"). Bakhtinian dialogism relies on several interrelated ideas of which a few have been influential in the development of this project.

From Sign to Utterance (Speech Performance): Revisited

Volosinov (1986) pointed out that every sign is constructed in social interaction and that all participants in such interactions are themselves socially organized (p. 21). As a result, every sign includes the ideological and existential moment of the participants in the interaction. In other words, *the meaning of a sign cannot be separated from its* use *in a socially constructed moment.* This is the reason Volosinov argued that the smallest unit of meaning is the utterance not the sign. Signs outside of dialogue are without social location and, therefore, without meaning *in themselves.* On the other hand, signs embedded in dialogue (i.e., utterances) carry the meanings of the individual participants as well as the socially (i.e., historically) organized action. While French poststructuralism rejects the emphasis on the signified found in Saussurian linguistics, it embraces the Saussurian emphasis on the sign (i.e., the signifier/signified) as the smallest unit of meaning. Such an emphasis on *langue* without *parole* leaves poststructuralists to conclude that meaning is radically "deferred" (Derrida, 1973). Volosinov's insistence that meaning lies only in utterance (i.e., *langue* and *parole*) suggests that any particular speech act has "once-occurrent" meaning in the "Being-as-ongoing-event." The differences between these two positions (i.e., the French and the Russian) are in some ways quite minor since both reject the idea that particular texts carry transcendental or fixed meanings, but they are in other ways profound in that the Bakhtinian view suggests that comments made in dialogue are filled with meaning and meaning with politics and not mere empty signifiers.

From Text to Performance

Clifford Geertz (1972) helped us realize that ethnography is not only a text in itself but that the object of the ethnography is also a text. That is, culture itself can be understood to be a text that is read by cultural participants and it is the job of the ethnographer to read the text "over their shoulders." But understanding culture as text privileges fixed meaning and so some who have been influenced by French poststructuralism have begun to emphasize "performance" rather than "text." Similarly ritual critique, as developed here, emphasizes performance rather than text. In the case of ritual critique, however, performance is understood to be a gesture in dialogue rather than a sign whose meaning is forever deferred (if influenced by Derrida) or as enacted discourse (if influenced by Foucault). As a gesture in dialogue, performance is an utterance and carries meaning derived from both the individual participants as well as the socially (i.e., historically) constructed interaction. Performance, then, becomes the central object of analysis.

Performance As Reported Speech

In *Toward a Philosophy of the Act*, written around 1920, Bakhtin (1993) presented the earliest version of one basic problem that remained central to nearly all of the subsequent work of the Bakhtin Circle and becomes central to my reconceptualization of method. The problem lies in the fundamental alienation of the "performance" from the "account." For Bakhtin, any particular act can only be understood within the whole of an individual's Being, which itself is an ongoing, constructed series of events. Since each act is itself a "once-occurrent event of Being," to abstract it out of the total once-and-future history of the individual is to relocate the event into a totally different realm of meaning. In other words, any retelling of an event is not the event (performance) but a retelling (account).[2] While the performance only gains meaning in its relations within the ongoing life of the individual, the account gains meaning in its location within an abstract set of relations such as "science" or "philosophy" or "art."

A unique form of the radical disjuncture between performance and account can be found in the concept of "reported speech" discussed at length by Volosinov (1986). Reported speech is the account of a particular utterance within the speech act of another speaker. When I quote directly the words of another author, I am using reported speech. Reported speech should not be confused with the original speech act and, yet, as incorporated within my speech act, it can bring with it some of the original characteristics that help construct its meaning.

Reported speech is regarded by the speaker as an utterance belonging to *someone else*, an utterance that was originally totally independent, complete in its construction, and lying outside the given context. Now, it is from this independent existence that reported speech is transposed into an authorial context while retaining its own referential content and at least the rudiments of its own linguistic integrity, its original constructional independence. The author's utterance, in incorporating the other utterance, brings into play syntactic, stylistic, and compositional norms for its partial assimilation—that is, its adaptation to the syntactic, compositional, and stylistic design of the author's utterance, while preserving (if only in rudimentary form) the initial autonomy (in syntactic, compositional, and stylistic terms) of the reported utterance, which otherwise could not be grasped in full (p. 116).

While there are many implications for Volosinov's discussion of reported speech, in this particular instance, the most important is its suggestion for how a scholar should understand both the processes of investigating and those of representing instances of performance because, while such representations may be many things, they are certainly examples of "accounts" that utilize reported speech as the primary mechanism for construction of meaning.

While there exists a radical disjuncture between the worlds of performance and account, these two realms can be brought together in a dialogue (of sorts) between the two. As Michael Holquist explains in the forward to *Philosophy of the Act*, "The act is a deed, and not a mere happening..., only if the subject of such a *postupok* [i.e., "performative act"], from within his own radical uniqueness, weaves a relation *to* it in his accounting *for* it" (Bakhtin, 1993, pp. xii–xiii; emphasis in the original, bracketed insertion my own). Through the attempt to weave a fabric of the two (performance and account), we make moral action possible by creating an "answerable act" or "deed" that is open to judgment. So while the performance and the account inhabit two different realms of truth and meaning, moral action requires their engagement of each other.

The task for the scholar then is how to approach the field study itself and then how to represent its findings in such a way as to acknowledge moral responsibility. Whatever methods are used, they must be considered in light of the two separate realms of performance and account. As a researcher in the field, I am an actor in a dialogic performance. I am a participant in the performance I am observing even if only as a spectator. As a scholar writing up my findings, I incorporate reported speech in a monologic utterance that represents (i.e., re-presents) a dialogic performance. How I dealt with the second set of problems (i.e., constructing the account) is found in the concrete example in chapter six. How I dealt with the first (i.e., participating in the performance) is briefly presented next.

In the Field

The fieldwork for the high school study began in two dramatically different high schools. One was a well-respected, economically stable, suburban school and the other an economically vulnerable, urban school with a reputation that reflected its lack of privilege. I had free reign to wander the schools and I spent every spare moment I could find in one or the other. I spent my time quietly observing every aspect of both schools from hallways to cafeterias to study halls to teacher's lounges to libraries to classrooms of various subject matters. While I did not ignore spoken words, I focused primarily on physical gestures including clothing, body locations and movements, vocal inflections, and large-group massing and movements. I was looking particularly for some evidence of ritual. Ritual is an especially interesting type of performance because its repetitive form provides a continuity across discontinuous instances. That is, since ritual has recognizable and expected form, it makes itself visible across geographic, temporal, and social locales. After recognizing several potential ritual practices, I selected a few to focus my study. From that point on, I restricted my observations to situations that were likely to produce such ritual performances. Many observations of these rituals allowed me to construct characteristic elements of the repeated forms of the rituals and then to begin to explore possible meanings. When I felt confident of having fully absorbed the ritual aspects of the interaction patterns found in the original two schools, I began to observe in three other high schools as checks on what I had been observing in the first two. By attempting to place myself in situations that might possibly call for similar ritual performances, I was able to see if the basic forms of the rituals appeared in completely different high schools and, if so, what variations might occur.

The Account

I make no claim that the abstracted ritual form that I detail in either chapter five or six and its possible symbolic meanings exist in the "performances" themselves. The form and its potential symbolic meanings are located in my "accounts," which themselves exist as utterances in an academic dialogue. My use of narrative anecdotes are similar to reported speech in that they provide injections of other voices though these voices are molded and fit into an otherwise monological text. The special value of my particular account lies only in its presumable contribution as an utterance in the larger dialogue of educational scholars and must not be confused with some mythical "truth" about some mythical "real world." On the other hand, this process of constructing an account of my own participation in the ritual performances within these schools also allows me to bring meaning to and accept moral responsibility for my actions through the weaving of a web that connects my deeds and my words.

Taken together chapters four, five, and six reveal a progression in my approach to researching ritual. Ritual critique provides a method that has all the advantages of poststructural and postmodern approaches to ethnography but without abandoning a recognition of material history in the formation of societies. It never confuses the researcher's account with the actual performance, but also maintains that a real political meaning imbues the performance. Performances cannot mean anything. While they are complex, dialogic, and multivoiced, they do carry hegemonic ideology throughout. The task of "the critic," as opposed to "the ethnographer," is to find a way to present the multiple voices in dialogue while also revealing the potential distortions between these performative meanings and the material lives of the oppressed and disempowered. Chapter six provides the fullest realization of this method as it struggles with providing both the multiple concrete instances of the ritual performance against a background of real politics.

4

Nonrational Classroom Performance

Ritual as Aspect of Action

With Peter M. Magolda

When people argue for the importance of ritual in contemporary education, they are usually referring to formal ceremonies that can be used to help forge common ideals and identities. The daily morning ceremony at the Harman Elementary School located in a Midwestern city is one such example.[1]

Life at Harman Elementary School

When asked to describe her school community, Mrs. Freeman, a teacher at Harmon Elementary School, explained:

> We begin each day with our morning ritual involving the entire staff and student body, along with parents who have brought their children to school. At 7:50 a.m., the bell rings, which signals students to line up on the yellow line labeled with their room number. Teachers take their places near their class and other staff members assemble (minus kitchen and clerical staff). Mrs. Robinson [the Principal] is already posed on the steps with intermediate students lined up to her left and primary students to her right. She greets everyone and we, in unison, greet her. At this time, three volunteers from a pre-designated classroom have already joined her to lead the assembly in our morning routine/ritual. The first child identifies him/herself by name and room number then leads us in the pledge. The second child proceeds accordingly with introduction, then leads us through the Harman School Mission (which staff, students and parents had a part in writing).
>
> The Harman School Mission,
> is preparing students today,

for a successful tomorrow,
by developing,
academic excellence,
and positive self-concepts,
to foster values,
and achievement for all.

The assembly repeats each section of our mission statement after the student leader. The third student, after introductions, leads us in the song, "Lift Every Voice and Sing" [also known as "The Black National Anthem"] after receiving the beginning key from a child with a recorder. Afterward, Mrs. Robinson thanks the student leaders and compliments the student body for having nice, straight lines. Then in a loud voice, she says, "What are we here for?"

Students respond, "To learn."

Mrs. R.: "What is school?"
Students: "Our job!"
Mrs. R.: "What is homework?
Students: "Our responsibility to our job!"
Mrs. R.: "How can we do our job?"
Students: "We can do it well!
Mrs. R.: "You are smart students and you have excellent teachers and staff members who care about you, and together we can—what?"
Everyone: "We can do it well!"

Mrs. Robinson concludes with special announcements, her expectations regarding behavior, her promise to come around to visit some classrooms, and then wishes everyone a great day. Classrooms are dismissed one at a time in an orderly fashion as she calls the room numbers. Students are expected to maintain silence and straight lines all the way to their classrooms.

—Personal note to one of the authors

Rituals such as this one—large, formal ceremonies—may be important mechanisms to be used in trying to transform urban schools. But in our opinion, as important as large, formal ceremonies may be, it is in the small rituals of ordinary, daily school life where the real work of creating community (or in resisting it) occurs. We are talking about what Goffman (1967) called "interaction rituals": especially those little actions between individuals that work to symbolically affirm or challenge the location of the individual in the status quo that he called "minor ceremonies" [or that Grimes (1990) calls "decorum"].

The rules of conduct which bind the actor and the recipient together are the bindings of society. But many of the acts which are guided by these rules occur infrequently or take a long time for their consummation. Opportunities to affirm the moral order and the society could therefore be rare. It is here that ceremonial rules play their social function, for many of the acts which are guided by these rules last but a brief moment, involve no substantive outlay, and can be performed in every social interaction. Whatever the activity and however profanely instrumental, it can afford many opportunities for minor ceremonies as long as other persons are present. Through these observances, guided by ceremonial obligations and expectations, a constant flow of indulgences is spread through society, with others who are present constantly reminding the individual that he must keep himself together as a well demeaned person and affirm the sacred quality of these others. The gestures which we sometimes call empty are perhaps in fact the fullest things of all. (Goffman, 1967, pp. 90–91)

Compare the Harman school example with a tale about a group of college students' first day of class as recorded by one of the authors. The setting is Midland College, located in a small, Midwestern urban community. You will find much more difference in the nature of the rituals then in the fact that one occurs in an elementary school courtyard and the other in a college classroom.

LIFE AT MIDLAND COLLEGE

"Is this 408?" the young woman carrying the knapsack slung over her shoulder asked. "No, 404" a nearby male student responded. The woman, scanning the piece of paper clutched in her hand, confirmed that she was in the wrong room and quickly exited. Without missing a beat, the male, while sticking his finger into a hole in the black slate-top laboratory table, turned to a woman sitting next to him and asked, "Is this where the Bunsen Burner goes?" The woman shrugged her shoulders, as the man continued his preoccupation with the hole in the table.

The room looked like a stereotypical high school laboratory that doubled as an equipment storeroom, not a college science laboratory. No high technology gadgets or supercomputers were visible, only rows of twelve-feet-long tables with the electrical outlet boxes affixed to tops with holes spaced equidistant from each other used to attach lab apparatus to the tabletop. Periodic table, spectrum, and planetary charts lined the walls. The clutter of equipment—telescopes, discarded computers, tripods, yardsticks, stools, globes, overflowing storage cabinets stuffed with scales, test tubes, fulcrums—lined the perimeter of the room, conveying that storage space was at a premium. Students maneuvered around the equipment as they circled the room to greet friends.

The students' first day of class attire was remarkably similar. Most were dressed in casual attire regardless of their age, gender, physical attributes, socioeconomic status, and ethnicity. Faded denim jeans, t-shirts, backward caps, and designer athletic shoes were the essential fashion components of the men's uniform. Men made no effort to conceal their allegiances to their favorite athletic teams, music icons, and fashion designers. Hornets, Bulls, Cowboys, Bengals, Stone Temple Pilots, U2, and Nike logos were prominently displayed on shirts and caps. While most men pledged allegiance to national sports teams, alternative music acts, and high profile sports apparel manufacturers, a few paid homage to nearby high school and college teams. Women's attire was also relaxed but slightly more color coordinated and tidy. Cool summer white, beige, and mauve were the colors of choice for blouses, augmenting denim and khaki shorts and open toe sandals. Two women sported the "Just Do It" slogan on their t-shirts, but most women's designer allegiances were more subtly displayed. Backpacks, slung exclusively over one shoulder, transcended gender; everyone had one. These "uniforms," which to a causal observer might appear as anything but uniform, signaled that these individuals were students and school was in session.

The buzz of multiple concurrent conversations filled the air as I tried to select a lab table to call "home" for the upcoming semester. Three of the tables were already full with four students, the maximum number allowed for each team. I bypassed these groups in favor of a table where three students, two women and a man, clustered.

I introduced myself to the three students mulling around the lab station. They reciprocated; "Hi, I'm Gail...Marlon...Iris." This station, located in the middle of the room, offered an optimal vantage point for me to observe other lab teams' activities as well as my own team. The station was less than optimal for copying notes from the blackboard at the far end of the rectangular room. I attempted to read the posters and flyers haphazardly tacked onto the bulletin board adjacent to the blackboard in the front of the room. I ascertained colors and headlines, but not the smaller print. Gail, noticing my squinting, assured me that I could copy her notes if I had trouble reading the board. Her hospitable nature influenced me to join the group.

I dropped my briefcase on the tabletop, sat down on the wooden stool, discretely opened my briefcase, and retrieved the syllabus that

Dr. Enid, the instructor, had given to me the previous week. I reviewed the syllabus and my notes scribbled in the margins:

Teacher Education (EDD) xxx—"Physical Science"...topics: physics, motion, energy, wave motion and sound, electricity, chemistry, lights...lab and lecture course...lectures—Tuesdays and Thursday mornings for 75 minutes each...lab meets weekly on Wednesday afternoons for two hours...EDD xxx is the first course of a two sequence science course required for all teacher education majors...non elementary major can use the course to fulfill general education requirement...enrollment = 24 students...no science background needed...

Gail and Iris seated across from me, conversed. Gail, dressed in a gray summer top with shorts, shook her shoulder length blond hair from her face as she spoke. Their fluid conversation suggested that they already knew and liked each other. They exchanged information about their upcoming semester classes and work schedules as they called out to classmates whom they recognized. Eventually, the conversation turned to EDD xxx. They compared notes about the mythology of the class. "I hear this course is tough, really tough; Dr. E. is no nonsense," Iris commented. Gail added, "I heard that A's were impossible to come by."

Marlon, seated next to me, unloaded his backpack. He pulled out the required text, a calculator, ruler, notebook, Bible, pen, and a roll of candy. He shared his scouting report about the class. "My girlfriend took this class last year and did really good [sic]. This is a really impossible course, I hope I survive." Gail and Iris resumed their conversation, pointing out different members of the class, providing brief biographies on each. "He is in my 204 class...She was in my psych class last semester...I thought he transferred to Centerville [college]..." I divided my time between listening to Iris and Gail's conversation and resuming my classroom observations. As I turned around to get acquainted with the lab groupings behind me, I noticed that Dr. Enid had arrived and was unpacking her belongings. I thought that her arrival would subdue the students' conversations, but I was mistaken.

*   *   *

We are interested in the small everyday rituals evidenced here because we are convinced that nonrational social mechanisms contribute much more to the construction of the social than is normally given credit. Perhaps contemporary social theorists have been overly influenced by a modern faith in the rational basis of action leading them to confuse

Weber's observations that modernity demands rational legitimacy with the belief that, therefore, individuals in modern organizations are too wise to be influenced by the nonrational. However as Bocock (1974) points out, Weber

> tends to see the non-rational as disappearing in modern society, rather than as being changed in form, but still very much present, as it was in other historical periods. He assumed that the growth of rational action in modern European society would entail the decrease of the non-rational in human lives. This is not so. We can now see..., that even the most rational types of action have non-rational sources. This does not necessarily reduce their rationality. But it does mean that the non-rational in human life has not simply disappeared. It is still at work in modern man. (P. 34)

We agree with Bocock that the nonrational is alive and well in human action. Perhaps what is most misunderstood is the realization that rationality and nonrationality may work hand-in-hand, side-by-side. The intertwining of rationality and nonrationality becomes particularly clear in large ceremonies such as the Harman School example presented at the start of this chapter. Notice the rational, cognitive aspects of their morning exercise. Certainly we could devote an entire chapter to investigating the rational basis for each of the various parts of this ritual. In particular we could analyze the meaning of such symbols as the school creed, individual introductions, and straight lines. But to do so would miss perhaps the most important aspect of this ritual, which is found not in the meaning of the chants and songs or the wisdom or ideology of the authoritative statement of the principal, but is located in the nonrational effects resulting from the whole school gathered together to participate jointly in these acts.

By joining together, these students and their teachers help construct social solidarity. We agree with Kertzer (1988) when he writes, "Solidarity is produced by people acting together, not by people thinking together" (p. 76). The feelings of community that arise through ritual result less from the sharing of some common idea and more from the sharing of some common experience. But while these performances help construct solidarity, they not only lead to the construction of a single, egalitarian "community," they may also work to reconfirm social hierarchies (Warner, 1941; 1959) or to increase social conflict (Gilmore, 1975), even to assist in revolution (Kertzer, 1988). Ritual is important to study because it is one of the major social mechanisms that utilize nonrationality to construct schools as places of community

(Hays, 1994) or of domination (Bernstein, 1977) or even of resistance (Hall & Jefferson, 1976; McLaren, 1999) or of struggle.

Unfortunately, as long as ritual is equated with large ceremonies instead of including the ordinary activities of ordinary days, we will tend to both underestimate and misunderstand the power of ritual in classrooms. While it may be easy to see both the rationality and non-rationality of formal ceremonies such as the Harman School morning ritual, it is in the informal rituals such as found in our Midland College example that this power may be most potently situated. In the grindingly ordinary and mundane world of everyday school life that appears so banal and irrelevant, we may find the key to school's inertial power.

When people first start to think of ritual as formalized, symbolic performance, they often attempt to categorize specific acts as ritual (e.g., Mrs. Robinson's daily interactions with students) or not ritual (e.g., Midland College students' greetings). We believe this to be unproductive. A more useful approach is to attempt to determine to what extent any particular act exhibits characteristics of ritual. There is no reason beyond misguided intellectual gamesmanship that requires an act to be pure of type. Most actions in life are complex, multi-voiced, and multifaceted and ritual acts are no different. We are much more interested in observing an act and determining to what extent ritual characteristics play a part in the action. As Middleton (1977) puts it:

> When we speak of religious, ritual, ceremonial, and so on, this is usually to distinguish and define various types of social behavior. In my view this approach is too rigid a one and distorts what actually takes place. It would be more accurate to consider religious and non-religious, or ritual, or ceremonial, rather aspects of behavior. It would seem impossible to find any organized, conventional or expected behavior in any society that does not contain some element of more than one of these aspects. Even the most technical behavior contains some touch of the ritual; and even the most religious act some aspect of the technical. (P. 73)

Ritual continues to have its effects on contemporary social life not because it is bordered and separate from everyday life (as is theorized in much traditional literature based on tribal societies), but precisely because it is integral to and, therefore, remains invisible to ordinary analysis. To clarify these ideas, we continue with the Midland College classroom narrative begun earlier. As you read through this second part of the Midland College narrative written by one of the authors of this chapter from his field notes, you are not likely to see much that is traditionally known as ritual and, yet, they contain many examples of formalized, symbolic performance. After completing the second part of this rather lengthy example, we will elaborate on some of the important insights that can be gained by learning to focus on the ritual aspects of the actions.

MORE LIFE AT MIDLAND COLLEGE

As Dr. E prepared to formally begin the lab, various lab quartets began to emerge. Two lab teams, each with four students, occupied the twelve-foot lab table closest to the front of the room. These two teams situated themselves as far apart from each other as possible, allowing each other maximum space to work and talk. Book bags, soft drink cans, caps, and textbooks formed a natural barrier that separated the two teams. Three of the students appeared to be over forty years of age, while the remaining five appeared to be traditional age students probably between the ages of nineteen and twenty-two. The next two tables also housed eight students each, divided into teams of four. The table furthest from the instructor had only one foursome; the undergraduate teaching assistant (TA) occupied the other half of the table.

The lab seating arrangement, which required half the class to face the front of the room while the other half faced the rear, was ideal for conducting lab experiments or playing poker, less useful for centralized instruction. Having secured a seat that faced the back of the room, I practiced glancing over my shoulder to observe the teams that were closer to the front of the room and the blackboard. I convinced myself that my neck would endure this awkward arrangement.

Students' conversations continued as Dr. Enid wandered the room, gravitating toward an empty seat, calling out "this group needs a fourth." After a pregnant pause, no one moved toward the vacant seat. Iris, Marlon, and Gail, sensing the possibility of being split up, forged an "under their breath" pact to remain a team and not yield to the instructor's consolidation agenda. A reluctant student from the back of the room collected her belongings and moved toward the vacant chair. Dr. Enid moved to the next vacant seat and again invited the students in the back to "move on up." Students sat motionless, avoiding eye contact with the instructor. Sensing an impasse, Dr. Enid commented, "typically, at least two students usually drop this class; we'll redistribute later." She continued to wander the classroom, stopping at different tables when addressing the class. She reminded the class, "If you don't get along with your team, tell me confidentially and we'll file for a divorce." Students nervously chuckled at the humor.

The absence of a formal welcome to the seminar surprised me, since it was the first laboratory of the semester. But as I later learned, the class had met the previous day for lecture and at that time, Dr. Enid reviewed the syllabus, introduced herself to the class, discussed expectations, and explained that during the labs, students would work in teams of four. This explained how students knew about the teaming expectations prior to the start of class.

Brief introductions followed. Dr. Enid asked students to "pair-up" and exchange information about each other. After the dyadic encounter, each student would introduce his/her partner to the entire class. As the duos formed, the instructor announced that she was circulating a seating chart. Students were to fill in the name that they like to be called on the diagram. I paired up with Gail. I learned that she was a sophomore and has attended another nearby school the previous year, but hated it and transferred. She indicated that she was from Cincinnati, worked part-time, lived with her boyfriend, and had attended a local high school. I revealed that I had lived in the area for ten years, was married, and taught in a school of education. Dr. Enid interrupted our exchange, instructing the class to begin the public introduction process. As expected, the introductions began with the person sitting in the first seat at the first lab table introducing her partner. The introductions proceeded in linear, row-by-row fashion. The no frills introductions were predictable:

> This is Kevin; he's a sophomore from NW high school . . . This is Bill, he likes baseball and coaches . . . This is Edith; she plays in a band . . . Sarah has four kids and works . . . Paula works in daycare and really likes kids . . . Sam coaches "Athletes In Action" teams . . . This is Peter and he is a professor and will in this class . . .

Dr. Enid augmented Gail's brief introduction of me. She provided the basics: who I was, what I was doing, when I was going to do it, and so on. Expecting no questions, the instructor urged Marlon to continue with the acquaintanceship experience by introducing Iris. As the process unfolded, I gathered demographic information about the class: twenty-eight students, twenty-two women, eight men, two older men, one older woman, one African American woman.

With logistical matters temporarily resolved and introductions completed, Dr. Enid briefly discussed the merits of group work. Unlike other teamwork pep talks that extol the virtues of teamwork by conjuring images of sports idols or successful corporate icons, Dr. Enid relied on existing scientific scholarship as evidence to support her preference for lab groups.

> Recent research shows that students learn better in groups...at times individuals can't comprehend a problem and peers are more effective than teachers in explaining a scientific concept...We all benefit from group learning...She then explained her expectations for individuals and teams: Since we will be working in groups, there are certain things you must follow. There are things that will appear on tests that might not be part of what you did alone in your group. Every student needs to know ALL parts, beyond your particular assignment.

Dr. Enid, a slender woman with medium length curly black hair and an olive complexion, dressed in a comfortable professorial attire—a paisley cotton skirt and blouse—spoke clearly and articulately, with a tinge of an unidentifiable accent. As she moved from table to table distributing a handout entitled "Roles in the Cooperative Team," she explained the four laboratory team roles—recorder, content checker, technician, and facilitator—and how each week students in the group were to assume a different role.

In fable fashion, Dr. Enid told the story of a team who had problems with a particular member and did not address these concerns with the person nor did they bring the concerns to her attention. The negative consequences for the individuals and the groups were obvious. She continued, "I assume you are all mature adults and will do what is right." A laundry list of suggestions to succeed was presented: attend classes, read carefully, work all the problems, and don't wait until the day before a test or quiz to study. In keeping with her "students are adults" theme, the instructor informed the class that she did not take class attendance, but warned that it was in students' best interest to regularly attend class—"Students [in the past] who consistently missed classes consistently earned D's or F's." While previous sage comments focused on lab hazards, Dr. Enid tone and focus dramatically changed when she introduced Anne, her undergraduate teaching assistant. "Anne is one of my best students ever...an ideal teacher...I'm proud of her." The moral of these stories were obvious—work hard, be serious, don't procrastinate, and be like Anne.

Dr. Enid concluded her introductory comments with a soliloquy often recited in undergraduate classes. As she stood in front of her lab station, she reminded the class that there were "no stupid questions." She continued, "if you are here to learn and you want to learn, don't think your question is stupid, just ask...By asking, you help yourself and others." Swiftly, Dr. Enid turned away from the students toward the board, signaling that she concluded her introductory comments and it was time to get to work. She called out, "I hope you can convert to metric," as she picked up a piece of chalk.

Students, like myself, facing the back of the room, scraped their chairs against the linoleum floor as they repositioned themselves to face the blackboard. The sound of snapping three ring binders, shuffling papers, unzipping book bags, and paper being torn from a notebooks filled the air. As students prepared for the mini-lecture, Dr. Enid copied a quick reference table onto the blackboard: "mm = millimeter; dm = decimeter; cm = centimeter; hm = hectometer; km = kilometer." Dr. Enid's veteran teacher status was evident as she strategically situated herself so that she could write on the blackboard, maintain eye contact with class members, and refer to notes sitting on the lab table that separated her from the rest of the class. She called out, "What is the conversion factor in metric?" A student, near the front of the room called out, "10." Immediately, the instructor replied, "Who agrees." A flock of hands swayed in the air. Dr. Enid solicited alternate responses. One of the two students who failed to raise their hands, quickly glanced at her notes, then looked up and said, "Never mind." The other dissenting voice remained silent as the lecture continued.

Within minutes, formulas filled the board—"large → smaller unit (x)...smaller → (÷)." The professor provided a commentary to accompany the formulas:

> Let's think about it...How do you get a larger number from a smaller number [pause] multiply...Therefore...OK...If you forget, write it down...Practice over and over again...Can you generate a prediction from what we have done so far?...Everyone understand this?...Division means moving the decimal to the left...Who disagrees?...Everyone comfortable? ....OK, it seems like everyone has got it; let's start the lab.

This brief lecture and intensive and interactive drill kept students alert. The question-then-answer-followed-by-another-question format kept students busy scribbling in their notebooks. Dr. Enid's nonthreatening dialogue solicited solutions, counter-solutions, and multiple rationales from over half of the students. Seldom did Dr. Enid bemoan incorrect responses. The hurried pace, evidenced by the flipping of notebook pages and the constant collective head bobbing of students—glancing at the board, then their notebooks and then the board—was exhausting. As the class paused to shift from the lecture to the team assignment, I remembered Iris's pre-seminar prediction of the class, which thus far proved valid—"this course is tough, really tough."

As the focus shifted from the front of the laboratory to the various work stations, the pent-up silence of students erupted as the groups began to sort out their tasks. Iris, Marlon, Gail, and I informally negotiated roles. Initially, I thought that my professor status would advantage me in this undergraduate seminar, but the pace and intricacies of the initial "review" tempered any sense of overconfidence I possessed.

Gail asked, "Who wants to do what?" Marlon replied, "I don't care," as he dropped his pen through one of the holes in the lab table. Iris, perusing the two-page lab handout, noticed that a yardstick and paper clip were required. She asked about their whereabouts. Marlon shrugged his shoulders. A few moments later, Anne arrived at our table to deliver the paper clip and yardstick. Marlon announced that we already had one. While the metric review was fast-paced and logical our small group negotiation session commenced with warp speed in a staccato fashion. The conversation resembled an MTV video. One moment students discussed the lab expectations, only to instantaneously shift the focus of the conversation to television. In a split second the group reverted back to the lab discussion. One moment Marlon was measuring the length of a textbook, the next he assumed a swashbuckling stance holding the yardstick, like a sword in front of him pretending to be Luke Skywalker, declaring that the force was with him, only to immediately resume his measuring duties—converting the length of the textbook from centimeters to decimeters.

Lab teams dispersed to all corners of the room, resembling "orchestrated chaos." As our group measured our paper clip and converted the measure from millimeters to meters, another team measured the length of the pane of glass in the door, while a third group measured the linoleum floor blocks. Unlike myself, Iris, Marlon, and Gail had their calculators and notebooks in hand. Seconds after the measurement was ascertained and announced, the conversion was calculated and recorded. As technician, my duties were minimal, since the equipment was delivered. Thus, I concentrated on brushing up on metric conversions and recording field notes.

The lab required each team to estimate the length of an object before measuring it. Our team's estimations got better over time. Dr. Enid playfully chastised one group for measuring before estimating—"Read the Instructions." Marlon escalated the group's commitment to "estimating before measuring" doctrine by declaring himself the "Guessmaster." As the tasks become routinized—estimate, measure, convert, record, check, recheck—Gail assumed the role of taskmaster. Only after our group successfully completed a segment of the assignment did she allow tangential conversations (e.g., laundry frustrations, expensive car insurance, and unreasonable parents) to resume.

Numerous teams have trouble solving the final problem—Dr. Enid reconvened the classes, directing students' attention to the front of the room; this was no easy task. She read the problem aloud:

> Mr. Wonderful wants to buy wallpaper for his bedroom. The following diagram shows the dimensions of the room (diagram included). What would be the total area of wallpaper that he will need? Now convert the area in meters (appropriate power) because the paper is sold in meters only. His wallpaper got damaged in flood—during which the room got filled with water. How many liters of water could fill up the room?

Step-by-step with guidance from the professor and focused dialogue between the professor and students the problem was solved.

> Does everyone agree with Jennifer?...I am not sure, tell me why...OK...How about surface area?...We know the area in the front, what about the back?...How did you get that?...OK, what do you think?...So, the total is?...Let's do another one to brush up...Check my calculations...Anne will introduce the next exercise...

As the focus shifted back to the laboratory teams, the stream of consciousness conversations resumed. Marlon told the story of a high school prankster who inserted a paper clip in an electric socket and shorted out the classroom electric service. He concluded his story, "He was Jewish; no, a Jehovah Witness." Iris countered with a story about how a coworker was so bored at work that she picked all of her nail polish off her fingers. Our team's stories were interrupted by the sound of a person from the next table smacking his yardstick on the table. Only momentarily stunned, our team resumed exchanging stories. Gail told the story of Dr. Epps, her former psychology teacher, who incessantly talked about his children in class. She concluded her story with the line—"too bad none of the stories about his kids were on the tests." No sooner had Gail's story ended when the lab task again took center stage:

> 16.5...Don't forget, convert decimal to fractions...I hate calculus...3.8...As I record, I am not going to tell you...In the old days, my father complained he had to do this by hand...My mother's smart...I have Defranko for Spanish...Is 3.26 repeating?...any unit?...$2\pi r2$ – diameter...imagine a cube...I've got it!...Volume = 100 centimeter cubed...Hey, the ratio decreases...

One need not glance at the clock hanging on the wall to ascertain that the class was coming to a close. The collecting of personal belongings, the dispensing of refuse, the zipping of book bags signaled that 2:50 p.m. was approaching. Dr. Enid reminded the class of their assignments for tomorrow's lecture and that they needed to meet outside of class to complete the lab assignments due the following week, as a stream of students exited the room. As I departed with Marlon, he again asked, "Are you really coming back?"

ANALYSIS

If ritual is performance, then it makes sense to analyze all aspects of a performance including the staging and the costumes. The stage speaks much to the geographic form of a ritual. There is, of course, instrumental reason for having a science laboratory classroom consist of tables with electrical outlets and features to facilitate the attachment of apparatus, but this particular design is also symbolic of a particular understanding of "science" and "lab." We can imagine other possible stagings. For example, the room could be made up of individual desks on one side of the room for lecture and lab tables on the other side of the room. Or we could imagine individual lab desks for each individual student. Or we could imagine a long and elaborate lab desk at the front of the room with the rest of the room made up of desks for students to sit and observe a lab technician conduct experiments. If none of these alternatives seems reasonable to you, it is only because the particular arrangement of multiple lab stations for a cluster of students to work in pairs or small groups is what we have come to understand a lab classroom to be. Why do we equate science with apparatus in the first place? Why not understand science to be the theoretical understanding of the natural world and the laboratory investigation as technology rather than science? In this case, the room that "looked like a stereotypical high school laboratory that doubled as an equipment storeroom" suggests a symbolic commitment to the idea that science is a hands-on affair that requires special apparatus to answer the questions of the natural world. So when the students sit in this room on the first day, they are placed on a stage in which science is going to arise right in front of them, using all of this exotic equipment as teams of individuals attempt to solve problems of the natural world. Science is obviously something that can best be conducted if properly equipped.

On this stage gathers a cast of characters carefully clothed in costumes. We find the students dressed in informal clothes including shorts, light tops, baseball caps, and backpacks. Is such personal style a formalized, symbolic performance? Most definitely so. Clearly the informal dress and backpacks are symbolic of group identity as can easily be seen by looking at the description of the two non-students in this narrative—the lab instructor and the ethnographer. The ethnographer does not unpack his *backpack* but instead drops his *briefcase* on the table. Is it only an instrumental realization that makes carrying a briefcase inappropriate for a student while perfectly appropriate for a professor? And observe Dr. Enid's "comfortable professorial attire" made up of a paisley cotton skirt and blouse. Of all of the ritual performances, the symbolic display known as "style" may have the most important effects in the construction of the social milieu. The Birmingham Centre for Contemporary Cultural Studies, particularly the work of Hebdige (1991/1979; 1988) has helped us see the powerful politics played out in youth subculture styles. It is not by accident that students at one university are able to recognize the style of students at a nearby university even when the two universities are very similar in student demographics. If we come to understand the wearing of clothes and personal grooming as a process of "costuming" ourselves instead of merely an instrumental act and that such costuming carries with it symbolic meaning then we can understand style as, at least partially, a ritual performance rather than merely a personal statement of preference.

In ritual every person involved participates in the ritual even if just as an observer. In EDD xxx, Dr. Enid has consciously constructed a particular conversational pattern. In her classroom, we find a pattern that combines student-to-student conversations with instructor-centered questions and answers. This authority and control could be used to symbolically reinforce the knowledge and wisdom of the "scientist" (in this case the instructor) and of "science" (a text), but Dr. Enid symbolically redistributes the power back to the students through such actions as stating that there are no stupid questions and by using a question and answer format in which the students are not commended for right or wrong answers but are challenged to commit to or reject the answers of other students. "What is the conversion factor in metric?" she asks. "Ten," one student answers. "Who agrees?" the instructor responds. Now to symbolically redistribute the power is not the same thing as to *actually* redistribute the power. We are not so naive as to believe that in this particular class, this instructor has actually been capable of (or even desirous of) giving up her own power to mythologize and ritualize science, but the symbolic redistribution is not unimportant in that it states *publicly* again and again that ordinary persons are able to and expected to participate in the making of science. One of the important aspects of ritual is that its performance is a very public statement, at least as powerful as, if not more powerful than, the meaning of the words spoken.

In fact, in this environment, science is something that can fit into the fissures of ordinary life. Look again at the conversation during the lab experiment. The conversation and actions are like an MTV video with quick ruptures and disjunctures where linear lines of thought and discussion do not exist. Instead we find the doing of science fits in nicely with playacting the movies, mythologizing other courses and instructors, and narrating one's life. Science is not more than a small intrusion easily incorporated into the ordinary flow of everyday life. We are reminded of Cusick's (1973) wonderful observation that middle-class suburban schools are designed to teach students how to use half of their mind on work and keep the other half entertained since that is exactly the kind of life that will be expected of them in the bureaucratic positions that most of them will come to hold as adults. In this case, students do not need to fully concentrate on the task of doing science and they don't. Ritually, science is just another thing to talk about to pass the time.

There are many other ritual aspects to actions in this narrative. There are the introductory rituals between individuals and the class as a whole that create such remarkable bonding that after knowing each other for only a few moments, our observed quartet decide that they will do what they need to do to not break up the group. There is the ritual mythologizing that occurs when students and the instructor tell stories about past experiences in this course. There is the instructor's narrative claim to "scientific research" as justification for teaching in groups (a ritual of storytelling). There are the characteristic posture and demeanor of the instructor when standing at the board and when signaling a change in pace. There is the rigidly ordered pattern of the research experiment—estimate, measure, convert, record, check, recheck. All of these acts are likely to consist of at least some formalized, symbolic performances that will act on the individuals in the course in ways that will leave them with lasting lessons about the meaning of this course, science, and college in general and that is at least as important as the cognitive measures learned and formally measured.

CONCLUSION

We are convinced that these nonrational lessons learned through the ordinary ebb and flow of everyday school rituals are not just an interesting aspect to schooling, but are, in fact, central to understanding our schools. When we understand that ritual permeates nearly all action, then we realize that we must start treating the nonrational aspects of ritual more rationally. This becomes particularly crucial when we begin to realize that ritual has the remarkable ability to connect the emotions of the body to the cognitive commitments of the intellect thereby either reinforcing them or resisting them (see the discussion of "enfleshment in McLaren, 1999; Rappaport, 1978, p. 86). When we realize that ritual only creates solidarity when the participants in the rituals come to believe in the symbols that mark the rituals, then we can begin to understand why so many children, particularly poor ones, reject school knowledge before it even occurs. When the nonrational rituals of school ignore or contradict a child's own identity and commitments, we should not expect much learning to occur. In the extended example presented in this chapter, we can see how a very ordinary science class is riddled with nonrational commitments through ritual aspects to the class action. These students are already successful students since they are in college. Rituals that permeate this class's experiences do not fundamentally challenge the students' own identity or their own sense of morality. Through this examination of the mundane, we can see how urban public elementary and secondary schools face a very different situation. Where the college students easily incorporate the rituals of the classroom into their own sense of identity and morality, many of the students we find in urban classrooms find the rituals of everyday classroom life challenge their identity and sense of morality. Once we realize that the rationally planned classroom activities cannot be separated from the nonrational ritual actions, we may begin to understand the cultural politics that play out in our urban schools and we may begin to rationally plan the nonrational ritual aspects of our classrooms as carefully as we do the rational cognitive goals. We may even begin to learn how to construct urban schools that work to transform rather then reproduce the inequities that are so evident in our urban schools.

5

ON SEMINARS, RITUAL, AND COWBOYS

Damian sits slouched in his chair, hands folded in his lap, Timberlands thrust under the table, his body forming a slightly sagging diagonal line. On his head sits his more-than-dirty white hat, brim turned backward, plastic strap pressed across his forehead. John Dewey's "The Child and the Curriculum" lies dutifully open on the table in front of him taking its place in the circle of texts that trace the perimeter of the table. Damian's face lacks emotion. In fact, it signals no information whatsoever. It is blank. Is his mind blank as well? I can assure you that it is not. His mind is actively presenting multiple words and images for his own contemplation. A film-loop projection of last night's argument with Sheila dominates the images. Endlessly he watches her rage-contorted face and hears her high shrill voice—though he has forgotten what her words were. Screw it! There's no pleasing some girls!

But his argument with Sheila is not the only thing entertaining his mind. For example, he can't stop humming that Goo Goo Doll's tune that he heard on MTV this morning. Nor can he put out of his mind John Rzeznik's tattoos. Damian has been contemplating getting a tattoo for several weeks now and he isn't sure if watching the Goo Goo Doll's increases his enthusiasm or his distaste with the idea.

And there isn't just contorted faces, guitar licks, and tattoos to occupy his mind. There is Tina. As always, Damian is sitting next to Tina. Tina was the very first person whom Damian noticed when he had entered the classroom on the first day. Noticing Tina did not make Damian unique. Everyone noticed Tina. Tina is the kind of young woman who puts a lie to the idea that men today are obsessed with Kate Moss look-alikes. Tina's body overflows with sensuality. Damian enjoys telling his friends that Tina has a "generous" body and that she could have had a role in the movie Dirty Dancing. But it is her bleached, waterfall hair splashing out all over in irregular tempo that distracted anyone nearby. It is not just the guys who notice Tina; the women do too and not with approval.

So the fact that Damian immediately noticed Tina upon entering the room on that first day does not separate him from his peers. What distinguishes him is that Damian did not hesitate to walk over and take the seat next to her. And since students nearly always return to the same seat every subsequent class, Damian sits next to Tina and her delicious distractions every class. So that besides high pitched screams, repetitive drumbeats, and tattooed arms, Damian's mind contemplates strategies for the seduction of Tina.

But you might wonder whether Damian is paying any attention to his class or if he is only thinking of irrelevancies. If so, you may be surprised to know that despite all the attention to women and song, Damian is also tracking the class action. Damian is a pretty good student. Well, OK, he is only an "A–B" student. But what is wrong with that? After all, he has known plenty of smart people who have been total losers as teachers. Like Mr. Compton his high school English teacher who never caught on to the ways in which the class would ask him questions about everything under the sun and avoid the topic of the day. But while you don't have to be a rocket scientist to get through ed school classes, Damian is determined to graduate in four years. His parents have made it clear that they are only paying for four years of college. He will have to pay for every additional semester himself and he already has twelve thousand dollars in student loans to pay back. For this reason, that part of Damian's mind not occupied with other more intriguing things has been following the class conversation. Class participation is calculated into the final grade and though he doesn't know exactly how it will be counted, Damian makes sure that he contributes at least one comment in every class. At this particular moment there is a pause in the conversation. Damian decides now would be the time to "contribute."

"Professor Ulrich," he asks, "What does Dewey mean when he talks about the progressives?"

You may be skeptical that this description captures Damian's actual thoughts. Let me assure you that it comes quite close. I know because Damian is a figment of my imagination. So are Tina and Professor Ulrich. They are fictitious constructions compiled from twenty years of college instruction as well as one school year visiting undergraduate and master's seminars of some of my colleagues in widely different areas of the university. I became interested in thinking about seminars when I happened to attend two different classes within a couple of weeks of each other. In observing these two seminars I became intrigued by both their similarities and their differences and began to wonder to what extent the similarities and differences might be understood by looking at the nonrational aspects of seminar classes. Relying on my colleagues' good natures, I invited myself to seminars all over the university. I enjoyed my visits and was pleased to find a very high quality of teaching. My purpose, however, was not to judge the quality of my colleagues' teaching, but, rather, to try and capture any basic interaction patterns with ritual aspects that might be constructed from this nonscientific sample of college seminars.

Since I use the term "ritual" to refer to an aspect of nearly all social action rather than as an attempt to construct a typology of action or attempting to discover whether any particular act "is" or "is not" a ritual act, I'm more intrigued exploring the ways particular acts might have *aspects* of formalized, symbolic performance. Part of the reason I have a beard is because it is easier and more comfortable than shaving every day. That is an instrumental reason. But undoubtedly part of the reason I have a beard is also because it provides part of a good symbolic costume for my performance as an American intellectual. It would be inappropriate to suggest that my beard is *merely* a ritual act on my part. But it would probably not be inappropriate to suggest that my beard has an aspect of ritual connected to it. In a similar way, Damian's characteristic diagonal slouch probably occurs because he finds it physically comfortable, but it probably also occurs because he finds it ritually comfortable. His posture signifies something—perhaps a casual distancing from the academic ritual itself—and so there is an aspect of ritual in his posture. In this essay I will identify interaction patterns found in seminars that have ritual aspects to them. Understanding the ritual aspects of these interaction patterns will, I believe, help us gain a better understanding of some rather common experiences of students and faculty attending seminar classes at the undergraduate and master's levels. In doing so I hope to raise some points about seminar teaching at the undergraduate and master's levels and about individualism and anti-intellectualism in American education.

* * *

One evening I attended a seminar for undergraduates. While the course was in the business school, the students were primarily from outside business and were taking it as part of their liberal education requirement. The staging of this class struck me as significantly different the moment that I walked into the room. Unlike the other seminars I had attended, this one took place in a classroom without a central table around which the class could gather. Instead this room had two rows of five tables fastened to the floor with three chairs at each table. This classroom staging is so frequently found in business schools and so seldom found in any other school that I can't help but think there is some symbolic meaning behind such a stage setting. Perhaps to business school insiders this organization implies something else but, as an outsider, this format seems to imply a combination of hierarchical and cooperative relations. The hierarchy is found between the instructor who stands at the front of the room and the students who sit at the table facing the front. The cooperation is potentially found in each table functioning as a team in competition with the other tables. I suspect that despite the potential for cooperative competition, most instructors fail to exploit this stage setting and end up interacting with students like instructors in other divisions where students sit in individual desks and face the front of the room. Whatever this seating pattern's typical symbolic meanings to those in the business school, when I sat waiting for the class to begin, I wondered how the instructor was going to overcome this staging. How could the instructor construct a "seminar" without a "seminar table" or without moveable desks pulled into a circle that symbolically constructs the appearance of the equality of participation that was found in Professor Ulrich's seminar?

As students arrived they each took their place in an assigned seat two to a table. Two tables had only one student. At all but two of the two-student tables, the students opted to separate themselves from their table partner with the third chair. I was surprised to find that as students took their seats, they got out their books, papers, and pens and kept to themselves. Little informal conversation occurred. It was clear to me that individualism was to be the norm here. There were sixteen students equally divided male/female. All students appeared to wear jeans of some sort (though not all jeans were blue). To my other-generation eye their styles were remarkably similar. Three wore flannel shirts, four wore sweatshirts, three wore t-shirts, five wore sweaters. All of these students presented an informal, casual, yet neat appearance. The one distinctly different style was one young male who wore a brightly colored hockey shirt presenting an obviously "jock" style.

The answer to my question about how the instructor would overcome the class staging was answered immediately. He took a position standing in the center aisle around the second row. Through the period, the instructor would move up and down the aisle though he stayed near the first two rows most of the time. This position allowed him to diminish the hierarchical implications of the fixed tables and chairs, but it required him to maintain the hierarchy symbolized in his

remaining standing while the students sat. Still, his strategy of standing and moving along the center aisle did allow him to both literally
and symbolically move from the head of the room to its center. As
became clear, the instructor not only was physically centered in the
room, he was also at the center of the conversation. His physical and
discursive centering suggested to me a wagon-wheel. The instructor
was the hub and the students sat on the outside and the action took
place across the spokes.

After the introduction of the guest, the instructor asked simply,
"Who'll get us started." One student quickly responded, "I've got a
question." He then requested clarification of a concept used in the
night's assigned reading. The instructor responded by explaining the
concept. When he finished his explanation, three hands shot up into
the air. The instructor called on a woman who asked a similar kind of
clarification question. Again the instructor responded by explaining
the concept but then he inserted some new information by displaying
a graph from a book. Another woman asked a question that implied a
particular reading of the text. It was clear that other understandings
were possible, so rather than answering the question right off, this
time the instructor responded to her question with a question. "Are
you sure? Find it in the book," he said. After she found it (with some
help from a few other students), he responded to her question. That
was, however, one of the few times that the instructor or students
actually focused the attention of the class on the written text itself. For
the most part, the initial question appeared to have derived from the
text, but the instructor's elaboration and concrete examples did not
seem to address the specific text itself.

For most of the class, the pattern remained the same. The instructor would prompt the students to raise a question or make an observation. A student, after raising her/his hand and being called on by the
instructor, typically asked a clarification question that the instructor
then responded to. Occasionally the instructor would turn the question back to the students and there would be one or two attempts to
address the question by the student or by another student in the class.
Typically the first or second student response would be close enough
to the instructor's sense of things to enable him to elaborate that
response showing how it answered the question or raised new relevant
questions. Throughout, the instructor would connect the ideas presented to other ideas in the course or in other courses or disciplines.
He would raise examples from popular culture (particularly advertis-
ing) and put the problem out on the floor for students to attempt to
address; then return to student initiated questions about the reading.

By the end of the class, every student had contributed. There was not a small set of students who dominated the conversation. It was nicely balanced throughout. When the students ran out of questions, the class ended.

This wagon-wheel pattern—the instructor at the hub, all eyes focused on the hub, all questions directed to the hub, all statements filtered through the hub—suggests that the nonrational, ritual learning of this seminar takes on some particular meanings. Obviously, one thing students ritually learn is that the instructor is the center of learning. Without the hub, the wheel would not turn. On the other hand, they also learn that each spoke of the wheel is important. While a wheel can turn with some of the spokes broken, it cannot support much weight for very long with too many broken spokes. Each student seemed to understand that s/he played an important part in the success of the learning experience. They all had apparently read the material and had come to class with some questions to ask. They all seemed to feel that they could safely present their own interpretation and could, without fear of failure, try to solve the problems placed before them. The students certainly understood that learning was more than just receiving the word from the instructor. Learning might primarily involve the instructor but there is an important and relevant role for each of the students as well.

After the class the instructor, while generally pleased with the performance of this semester's class, expressed to me some frustration with the apparent inability of the students to address each other, the inability of the class to allow him to move out of the hub. He consciously attempted to redirect questions and comments back to the students, but clearly could not easily break the wagon-wheel pattern. I heard other instructors express the same frustration after I had visited their seminars and I often find myself engaged in futile efforts to remove myself from the hub of classroom discussion in my own classes. This is especially so when I'm dealing with undergraduates or with large classes (over twenty students). I feel that I am the hub or perhaps the railroad switchman taking things in and shunting them back out on a different line. But in watching this seminar's nonrational social mechanisms at work, I feel less dissatisfaction. While we may not think that we have arrived where we need to be (students taking control of their own conversation around texts and topics), clearly the wagon-wheel pattern is a far better interaction form than the banking pattern that Paulo Friere so masterly named in his *Pedagogy of the Oppressed* (1968). A pattern that Friere suggests assumes education works like banks, teachers deposit information in students' minds and after several years of earning interest on those deposits, the students are able to withdraw their fully matured educational "bonds" to use for their own and others' benefits.

*   *   *

Tina can't believe Maggie and Kendra are serious. What had started out as a late afternoon get-together at the old neighborhood pub has become a gang-up-on-Tina bash. The three have been best friends since junior high where they had met in first-year French class and had come to be known as Le Trio Gateau au Fromage by a certain set of boys. The boys assigned a particular flavor to each of the girls—"Cerise" to Maggie for her red hair, "Chocolat" to Kendra for her creamy chocolate skin, and "Cannelle" to Tina for her spicy personality. The boys meant the names as a compliment and the girls accepted them as such, often calling each other by these nicknames. They had spent all of their free time together, all the way through high school, though only Tina had continued with French. The friends shared intimacies that none would dare reveal to anyone else. It is true that since Tina has enrolled at the university, she hasn't had the time to hang out with her best friends, but surely they realize that succeeding in college is important to her and that it will never change her commitment to her old "partners-in-crime."

"Look at you!" exclaims Maggie, "Who do you think you're foolin' wearing those American Eagle sweaters? You don't really think that those sorority barbies are fooled, do you?"

"Face it," Kendra adds, "In their eyes you are from the Knob and you'll always be from the Knob."

"They're just laughing at you,"

"And those frat guys are only interested in one thing from a girl like you."

"And it ain't that giant brain of yours."

They bend over laughing, but Tina notices that their eyes belie any vocal expression of merriment.

Tina, who has always been the talkative one of the three, has remained silent throughout the harsh teasing. She has been so looking forward to seeing them again. This old pub has been serving them since they were high school seniors. Knowing that these local kids were not working for the state alcohol agency and knowing their parents personally, the owners were more than happy to serve them as long as they drank in moderation. She has so much to tell her friends about what she is learning. She has always been the one interested in school and was, in fact, recognized by her teachers and her peers as the "smart" one. But Tina has sometimes felt like Rita in the movie Educating Rita *and has no one at the university to talk with. At least not in the way that she needs. And now her friends have turned on her the moment she begins to talk about her classes.*

Well, she shouldn't be surprised. Maggie and Kendra have always made fun of her interest in school and her desire to make something of herself. But she is damned if she is going to sit here and take this abuse.

"You're wrong!" she explodes. "You're wrong about me and you're wrong about them. They've all been nice to me. There is this guy I have in one class. His name is Damian and he always sits next to me and talks to me and has never said anything inappropriate to me. He sees me as more than a body. And those who you call 'sorority barbies,' " mimicking their sarcastic voices, "have been nothing but nice to me and what do you think the bimbos around here think of me? Do you forget the way we were treated in high school? And when has any jerk from around this place ever been interested in anything about me but my chest!"

"At least they're honest about it," laughs Kendra.

But Tina doesn't succumb to the laughter. She is too hot. It's not important for us to hear all that she gives back to her two friends. It's enough to know that by the time she finishes defending her new university classmates, not only are her old mates sitting in silence but so is everyone else in the place. Without waiting for their response, Tina gets up and walks out.

You don't have to worry about their friendship, however. Old friendships forged in youth are often strong enough to survive tiffs such as this. In any case, they will remain friends for many more years even through marriages, kids, and divorces.

Perhaps their friendship is aided by an incident that takes place a couple of weeks later. Some of the juniors in Tina's education seminar had participated in a field experience at Maggie's old elementary school. While they were there one of them had witnessed an argument between a white and black student that was apparently marked by racist language. The students in the seminar engage in a conversation that disparages the whole community. Their opinion is summarized in one outrageous statement by Jennifer, a sorority girl who had always been nice to Tina.

"But what do you expect from them?" Jennifer concludes. Tina has been uncomfortable throughout the discussion but when Jennifer asks her question, Tina can hold back no longer.

"Them? Them?" Tina repeats with a tight intensity in her voice. "What do you know about 'them'? You know nothing of them. I come from that area and my best friend went to that school. I get sick of people from the outside thinking they know what we need and what we want and telling us what to do. Just because you come from the posh

side of town doesn't mean you know better than we do about how things are with us. Isn't that what Friere was talking about in that reading last week? What you need to do is not dismiss the people as ignorant, no matter who they are. But to get them to recognize their own issues and to figure out their own solutions."

Jennifer apologizes, but she is hurt. It was just like someone like Tina to take it all so personally. She didn't mean anything by it. Jennifer just wishes people didn't get so emotional about these things. It just doesn't pay to raise these kinds of things with others. It is best just to talk seriously among your friends. Won't she ever learn?

Gene Autry died shortly before I began this study. Gene Autry, the cowboy with the white hat, ever-ready six-gun, and voice sweeter than a meadowlark. The Lone Ranger had his silver bullets, but Gene Autry had the golden voice. Gene Autry, The Lone Ranger, Roy Rogers, Hopalong Cassidy were all important figures in the lives of those of us who are of the first television generation. Television in the 1950s may be primarily remembered for its live TV shows such as Milton Berle, Jackie Gleason, and Dinah Shore, but for those of us who were just children, particularly, perhaps, those of us who were boys, 1950s television was largely cowboys with their stories of good guys/bad guys living in a fantasy West inhabited by white Americans struggling to tame the wild land of taciturn, noble and exotic Indians and lazy, ridiculous, and exotic Mexicans. But what was so memorable of Gene Autry compared to those other cowboys was less the obligatory pistol-shooting horse chase or the stereotyped Others and more the campfire and the bunkhouse. For me, Gene Autry movies were memorable for the moments in which the men would gather around and join Autry in singing. Even as a child I was aware that these cowboys had voices much nicer than any group of people I had ever heard sing around a campfire while toasting marshmallows. But what may be important to understand about these moments is less the Hollywood quality of their voices and more the ritual expression of solidarity that such moments expressed. Think about the cattle drive, about the vast empty spaces in the West, about the need to develop community for these descendants of Europeans in this foreign land working all day separated from others except when settling down for the night. Isolation had to have been the nineteenth-century reality that provided the seeds for the nostalgic twentieth-century celluloid theme—the glorification of the individual. The construction of man (in the generic sense but also in the specific sense given the male-centeredness of these shows) as a unique individual who, with hard work and courage, was capable of overcoming the most overwhelming of odds in the name of decency and justice. But while rugged individualism may be the primary narrative theme, these moments in Autry movies, where the individuals come together and join in a cooperative song, belied this central theme and suggested that even in the most isolating situations people gain when they join in rituals of solidarity.

I'm thinking of Gene Autry and his campfire songfests because of some of the seminars I attended in which a recurring pattern I came to call the singing-cowboy pattern could be observed. I attended one master's seminar in one of the "social and behavioral sciences" on a day in which individual students were presenting ideas for their future master's thesis. There are many positive things that I could say about this seminar; not the least was the interesting and varied topics being proposed and the way in which nearly all of the students actively participated through questions and comments in helping to strengthen their peers' projects. But my interest lies less in the "content" of seminars than in the "performance" and, in the case of this seminar, the performance was even more fascinating than the content.

There were fourteen students in the class, seven of whom were sitting around a long table with the other seven in chairs behind them and along the wall. The instructor sat in the traditional seat at the head of the table. While his position at the head of the table is clearly a hierarchical position, this instructor successfully removed himself from the hub of the conversation. His participation in the conversation was minimal serving primarily to signal the transition from one presenter to the next. Half of the students presented that day, giving each about fifteen minutes to explain their project and respond to questions and suggestions from their fellow students and the instructor. As the seminar proceeded I began to get a sense of the interaction pattern that had been established. For a short period one student was the center of the ritual. She (or in one case, he) would become the focus of nearly all of the sets of eyes. All of the bodies would shift their orientation toward the speaker. The speaker for her part would sit up and begin to speak in the ritual language of the discipline. While most of the words were knowledgeable to any educated English-speaking adult, many words were clearly specialized to the discipline. Perhaps more importantly than using the words themselves was the way in which the words were put together into a "narrative" structure. Certain elements were obviously obligatory and held to a particular form. Each student presented a brief description of their area of interest stated with few citations though with broad references to unspecified "research." Each student's description addressed the relevant literature and pointed out some area that had not yet been fully or satisfactorily explored. This description was followed by a short "statement of the problem" and a brief explanation of how the study would be conducted. One of the important elements, when relevant, was the tying of the student's proposed study to the research project of the faculty member with whom that student had an assistantship. The initial student presentation was followed by a series of questions and comments by the students and the instructor. The presenting student typically responded with an explanation, gentle rebuttal, or words of thanks until the time was up and a new student was anointed the temporary soloist and attention shifted to her presentation.

Because it is presented as the rational method of their discipline, the students' discursive pattern may seem purely instrumental without any important aspects of ritual. But I am inclined to think this interaction pattern is largely ritualized, perhaps because I happen to be one of those scholars in the social sciences who rejects the "modern" assumptions contained in this "scientific" discourse of standard research. But even without "postmodern" biases, the ritual aspects of this seminar should be apparent because its interaction pattern is so obviously culturally constructed. This became particularly clear to me when one student failed to fulfill her role in the ritual. When this student was called upon, she immediately deflected the call to take center stage by speaking in a tentative and stammering manner about her discomfort with her situation. But with all eyes on her and bodies oriented toward her and with the verbal encouragement of several member of the group, she began. But she did not get very far, before she explained that, unlike the others in the class, she was not "in the program" but she was just "taking the class" to get a sense of the program. She then went on to say that she was more comfortable responding to questions than in giving a presentation. The class then broke the singing cowboy pattern and offered a series of questions to the presenter that drew out what they wanted to know. In her response to the questions, it became clear that her problem did not lie in not knowing what she needed to know, but rather it lay in her not being comfortable in the ritual form of the disciplined conversation. She didn't know how to "properly" say what needed to be said. In her case, the rest of the students were very kind by generously taking up the slack and by asking questions drew out of her what they needed.

The singing cowboy pattern of individual presentation followed by brief series of dyadic conversations comes close to the Gene Autry bunkhouse songs even if the solo was passed from student to student rather than always being in the hands of the star. In this seminar we see the solo being passed around and we see the supporting voices in dialogue with each of the soloists. Perhaps even more than the bunkhouse, this seminar room was the site of a ritual of solidarity in which nascent members of this discipline had the opportunity to participate in a ritual of professional identity and solidarity. The singing cowboy interaction pattern of the seminar utilized ritual words put together with a ritual narrative and jointly performed with the solo parts being passed around and with everyone regularly joining in. Such a ritual of solidarity works to bind members to each other and to encourage them to believe in the rightness of the symbols that are being honored in that ritual (in this case, the words and narrative form of their discipline). The ritual seemed to work for all of the students except for the one student who just didn't participate at all.

One student, let me call him "Jack," attracted my attention at the beginning of the class. He was sitting away from the others and although other students arriving late sat next to him, Jack still remained at the end farthest away from the action. While the rest of the students displayed a similar ritual costume (jeans or other similar pants and very informal tops such as old sweaters, sweatshirts, T-shirts, and flannel shirts), two students appeared to be dressed slightly differently. One turned out to be the woman who was not "in the program" mentioned earlier wearing a print blouse with matching solid color pants. The other was Jack who was dressed in a long-sleeve T-shirt with what appeared to be a gray, collarless work shirt over the top of it. He wore "ordinary" blue work pants. He also had his blonde hair pulled back into a ponytail and sported a goatee. Unlike the other students, Jack's costume was not that of the budding liberal academic but that of a "friend of the working man." Throughout the entire three hours, Jack only made one brief comment and that while several persons were talking at once. During the break, Jack went off by himself and engaged in a conversation in another room with someone not in the class. Jack was the one student who appeared not to buy into the ritual. He did not appear to feel the individual effects of the ritual. He was not one of the group in solidarity. Perhaps like Tina in the earlier narrative, he didn't feel one with the group. While Tina was willing to try to ritually costume herself in solidarity with her university classmates, she couldn't give up her style completely. Like Jack, Tina's presentation of self as read by her largely middle-class peers as "aggressive sexuality" (her overly full hair and "dirty dancing," unrestrained movements) symbolically set her apart from the other university students. And perhaps Jack, unlike Tina, said as little as possible because to speak was to challenge the ritual solidarity that the singing cowboy interaction pattern works so well to create.

The kind of solidarity that the singing cowboy pattern can create was driven home to me when I observed a seminar for first-year master's students in another department in a professional school. The students were discussing Dick Hebdige's book *Subculture: The Meaning of Style* (1991) and were struggling to make sense of it. What first struck me as odd was the way in which these students of diverse racial, ethnic, geographic, and class backgrounds had washed out their differences in style in less than a month. They had adopted presentations of Self and patterns of conversation that promoted group identity and solidarity. True, there were some variations in what they wore, but all of them wore some version of acceptable attire for college students with professional aspirations. While one wore a baseball style hat and one a tie and one wore a denim shirt and another a pullover from Ambercrombie & Fitch, they all fit into the acceptable mold of slightly progressive American professional graduate students in the 1990s. This class dressed differently than the master's class discussed earlier, which had been in the College of Arts and Sciences.

Even more interesting than the ritual of solidarity expressed through the symbolic display of their dress was the implicit ritual narrative found in their conversation. It was a narrative of individualism very similar to that found in the old Western movies. In this case, their conversation seemed to claim that we are all unique individuals who can, and must, struggle to deflect the inappropriate (actually immoral) pressures of the group to enforce its cultural styles on us. This claim was being made even though it was obvious to me that this group of students, as much as any other that I observed, had allowed the group to construct their style. Though they may not have been conscious of their own submission to the ritual demands of the group, various examples arose in their conversation: the young woman who acknowledged that she stopped wearing cowboy boots because of the comments of one of her peers and the embarrassed apology of another for wearing an Ambercrombie & Fitch shirt saying that it was "left over" from her undergraduate days last year. The conversation centered around what it meant to be an individual and struggled to understand how we were to deflect the influences of peer pressure. While the narrative clearly assumed an autonomous individual, their actions suggested something more complex. Even the constant reflections on the uniqueness of one of the young men who had worn a skirt to class the week before was seen as evidence of individual choice rather than as a stark example of the way in which culture works to assure conformity and, therefore, to reassure solidarity. After all, he was the first male they had ever seen wear a skirt to class and I doubt that he ever wore a skirt to class again.

Their conversation reminded me of Herve Varenne's study (1978) of a small city in the American Midwest in which he concludes that the one unifying cultural trait of Americans is their absolute belief in their own uniqueness as an individual. And yet the book that this class was discussing (Hebdige's *Subculture: The Meaning of Style*) is an examination of how style is not the purview of the autonomous individual, but a social statement in the politics of culture. Hebdige's long interest in what he calls "spectacular" youth subcultures provides us with a deep understanding of the way in which style becomes a performance of opposition in youth disaffected by inequality. While these beginning graduate students easily grasped the oppositional nature of such English youth subcultures as Teds, Mods, and Punks, they had a more difficult time grasping the politics of it. And they had no sense at all of the politics of their own style. No realization of the way in which their mildly marginalized style markers (the odd tattoo, the occasional male in a skirt, the adaptation of inner-city black hip-hop culture found in their—only slightly—baggy clothes) *in their very mildness* does not really proclaim unique personal identity as much as it is a public performance of the American myth of the individual. As one after the other, in their own way, failed to address the artificiality of the individual/culture dualism assumed by that American myth, they publicly proclaimed their acceptance of it. What was important about their verbal performances was not whether or not they actually grasped the ideas of Hebdige's book, but the way in which they all willingly participated in the ritualizing of their graduate experience and their Americanness. While the instructor and visitor both attempted to disrupt the American mythology of individuality, they were both very eager not to disrupt the growing solidarity that was being performed by these new graduate students in their new ritual roles as members of the academy engaged in an intellectual discussion around the merits of a book.

This seminar came closer than any of the others that I observed in fitting the pattern of a dialogue among equals. The instructor maintained a conspicuous silence, only contributing after long pauses, and then, only to get the conversation among the students started again. But this conversation did not have a Tina present. It did not have someone to speak strongly and aggressively for a different view. Nor did it have a Jack, someone whose very separation from the group introduces a ritual anomaly. In this seminar, the solo was passed around among equals and the chorus never failed to harmonize.

Arthur Levine and Jeanette Cureton (1987) claim that college students at the end of the century were more likely to construct an identity that distinguished them from other students than an identity that bridges those differences. This is in contrast to students of the late 1970s who tended to describe themselves with common "generational characteristics or values" (p. 79). While I have no doubt about the empirical findings the authors describe, I do have a different idea about what these findings mean. Levine and Cureton interpret their findings to mean that the college students of the 1990s, unlike those of the past, had a "preoccupation with differences" (ibid.), but I am inclined to think that students of the 1970s also had a "preoccupation with differences." The contrast between the students of the 1970s and those of the 1990s was not their preoccupation with differences, it is that in the 1970s the differences that occupied students' attention were generational whereas in the 1990s they were ethnic, racial, religious, and class-based. I suspect that college students in the 1990s and in the 1970s faced the same problems that the Americans in Varenne's study did: how to resolve the contradiction between the culturally demanded commitment to uniqueness and the culturally necessary need for commitment to the group. Of course Varenne was not the first Frenchman to recognize this American contradiction. Alexis de Toqueville (1863) found very similar contradictions in the American culture of the mid-nineteenth century.

How do you construct a culture that worships the individual while making invisible the realization that worshiping the individual is a cultural, not individual, construct? The class that I observed studying Hebdige was caught in this dilemma. As Americans, they wished to voice ritual support for the idea of the individual, but as strangers brought together from around the country into a common professional graduate program, they also felt the need to construct ritual solidarity with each other. This particular class was able to accomplish this by not understanding the text that they were reading. By failing to grasp the fundamental politics of style that the book is centered around, these students were able to ritually (and "magically") resolve that dilemma. On the other hand, Tina's and Jack's "errors" lay in their failure to subordinate their unique subgroup identity to the ritual of solidarity that constructs the class. By challenging the claims of a fellow student, Tina ritually proclaimed that her subgroup was more important than the class group. In a similar way, Jack, through his failure to participate in the rituals of solidarity of his seminar group, accomplishes the same end. The ritual of solidarity found in the singing cowboy interaction pattern would be difficult to maintain with a couple of Tinas or Jacks present. Perhaps this is why the singing cowboy pattern is more likely to be found at the graduate level where the students have a vocational identity that is likely to supersede all other identities in the neophyte. Perhaps the wagon-wheel interaction pattern is more conducive to the ritual construction of solidarity when there is no common identity inherent in the class. If Americans can't construct ritual solidarity around group identity, than the solution may be to construct it around the myth of the individual. Perhaps the wagon-wheel pattern is as much about this need to avoid disruption and the need to commit to individualism as it is about intellectual disinterest. Then again, perhaps intellectual disinterest is itself part of our ritual construction of the individual.

*   *   *

One of the most common complaints among faculty on our campus is the lack of "intellectual vitality" among our undergraduates. There have been reports and formal and informal meetings that focus on our undergraduates' apparent anti-intellectual character. At one meeting held in the president's home one of my colleagues dramatically proclaimed, "When we were undergraduates, we believed that our education was found in the classrooms, in our studies. Today's students appear to believe that their education is found, not in the classroom, but in their diplomas." My institution is not the only one to complain of student disinterest in intellectual pursuit. Even the president of the fictitious Waldon College in Doonsberry complained of students' "lack of curiosity." Levine and Cureton (1987) suggested that students overwhelmingly understand their education as a consumer good to be purchased and used rather than as something to build and enrich. They quote a Georgia Tech student as saying "Academics are a means to an end. There is no emphasis on learning for its own sake" (p. 115). Levine and Cureton go on to argue that learning is primarily linked to material gain.

> Even more dramatic than this continuing trend toward vocationalism, however, is the plummeting value placed on nonmaterial goals, such as learning to get along with people and formulating the values and goals of one's life. Whereas these personal and philosophic goals were the principal reasons for attending college in the 1960s, today [in the 1990s] they are at the bottom of the list. (P. 116)

To be certain, much of student ennui with academic study is caused as much by poor instruction as by any generational flaw in the students.

Furthermore, much of faculty complaining is really conservative snip-
ing at the gradual loss of influence of their elite canon (e.g., see Bloom,
1987). But despite these caveats, there is enough evidence to suggest
that American college students really are suspicious of (or at least bored
by) intellectualism. It is true that Levine and Cureton (1987) found
that 83 percent of college students consider themselves "intellectual,"
but they also point out that student rejection of learning for learning's
sake makes it likely that students equate "intellectualism" with "hard
work" rather than something to do with engaging the intellect. While
I may not agree with the implication that intellectualism should be
equated with learning for learning's sake, I think they are right even
today to suggest that "Most students work hard, or think they do, but
tend to confuse hard work with intellectualism" (pp. 132–133).

    At the center of American culture lies a dilemma: a cultural construct
(something shared by the group) committed to radical individualism
(the belief that one should stand apart from the group). To overcome
this dilemma, Americans must regularly participate in rituals of solidarity that ironically celebrate autonomy. Through participating in
such rituals, Americans develop commitments to the antipodal values
of community and individualism. This dilemma inserts itself into the
American seminar. Intellectual discussions contain a double jeopardy:
when we challenge others' positions, we symbolically reveal our lack of
solidarity; when we fail to challenge others' positions, we symbolically
reveal our lack of autonomy. Succeeding in ritually displaying one side
of this dilemma ritually challenges the other. However, performing
rituals to individualism magically resolves this dilemma by encouraging us to emotionally bond with others around our commitment to
individualism. The singing cowboy interaction pattern facilitates such
performances. By rotating the solo part, students perform their "individuality." By singing harmony in the chorus, students perform their
"solidarity." After all, if tough cowboys can croon about the rugged
West of the past, than deserving and hardworking students can warble
about the arduous America of the present. For graduate students, who
are preoccupied with constructing a professional identity, the singing
cowboy interaction pattern works particularly well. The soloists are
able to proclaim their individualism, while the chorus harmonizes a
professional identity.

    But for undergraduates, who are more likely to reveal a wide variety
of subculture identities and less ready to commit to a strong professional
identity, the singing cowboy interaction pattern makes them vulnerable
to social disruption. Without some unifying identity around which to
coalesce, the chorus fails to harmonize and the soloists fail to soar.

For many undergraduates, ritual performances of boredom or detachment might be a better strategy. By carefully presenting performances of detachment, no one needs to publicly proclaim their ideological orientation and, therefore, publicly challenge someone else. By utilizing a wagon-wheel interaction pattern, these students ritually affirm the myth of the individual while failing to put at risk the myth of the community. Through the wagon-wheel interaction pattern, they may *perform* both detachment and participation at the same time; thereby maintaining the magical resolution of the American cultural dilemma.

Instructors interested in making undergraduate seminars look more like graduate seminars must find a different way to overcome the dilemma created by our cultural commitment to individualism. At present, that dilemma may be "magically" resolved through the ritual aspects of the wagon-wheel interaction pattern that makes our commitment to individuality possible by allowing the students to avoid direct confrontation with each other. One possible solution to this strategy is to seek some kind of identity marker powerful enough to subsume the subculture differences that threaten to disrupt the solidarity of the class; or, put another way, magnetic enough to attract different subcultures to the same marker but flexible enough to allow their unique subculture identities to remain. These subculture differences include such obvious categories as race, ethnicity, gender, class, and sexuality, but are much more likely to be located in subtly coded appeals to broader youth styles such as hip hop, skaters, alternatives, rave, prep, skinheads, pachuchas, and so on. It is not so much that these college students are full-fledged members of such subcultures as that they symbolically proclaim sympathy for one or more of such spectacular subcultures. The identity marker needed to overcome subculture differences can be anything as long as it is not an appeal to negate the students' primary identities. I am not suggesting the need for a common culture (Hirsch, 1987) or the need to celebrate the "unum" rather than the "pluribus" (Schlesinger, 1998). Any attempt to use my argument to suggest an anti-multiculturalist position misunderstands my argument. The trick is not to eradicate subculture identities, but to overcome the dilemma resulting from our cultural commitment to individualism. The undergraduate seminar instructor needs to facilitate the creation of an identity in addition to the ones brought to the seminar by the students, not in place of them. It must be an identity that allows the students to maintain their "individual identity" along with the new seminar identity.

The smaller the institution and the smaller the class, the easier the task of creating a new identity because students can come to know others as people instead of as mere symbolic representations of various groups. When people are known primarily through their symbolic plays of group membership, others are likely to interact with them . terms of these symbolic displays. Students are likely to call for and to participate in small ritual displays of solidarity with students displaying symbols of their own or allied groups and to call for and to participate in small ritual displays of opposition with students displaying symbols of oppositional groups. As people come to be known in more complex ways, their symbolic displays of group membership become less crucial to our understanding of them, reducing the need to ritually perform in opposition to them. In turn, this opens up the possibility of creating new common identities. Master's students (and some undergraduate professional majors such as engineering and architecture) may have their nascent professional identity around which to create this seminar ritual. But most undergraduate seminars, even most professional seminars, are likely to have to appeal to a different kind of symbolic identity, something more unique to the particular class itself. Of course, many instructors have been doing this for years (though without necessarily realizing what they were doing) through such things as cookouts at their home, meeting in the pub after class, or taking the class on overnight field studies. I remember one of my own classes that finally achieved a common identity when we continued to hold class for more than an hour while sitting in the hallway in the basement while a tornado passed south of the university. This common experience helped to forge a common identity that these students had with each other and with no one else. From that moment the class had its own identity and the subsequent discussions reached a new level of harmony. Each of those kinds of activities helps to develop a temporary group identity that can be ritually appealed to by the students in order to provide the necessary conditions for the move from a wagon-wheel interaction pattern to a singing cowboy interaction pattern. This would be an improvement from the typical undergraduate seminar because now the instructor is able to move out of the center of the conversation, but it is not the best solution because it only avoids the fundamental dilemma created by our cultural commitment to individualism.

While master's seminars are more likely to already have adopted a singing cowboy interaction pattern, the fundamental dilemma still exists. While master's seminars may be marked by more students talking to each other, they still avoid the direct engagement with each other that most instructors think is important to a seminar class. Master's instructors need to help their students recognize that the autonomous individual is a culturally constructed myth. The rotating solo with background harmonies of the singing cowboy interaction pattern needs to be recognized for what it is: a mechanism for deflating honest intellectual engagement emanating from different cultural and political positions. I'm less confident that I know how to satisfactorily move master's students in this direction. I suspect that the way in which this is typically accomplished at the doctoral level is through doctoral students' becoming identified with particular theoretical stances or with faculty who personify such intellectual positions. In other words, at the doctoral level, students may be able to have a pattern of fully engaged seminars because the engagement becomes a kind of performance of intellectual subgroups—the interpretivists against the positivists, the marxists against the neoconservatives, radical feminists against liberal feminists, and the postmodernists against everyone. If I were to name this pattern, I might call it the shootout-at-the-OK-corral pattern. To a certain extent, this same pattern may form the interaction of many faculty meetings and, so, one might wish to argue that it is the appropriate apprentice experience. But, to be frank, I am not certain that this is a solution that I like very much. To substitute ritual posturing around theoretical positions is, ultimately, no more intellectually justifiable than the rituals of individuality-within-unity found in the singing cowboy interaction pattern or the rituals of limited engagement found in the wagon-wheel interaction pattern. What the solution to this problem may be I can only speculate, but I keep thinking of the late Barbara Myerhoff's (1993) observation that ritual is a dangerous social mechanism to use because once it is seen for what it is—ritual—it loses its effect. Is it possible that by shining the spotlight of our rational, cognitive powers (limited as they may be) on the ritual aspects of academic dialogue, we might be able to move to intellectual engagement that is more than just ritual performances of theoretical identities? Or is that thought just as much a fantasy of my imagination as Professor Ulrich and Louis and Fyodor?

Professor Ulrich has spent the morning in the coffee shop. She often works there when trying to avoid her office and the demands of the bureaucratic university. This morning she has spent making notes for her next article. The two elderly gentlemen engaged in the lively conversation at the next table have been there almost as long as she, but the professor has ignored them while trying to capture the ideas running through her head. However, the ideas have finally run out. She takes a sip of cool coffee and her mind tunes into the adjoining conversation.

"Let me try to make myself a little clearer, Louis." The old man speaks with a thick Eastern European accent. "The advantage of the novel, as a form, is that it allows the author to bring in all of the other forms so

that in the one form we find the many. The novel is the one literary form in which heteroglossia is inherent. Think about the way in which the book you wrote on the Comstock load includes aspects of the epic, the comic novel, the melodrama, as well as letters, drama, poetry, and the characteristic speech of the social classes, the ethnic speech of many nationalities, and the historically located speech of the moment. The potentiality for exploring the heteroglossia of democracy flies out at you. Language is heteroglot through and through, Louis. In language, we find ideology in conflict and contradiction—between the present and the past, the entrepreneur and the worker, the natural-born citizen and the foreigner— all in their language. These languages intersect, create new languages, releasing and rebuffing other languages. What could be more indicative of democracy at work than the freewheeling conversations of the old American West? They are there, Louis, in your books. Or, at least, the potentiality is there."

The conversation pauses for a moment while the speaker sips his coffee and looks around the room. "I'm just saying that I don't think you recognize it. You seem, in fact, to try to deny it. But I'm telling you, Louis, I do like your work. I honestly do. I obtain great enjoyment from your books and stories. I find them, how do you say in English, endearing. Yes, naively endearing."

"Naive! You call my work naive? Listen here, Fyodor! My writing may be simple, it may be for the popular reader, but there is nothing naive about it!" The man addressed as Louis responds with a slight twang of the American West and the quiet intensity of a Gary Cooper. "As a teenager I worked a freighter all over the world from Borneo to Singapore to Calcutta. I've farmed wheat in North Dakota, mined copper in Arizona, and chopped wood in Oregon. Far from being naive, I have the wisdom of living life fully. My books are filled with that wisdom. And where have you been, Fyodor? Have you seen the world as I have? Have you worked with your hands as I have? Made your own way—the hard way? No, my friend, you may have written great books of literature, but you can hardly have experienced the world as I have. My books may be little more than popular penny novels—Westerns—but naive they are not."

The two old men stop talking for a while. Each drinks some coffee and takes bites from their muffins. Finally, Fyodor speaks, "All socially significant worldviews have their ideologies locked within their language and when placed in concrete dialogue with alternative languages, those ideologies become clear. All characters have the potentiality of stratifying language dependent upon their social significance as revealed in their nuances and accents. The potentialities and constraints of a nation can be found in the language of its literature."

"Your problem. Fyodor, is that you confuse complexity with intelligence and intelligence with truth. Like so many Europeans and intellectuals, you confuse words with action. What could be more naive than to think that democracy depends on words?" Louis's final phrase is spoken with thick disdain.

"But Louis, all languages are heteroglossic. They are filled with competing ideologies and worldviews. Isn't that what democracy is about? Bringing to the table the many different languages and letting them speak to each other—testing the limits of each, forcing them to regroup and reform, creating new voices?"

"What good is argument, Fyodor? I wish they would take their arguments elsewhere. Democracy isn't sitting at a table and arguing. It is every individual standing on his own two feet, minding his own business, and fighting his own battles. Words only confuse the truth. It doesn't matter the language you speak but the character with which you speak it and character, Fyodor, is the same in every language. "

"Is it, Louis?"

"Yes, that is one thing I am certain of. Good men and good women recognize good character in others. Oh true, we are all human and we all make mistakes, and we are living in difficult times but, Fyodor, a good man is evident through the things that he does, not the things that he says."

There is another long pause in their conversation. Louis takes their cups up for another refill. When he returns he speaks quietly,

"I'm afraid that you do not understand America. And my books are nothing else if not American. In America, Fyodor, there are people who work and there are people who talk. Americans trust those who work."

"I know, I know, Louis. I see ads too." Fyodor has amusement in his voice. "Just do it!' Right!"

Louis picks up on his tone of voice and smiles, "Right."

"But, Louis, what is a novel if not words?"

Louis looks up, "You're a good man, Fyodor, but you use too many big words. You may be a man of the world, but you will never understand Americans."

"Do you really think that your Westerns speak for Americans?"

"Yes," Louis responds, "They speak to and for all Americans whatever their age or ethnicity or color or income. We may speak with different accents and we may have different complexions, but when it comes right down to it, we all speak in one voice."

"And what is that voice?"

"To work steadily, carefully, and hard. To stand on our own two feet and depend on no one else. And also to trust only those few good men and

good women who speak when they have something worth saying and to watch out for all of the rest."

"Cowboys?" Fyodor looks pensive and skeptical, "Perhaps you are right. I may never understand Americans."

Professor Ulrich has wanted to jump in and reject Louis's claim of a unified American voice. How could anyone think that the language of the mythical West speaks for all Americans. Has he ever watched television or listened to the radio? As a nation we are constantly bombarded by meaningless chatter. Is that evidence of Americans' suspicions of those who talk? We are a polyglot nation. The European gentleman has a much clearer understanding of our nation's multivoiced and conflictual culture than that chauvinistic, jingoistic old writer of Westerns. Who could still think that, in this day and age, the patriarchal, white, and capitalistic language of the old Western could really speak for all Americans? After all, there are few genres in which women are more irrelevant and absent than that of the Western. But Professor Ulrich minds her own business and does not enter the discussion.

The coffee-shop conversation rushes through Ulrich's mind as she looks around at her class. They sit there quietly, wanting to please, but reluctant to participate. They act removed, suspicious of the situation. They aren't stupid. They just aren't engaged. Perhaps the often referred to anti-intellectualism of the American student and the "just do it!" mentality expressed in that coffee-shop Western philosophy are part of the same worldview. Maybe that is why she has such difficulty getting these students to engage the texts.

The silence in the seminar has stretched far too long for comfort. The students are looking down at their books—few making eye contact with Ulrich. A whispered conversation begins at the far end of the table. Jennifer is talking to the girl sitting next to her. Damian sits back in his chair with his characteristic hat turned backward and his characteristic blank face. Tina sits looking at Ulrich expectantly.

One of the better students leans forward. "Could you explain what the author means by hegemony?"

Professor Ulrich looks around the table and waits. No one speaks. Finally she asks, "Who would like to explain what hegemony means?" After a short pause, she resigns herself to the situation and launches into an explanation herself. While Ulrich is writing something on the chalkboard, she looks around at the students busily writing things down in their notebooks. She blinks both eyes and looks again. Is she going crazy or are they all wearing cowboy hats?

6

THE PUZZLEMASTERS

PERFORMING THE MUNDANE, SEARCHING FOR INTELLECT, AND LIVING IN THE BELLY OF THE CORPORATION

the forces of corporate culture have adopted a
much more radical agenda...
to transform public education from a public good,
benefiting all students, to a private good
designed to expand the profits of investors,
educate students as consumers, and
train young people for the low-paying jobs
of the new global marketplace.
— Henry Giroux, *Stealing Innocence*

THE GREETING AND LAST NIGHT'S PUZZLES

Algebra II
City Square High School
November 2000

The classroom sits bathed only in the dusky light of a winter's dawn. The seven islands made of desks clutter the room. Except for the whir from the air ducts and distant murmurs, the room is quiet. For the moment peace reigns in room 142. My mind snaps to the clatter of a doorknob and flip of a switch. As my eyes adjust to the fluorescent lights, Ms. Archer strides to the side of the room and places her stack of folders onto a teacher's desk angled to face the center. She begins writing on the plastic roll of an overhead projector.

"Good morning!" I say.

Startled, Ms. Archer looks up, then gives me a genuine smile. "Good morning!" she returns, "Are you going to sit-in today?"

I tell her that I would like to if it is okay with her and, of course, it is. Like nearly all of the teachers I have been observing this year, Ms. Archer always graciously invites me into her classroom. "We'll be working on how to solve a system by graphing."

We exchange a few more pleasantries and then I retreat to my chair in the corner to observe. Students drift in alone or in pairs until they become a stream of adolescents. I'm always amazed at the quietness of their conversations. Only a few give a yelp or speak loudly. To me they seem subdued for American teens, but this behavioral restraint (I have come to learn) is typical in the schools that I have been visiting. Then the reserve and my camouflage are busted.

"How ya doin'?" A large, male booms.

"Fine, how are you?" I respond.

He just nods acknowledgment and puts his books on a desk, and turns as a young woman approaches him and lays her head on his chest. He gives her a gentle, reassuring one-armed hug and they begin quietly talking.

Across the room a young woman says with incredulity, "I can't believe it. My father really does know how to do this stuff. I had trouble with the homework last night and he actually helped me!" Nearer to me, two girls (as these young high school women unanimously refer to themselves) examine a necklace, while next to them a boy fixes his earring. Another girl stands and wraps a jacket around her legs and then sits again. While three guys pester a girl at their table, a different young woman fixes the hair of her friend. Ms. Archer moves around the room handing out calculators.

"Good morning," Ms. Archer says in a voice just loud enough to rise above the conversations. The students settle down but do not seem to respond in any other way. "I hope everyone is feeling fine today."

"Are you going to collect homework?" a voice calls out.

"No."

"Good, because Bob got robbed last night and the burglar stole his homework." Friendly laughter arises from a group in the middle.

Standing at a podium next to the overhead, Ms. Archer briefly smiles and show says, "Here are the answers from last night's homework." She reads a dozen or so answers. There is low murmur while she reads the answers but everyone appears to follow. When she finishes, she asks, "Which problems do we need to go over?" One student calls out a number and Ms. Archer asks for a volunteer. A hand goes up and after being called on the student explains how to solve the problem. This happens twice more and then Ms. Archer announces, "Today we are going to learn how to solve a system by graphing. You will need a calculator so if you didn't bring one, make sure to get one from the cart."[1]

And so begins a typical day in a typical American high school. The opening stages of the interaction pattern described in this anecdote repeats throughout the day, not only at City Square High School, but at all five of the high schools that I observed during the 2000–2001 school year. While the "greeting" and the "homework review" might be considered rituals in themselves, I found them integral stages of one particular interaction pattern I came to call "the puzzlemaster." While I observed several other interaction patterns, the puzzlemaster was one of the most prevalent. The puzzlemaster appeared ubiquitous in mathematics classes and almost as universal in science classrooms, but I also found the puzzlemaster pattern in every other subject I observed (except for orchestra and social studies[2]). Since nearly every math class and almost as many science classes follow this pattern, the puzzlemaster pattern does not correlate directly with successful or unsuccessful learning. I observed both excellent and less-than-excellent teaching and learning in classrooms exhibiting the puzzlemaster interaction pattern. On the other hand, the puzzlemaster interaction pattern was the most likely interaction pattern to be found in the "best" classes. The better the teacher in non-math subjects, or the more academically able the students, or the more privileged the school, the more prevalent the puzzlemaster interaction pattern.

While the best teachers and best students in the best schools construct the puzzlemaster interaction pattern, less successful teachers and less successful students in less privileged schools also create the puzzlemaster. In other words, one can regularly find the puzzlemaster interaction pattern in many different classrooms in widely different sorts of high schools. Once, while sitting over a glass of Beaujolais in a Bloomsbury wine bar, the educational sociologist Basil Bernstein said to me,

> Everyone seems to be interested in how schooling differs. How it is different for girls and boys? How schools in Edinburgh differ from those in London. How working-class schools differ from middle-class schools. But what interests me is that whether I'm in London or Lisbon or Lagos or Hong Kong, when I step into a school, they all look alike. You know you are in a school.

Of course, as a Durkheimian, Bernstein's point should come as no surprise. After all, structuralism is about uncovering that which lies underneath the surface and governs that which is above. But even though my social theory is more influenced by the Bakhtin Circle than Durkheim, Bernstein's words repeatedly came into my head as

I visited classroom after classroom in schools that were in some ways dramatically different yet also so amazingly alike.

My interest in the ritual aspects of interaction patterns led me to wonder if some common theme might be revealed in the ritual aspects of this observed interaction pattern. Might the ritual aspects of the puzzlemaster interaction pattern suggest a commonality among schools that are in other ways so dramatically different? Before I can answer that and before I fully elaborate all of the stages of the puzzle-master interaction pattern, I would like to consider some interesting aspects of American schooling and its culture.

THE GREAT PANACEA

Nineteenth-century Americans maintained a keen sense of their country's unique role in world history. The first nation-state to declare itself free from aristocracy struggled to define a new identity. By the end of the nineteenth century, Americans had all but stopped thinking of the nation as a republic, preferring to think of it as a democracy instead. Today, of course, nearly all Americans would use the term "democracy" as the primary identity of their nation, but in the early days the idea of democracy was not only challenged by the idea of republicanism, but by piety as well (Cremin, 1980). Early Americans equated their country with the biblically promised "God's kingdom on earth." Even such famous "deists" as Jefferson and Franklin sometimes presented the country as the embodiment of scripture.[3] After the Second Great Awakening (1790s–1840s) many ordinary Americans understood their new country to be the realization of Christian virtues.

Because the great public discussions of the day engaged issues of republicanism, democracy, and piety, we might be led to think that America's self-identity was restricted to these iconic terms. But there was another identity central to America's construction of self, so central, in fact, that little argument was needed. America was a nation of commerce. In ordinary language, the United States was home to the "Yankee Trader." While politicians, clergy, and newspaper editors might debate the appropriate relationship between democracy and Christianity, the business interests were seldom questioned. Despite the American mythology that the colonies were settled by religious and social castaways, the American colonists were much more likely to come from the relatively well-off and relatively well-educated merchant and yeoman classes (see Anderson, 1991; Wright & Viens, 1997). While great scholars seldom articulated business interests in relation to other interests, few early American settlers were unaware that democracy and piety were handmaidens to the pursuit of capital. For strategic reasons, Jefferson replaced Locke's "pursuit of property" with the "pursuit of happiness," but in the hearts and minds of average Americans property was a central element of happiness. In many ways, then, the struggles among democracy, piety, and capital have been part of the American experience from the beginning. One fortunate (or unfortunate) aspect of these struggles was the eventual belief by those committed to each that schooling could play a key role in achieving their designs (see Kaestle, 1983).

Civic education became a central aim to those, such as Jefferson, committed to the development of democracy and republicanism. Besides being the prime mover in the founding of the University of Virginia, Jefferson authored the Bill for the General Diffusion of Knowledge—an early attempt to create a general public education system from primary to higher education. As Jefferson wrote in a letter to Colonel Charles Yancey, "If a nation hopes to be ignorant and free..., it expects what never was and never will be" (Ford, 1904, p. 4). On the other hand, schooling was not only suggested as serving a civic purpose, but as fulfilling protestant virtues as well. Literacy was the primary mechanism to put God's word directly into the hands of the individual. And when instruction in reading was combined with good character education, it was an excellent vehicle for teaching the Christian virtues as well. Any quick perusal of early reading books, such as the well-known McGuffey Readers, makes this absolutely clear.

While the very first "compulsory education" acts are often attributed to the Puritans of New England as a way to teach children to read the Bible, these Puritan laws did not survive very long into the colonial period. Not until the mid- to late-nineteenth century did state legislatures pass compulsory education laws. These laws were not passed, however, as a result of Christian advocacy as much as that of the combined pressures of the social elite and organized labor. The social elite feared youthful idleness and the unions disliked the exploitation of their children through cheap and dangerous child labor practices. The fact that child labor helped suppress the wages of adults also played its part in labor's concern. This unlikely coalition between society's most and least privileged pushed through the first compulsory education laws. But while labor may have been the primary movers, America's business leaders quickly turned to schools as a vehicle for producing a well-trained workforce. By the end of the nineteenth century, all the important cultural forces in America had identified schooling as one important tool to advance their interests. In the catchphrase of Henry Perkinson (1968), schooling in America became "the great panacea" serving all interest groups.

THE NEW RULES AND DEMONSTRATION

Physics
Greenwood High School
January 2001

Newspaper and candy wrappers whirl around the bare courtyard conjuring memories of the movie American Beauty. My wandering gaze returns to the classroom when Mr. Tolin says, "Now today, we are going to learn about Newton's Second Law of Motion. Who can remember what his first law was?" After calling on a couple of students, Mr. Tolin finally receives an acceptable answer and then proceeds to explain Newton's Second Law. After he finishes, one student expresses confusion. This is what Mr. Tolin is waiting for.

While Mr. Tolin restates Newton's Law, he moves to the side of his desk and slides a large wooden box a few feet centering it under one of many strings hanging from the drop ceiling around the room. Still talking about Newton, Mr. Tolin moves to the side of the room where he reaches into a cabinet and comes up with a sixteen-pound black bowling ball with two hooks drilled into opposite sides. While he continues to go on about Newton, all eyes watch him attach the bowling ball to the string hanging over the box and then attach another string to the bottom hook under the ball. As he steadies the ball, Mr. Tolin's speech finally coincides with his actions bringing the mystery of the bowling ball into the narrative of Newton's Second Law. "What will happen if I jerk on this bottom string real quickly?" he asks.

A few students guess that the bowling ball will break the string and fall into the box but then one suggests that the string under the ball will break first and the bowling ball will not fall into the box. After getting the last student to explain his thinking, Mr. Tolin reaches for the string. He pauses for dramatic effect. Then he jerks the string quickly and forcefully. The bottom string breaks. The ball remains where it is—swaying only slightly. A collective gasp arises from the students. Conversation breaks out around the room. Mr. Tolin quiets them down and then retells in terms of Newton's Law what just occurred as he ties a new string to the bottom of the bowling ball. He then asks, "What will happen if I pull on the string slowly?"

A few students speak out suggesting that the ball will now fall into the box. Mr. Tolin takes hold of the string and then very slowly begins pulling on the string. As he slowly increases the downward pressure the students collectively hold their breaths. As tension builds in the taught string, it also increases in the atmosphere of the room until suddenly the sixteen-pound bowling ball falls with a muted thud into the sand in the bottom of the box below. A microsecond of quiet is followed by a sudden sound of students excitedly talking.

SCHOOLING AND THE NATION-STATE

The panacea that was public schools became a central trope in the myth of the American experience. In 1972 Colin Greer called this myth "The Great School Legend." In his powerful little book of the same name, Greer revealed how prominent historians such as Daniel Boorstin and Henry Steele Commager explained America's democratic and economic success through its investment in a mass public school system. These historians explained everything from the taming of the West to the assimilation of immigrants to the expansion of the economic miracle through American investment in public education.

Ten years earlier, sociologist Martin Trow (1977) argued bureaucratic industrialization with its need for a literate workforce spawned a mass secondary school system. He further argued the increased complexity of technology required an expansion of mass schooling to the post-secondary level. Trow's argument provided "scientific" support for "The Great School Legend" while his structural-functional theory accepted unquestionably the desirability of the nation-state's investment in "human capital." Today, the nation-state's investment in schooling for economic development has become accepted truth.

But Greer not only pointed out the extent to which historians had accepted the "Great School Legend" as truth; he showed why it was merely myth. The rise of the United States as a successful modern state had more to do with wider social and economic factors then with schools. Greer, like other revisionist historians from that period (see, e.g., Callahan, 1962; Katz, 1970; Tyack, 1974), tells us a different story of public schooling—one that shows schools as complicitous in the reproduction of the status quo through its failure to successfully educate all members of society. Of course, since that period, reproduction theory has become one of the central explanatory theories of education (Bourdieu & Passeron, 1977; Bowles & Gintis, 1976; Morrow & Torres, 1995).

While Marxist and other critical approaches to reproduction theory are well-known to educational scholars, a less well-known critique of the celebratory school myth comes from Weberian conflict theorist Randall Collins. In his 1979 book *The Credential Society*, Collins directly challenged Trow's assumptions, providing evidence to suggest that the expansion of mass secondary education and the continuing increase in schooling credentials had more to do with cultural politics then with industrialization or increased technological complexity. Collins's work showed that the increased demand for educational credentials around the world correlated much more highly with the degree of cultural diversity in the nation than with its industrial or technological base. His evidence suggests that legitimating the superiority of elite culture formed the primary mission of mass public schools. By equating the culture of the dominant elite with the culture of the nation-state, schools legitimize the dominant group's culture and de-legitimize the cultures of all other groups; therefore, reassuring that the children of the elite continue to obtain the sinecures that they desire. In this way, public schools construct the myth of the nation-state. The *idea of the nation* itself constitutes the primary subject matter of the public schools. Andy Green (1990) argued that the formation of the nation-state is the primary explainer of the development of mass public education.

The argument over whether mass public schooling explained America's progress toward liberty, equity, and success or whether it reproduced America's inequitable and unequal structures continued throughout the second half of the twentieth century. Conservatives and liberals (while disagreeing on the details) agreed that the public schools deserve much credit for advancing democracy and equity. The progressive democrats, on the other hand, share the belief that the public schools inhibit democracy and reproduce inequality. While this argument has been an important one, recent events suggest it may have become irrelevant. At its most basic, the argument between the conservative/liberals and the progressive democrats focuses primarily on how the public schools have served social ends. Liberal/conservative apologists argue that public schools have served the democratic interests of the society by providing a mechanism for social mobility. Progressive democrats argue that public schools have failed to serve democratic interests of the society by failing to teach the majority of American children and, therefore, justifying the inequality of an inequitable economic system. In Greer's words (1972), "My point is not merely that schools worked poorly in earlier times, but that their failure has been, in fact, a criterion of their social success, then and now" (p. 152). But while these two forces disagree on how the public schools have served the society, both sides share the assumption that social ends are, in fact, the primary goals of the schools. Furthermore, these social ends are defined as in the national interest. The assumption that mass public schooling serves primarily the interest of the nation makes some sense. One can argue that mass schooling is closely aligned with the development of the modern nation-state in the industrial era. Whether one takes the liberal/conservative or progressive democratic position, public schooling appears aligned with the construction of a national identity. The argument between the liberal/conservatives and the progressive democrats is whether or not the public-school-constructed "American" identity serves the general interest (i.e., democracy) or the special interests (i.e., ruling elites).

Since the 1970s when the fundamental narratives of the above two competing positions were originally laid out, scholars have suggested that the experience of individuals within the schools is much more complex than either the liberal/conservative or the progressive democratic position might suggest. Ethnographies such as those by Paul Willis (1981), Peter McLaren (1999), and Signithia Fordham (1996) have helped reveal the way in which students resist the schools' attempts to de-legitimate working-class and minority cultures. Historians such as Kate Rousmaniere (1997), Vanessa Siddle Walker (1996), and Kathleen Weiler (1998) have shown the way that individual teachers, administrators, and students negotiate the constrictions of the socially imposed structures to create individually meaningful educational experiences. David Laboree (1997) has presented a particularly powerful analysis showing that despite the larger social purposes of policymakers, individuals have approached schooling in ways to serve their own private interests by understanding schooling as a private consumer good. In fact, Laboree suggests that it is this private interest that is the primary threat to good education today. My own work is sympathetic to these resistance and neo-revisionist theorists (see Quantz, 1985) and the argument in this essay shares much with Laboree's main point. We can no longer assume that large macro forces merely structure and that individuals merely act in response. Clearly the schools of today at various times accomplish all of these things. For some people, in some places, schools are a democratically liberating experience. For other people, in other places, schools are an oppressive experience. And yet, in this "postmodern" moment in educational scholarship in which such large metanarratives are being questioned by personal narratives of individual experience, are we unable to create any larger historical understanding of our present moment? Granted that individuals experience large social organizations in unique ways, can we not still make statements that place these experiences into broader historical context? In other words, at this time when neither the liberal/conservative nor the progressive democratic narratives seems to explain the widely differing experiences of schools, is there another narrative that might provide new insights? Particularly, what should we think of schooling in the present moment when the power of the nation-state (to which both the liberal/conservative and the progressive democratic narratives appeal) is becoming rivaled by the power of transnational corporations (TNCs)?

Transnational Corporations and the Nation-State

As multinational corporations with their global interests but national location become transnational corporations with not only global interests but globe-trotting rootlessness, the role of nation-state is rapidly becoming little more than a handmaiden to transnational corporations.[4] In the words of Masao Miyoshi (1993), "Wealth that generates right and might seems to have overwhelmed power that creates wealth" (p. 743). Or as Bill Readings (1996) put it, "The erstwhile all-powerful state is reduced to becoming a bureaucratic apparatus of management" (p. 47). While the recent economic difficulties reveal clearly that the nation-state has not yet become obsolete, its ability to control TNCs has been greatly reduced as the amount of economic capital controlled by TNCs begins to rival that of the nation-states. Leslie Sklair (1991) provides some empirical evidence of this shifting control of capital:

> In 1986, according to the World Bank, 64 out of 120 countries had a GDP (gross domestic product) of less than $10 billion. United Nations data for 1985–6 show that 68 TNCs in mining and manufacturing had annual sales in excess of ten billion dollars, while all the top 50 banks, the top 20 securities firms, and all but one of the top 30 insurance companies had net assets in excess of ten billion. (Pp. 48–49)

Certainly economic measures reveal a startling shift in economic power. Susan Strange (1996) states that

> between 1985 and 1990, the *average* annual increase in FDI [foreign direct investments] was 34 per cent, while the comparable (nominal) average annual rise in world exports was 13 per cent a year and for GDP, 12 per cent. In 1990, the total stock of known foreign direct investments was $225 billion. And sometime around the mid-1980s, it is generally agreed that the total of international production—output of the affiliates of TNCs outside their home base—overtook the volume of world exports of manufactures. (P. 47; emphasis in original, brackets inserted)

Strange's data are important because FDI bypasses governmental oversight in ways that traditional import/export shifts of capital do not. This ability to shift capital outside of governmental control places new powers in the hands of those who control capital.

The results of this shift of power are visible everywhere. Whereas at the beginning of the twentieth century, nation-states still had the political power to strip the large corporations of monopolistic power, by the end of the twentieth century such power appears to be sorely reduced. For example, while Microsoft may have been convicted of monopolistic practices, the remedy has been far short of what was done to Standard Oil at the end of the nineteenth century or even to Bell Telephone in the middle of the twentieth when they were convicted of monopolistic practices. Whereas both Standard Oil and Bell Telephone were broken up into smaller companies, Microsoft appears to have gotten off with little more than a slap on the wrist.

One does not have to accept the idea of "the end of the nation state" (as the provocative title of Kenichi Ohmae's book proclaims) to recognize that there has been a fundamental shift in the relationship of power between the nation-state and the transnational corporations. Ohmae (1995) points out that the right of nation-states to manage economic affairs resulted from the nation-state's control of military strength, natural resources, colonies, land, and political independence. But Ohmae also points out that military strength has become "an uncomfortably great burden to maintain," that natural resources are less important in a "knowledge-intensive" economy, that colonies are more of a drain on national treasuries than a boon, and that the "borderless economy" makes control of land less necessary and political independence less likely.

Nor does one have to believe that the nation-state is irrelevant to acknowledge that the transnational corporation is no longer as dependent on the nation-state as in the past. At the very least, today transnational corporations can opt out of national political struggles rather than enter into the messy business of political engagement. As Rodrik (1997) put it,

> Far-sighted companies will tend to their own communities as they globalize. But an employer that has an "exit" option is one that is less likely to exercise the "voice" option. It is so much easier to outsource than to enter a debate on how to revitalize the local economy. This means that owners of internationally mobile factors become disengaged from their local communities and disinterested in their development and prosperity—just as suburban flight in an earlier era condemned many urban areas to neglect. (P. 70)

As the locus of economic-exchange shifts from the nation-state to the transnational corporation there appears to be a fundamental shift in the role of the public schools. As one institution of the state, public schools are feeling the pressure to shift from building the nation-state to helping the nation-state serve the transnational corporation. In recent years the educational literature is filled with books and articles discussing the encroachment of corporation into public schooling. All of these writings make important points, but I believe that the situation is even more dire than these writings suggest. While they point out the degree to which corporations are infiltrating the everyday life of public schools, they tend to underestimate the degree to which public school people themselves have come to understand schooling as a corporate enterprise itself. What I am suggesting is that those people who inhabit public schools overwhelmingly understand their enterprise as providing a service to individual and corporate consumers.

THE IN-CLASS PUZZLE

Eleventh Grade General Science
Camelot Hills High School
April 2001

As the students quietly move down the hall carrying their worksheets, two students engage in a mock sword fight with meter sticks. They gather at the end of the hall by the two-storied glass entryway of the new mall-inspired high school. Miraculously the sun actually shines brightly—an unusual event in this cloud-covered Midwestern region. Only a couple of hours earlier, while driving to the school, I witnessed the dawn sun focus streaks of light through a hole in billowing black-purple clouds to a distant spot on the earth. I finally understood Renaissance Italian paintings with their god-symbolizing sunrays. And now these tenth graders held up 3 x 5 cards with pencil-point holes to capture the sun's rays and create its picture on paper. Working in pairs the students follow the worksheet measuring and writing down numbers and answers. The whole event takes but 10 minutes and then we return to the classroom. Mr. Conrad reviews the relevant formula and the students compare their answers. They are trying to find the size of the sun. As students shout out their findings, Mr. Conrad responds with encouraging comments such as, "You're in the ballpark," "You're in the infield," and "You're on the pitcher's mound." Or he softly suggests that a group "Check your math," or "Try recalculating it." Mr. Conrad then writes the formula for finding error on the chalkboard reminding students that they have been using this formula all year. The students calculate the percentage error in their original findings and discuss the possible causes of these errors. This emphasis on the measurement of error in their own original measurements is intended to emphasize the importance of approximation and uncertainty in science as opposed to getting the "right" and "absolute" answer.

SCHOOLS AND CORPORATIONS

Introduction

George W. Bush holds an MBA. He was the first American president to do so. While many presidents have held law degrees and at least one also held a PhD,[5] no president other than Bush has held a graduate degree in business. Not surprisingly Bush's schooling and experience formed the mindset behind his governance. He claimed to have run the executive branch like a corporation. In a *New York Times* article titled "Bush is Providing Corporate Model for White House" Richard Berke (2001) wrote,

> In the seven short weeks of his presidency, George W. Bush has transformed how the White House and elements of the sprawling government operate in ways that contrast sharply with those of Bill Clinton and other past presidents.
>
> It is no accident that a bust of Dwight D. Eisenhower is perched to the right of Mr. Bush's desk in the Oval Office. Not since the general's days in the White House, some veterans of past administrations say, has a president so reorganized a government to function with the crisp efficiency of a blue-chip corporation.

The shift from law to business as the background for the presidency symbolized a shift in our nation's understanding of the state. From an institution to mediate political interest groups and serve the common good, the state under Bush appeared more like a corporation to facilitate economic interests and serve consumer desires.[6]

While President Bush may have been the first president with an MBA, he is only the most prominent state official to take the corporate model as his fundamental mindscape. Governors, mayors, and legislators also frequently use the language of corporations. Even public school superintendents and principals utilize the language of corporations. For example, a local superintendent is reported as having stated that "the district is working hard to help its 'products' improve their achievement while holding down costs" (Kiesewetter, 2001, B3). While the language of democracy may fill the discourse of educational academics, the language of economics fills the discourse of schools.

Schools and the Industrial State

Of course, that public schooling works primarily for the corporate interest is hardly a new idea. For many of us, Joel Spring's *Education and the Rise of the Corporate State* (1972) revealed the full extent to which corporate thinking governed the development of the modern public schools. In 1972 Spring clearly showed that public schooling in the twentieth century had been organized to meet the needs of the industrial state. As Spring wrote in the opening sentence of that book, "The corporate image of society turned American schools into a central social institution for the production of men and women who conformed to the needs and expectations of a corporate and technocratic world" (p. 1). Since that time variations of this theme have become commonplace in educational critique. Recently the theme of corporate infiltration of public schooling has appeared routinely in academic publications.

Books such as Alex Molnar's *Giving Kids the Business* (1996) and Deron Boyles's *American Education and Corporations* (1998) detail the numerous ways in which corporations have burrowed into every aspect of schooling eroding the democratic potential of our schools. Boyles argued that corporations promote technorationality, consumer materialism, and intransitive consciousness. Technorationality reduces all problems to a mechanical means-ends reasoning that sets aside questions of the moral desirability of the ends. Consumer materialism promotes the idea that all problems can be solved through the consumption of commodities. And intransitive consciousness [a concept taken from Freire (1973)] removes any language of possibility that things might be otherwise. Henry Giroux has written extensively of the pervasiveness of the corporate interest in all forms of education (see especially Giroux, 2001). In a short little PDK fastback titled "Corporate Culture and the Attack on Higher Education and Public Schooling" Giroux shares Boyles's apprehension of corporate culture's effect on contemporary life. Giroux (1999a) writes,

> As the rise of corporate culture reasserts the primacy of privatization and individualism, there is an increasing call for people to surrender or narrow their capacities for engaged politics for a market-based notion of identity, one that suggests relinquishing our roles as social subjects for the limited role of consuming subjects. (P. 13)

Like Boyles, Giroux recognizes the amorality of corporate culture and he speaks eloquently to the danger of allowing corporate culture to drive public decisions:

History has been clear about the dangers of unbridled corporate power. The brutal practices of slavery, the exploitation of child labor, the sanctioning of the cruelest working conditions in the mines and sweatshops of America and abroad, and the destruction of the environment have all been fueled by the law of maximizing profits and minimizing costs, especially when there has been no countervailing power from civil society to hold such powers in check. This is not to suggest that capitalism is the enemy of democracy, but that in the absence of a strong civil society and the imperatives of a strong democratic public sphere, the power of corporate culture when left on its own appears to respect few boundaries based on self-restraint and those non-commodified, broader human values that are central to a democratic civic culture. (Pp. 13–14; see also Giroux, 2001)

I share completely Boyles's and Giroux's concern over the influence of corporate culture in our educational institutions, but I think I perhaps also share Giroux's apparent skepticism over the possibility that public schooling is a viable arena of democratic contestation. In recent years Giroux has turned his attention away from critique of the public schools and focused instead on the educational role of popular culture (see especially Giroux, 1999b, 2000, 2001, 2005, 2006a,b, 2008). This shift in Giroux's work away from formal schooling and toward the nonformal education of popular culture reflects the shift in power away from the nation-state and toward the transnational corporations.

Schools and the Transnational Corporations

Leslie Sklair (1991) argues that the transnational mass media promulgates a culture-ideology of consumerism to advance the interests of the transnational corporations and the emerging transnational capitalist class that controls them. "The socialization process by which people learn what to want, which used to occur mainly in the home and the school, is increasingly taking place through the media of the global communications industries" (p. 77). Sklair's "theory of the global system" is the most organized descriptive theory of the evolution of a world social system. One does not have to accept Sklair's assumption of a "system" to recognize the power of his central point: the locus of power is shifting from the nation-state to the transnational corporation and the culture reflects this shift. Like Miyoshi (1993), Ohmae (1995), and Rodrik (1997), Sklair reveals how the power of the nation-state to control the actions of the transnational corporation has been greatly reduced. By their size, wealth, and mobility, the transnational corporations not only avoid the sanctions of individual governments but they often control them as well. From the manipulation of politicians to the control of the media to the economic threat to move elsewhere, transnational corporations now wield more power than many nation-states can adequately control. While Sklair's 1991 book presented his "theory of the global system," his 2001 book provided empirical evidence to support his claim that the rise of the transnational corporation coincides with the permeation of a "transnational culture" and a "transnational capitalist class" all working to advance the interest of the "transnational system."

Whether we agree or not that the shift in the economic order has proceeded as far as Sklair, Miyoshi, Ohmae, and Strange suggest, certainly we must agree that as world capital becomes differently organized, nation-states are changing as well. With their ability to concentrate capital through the control of political power, nation-states in the industrial period provided the primary structures of the world organization. As the concentration of capital is moving outside the nation-state to the transnational corporations, the power of the nation-state to control the institutions that their hegemony created is diminishing. Nothing could be more symbolic of this shift then the September 11 attacks on Washington, D.C. and New York. While the attack on the Pentagon might symbolize an attack on the power of the nation-state, the attacks on the World Trade Center are more symbolic of an attack on the transnational corporation than of the United States. After all, its name was the *World* Trade Center, not the *American* Trade Center. And it truly was a center of world corporate activity. While Americans constituted the overwhelming majority of victims, over a thousand victims came from more than eighty other nations. Japanese corporations alone housed more then one hundred companies in the World Trade Center. More than a "declaration of war" on the United States, this act of terror represents an "act of war" against the world. The United Nations formally recognized the *international* implications of these acts in resolution 1368 adopted on September 12. Not only the victims but also the perpetrators represent transnational interests. These terrorists did not represent a nation-state or even an alliance of nation-states, but acted as a non-affiliated amalgamation of terrorist cells without nation-state allegiance funded by a multimillionaire in an organized effort that Peter Bergen (2001) called "Holy War, Inc." While the terrorist organizations clearly attacked the United States, the real object of their aggression may be the secular society that transnational capitalism represents. We now find ourselves involved in a new kind of "war" indicative of our

Returns Are Easy!

Visit http://www.amazon.com/returns to return any item - including gifts - in unopened or original condition. Full refund (other restrictions apply). Please have your order ID ready.

Your order of February 16, 2012 (Order ID 104-3111712-4554616)

Qty.	Item		Item To
1	Rituals and Student Identity in Education: Ritual Critique for a New Pedagogy (Education, Politics, and Public Life) Paperback (** P-4-B202B30 **) 023010116X	$29.00	$29.5
1	Scar Tissue Anthony Kiedis --- Paperback (** P-4-A75C7 **) 1401307450	$10.87	

This shipment completes your order.

Subtotal
Shipping & Handling
Promotional Certificate
Order Total
Paid via credit/Debit
Balance due

Have feedback on how we packaged your order? Tell us at www.amazon.com/packaging

new kind of world, in which nation-states provide the military services to fight a war that is primarily between transnational corporate capital and a particular version of transnational Islamic fundamentalism. This new world with its locus of economic power outside the nation-state affects every social institution including schools.

In his powerful analysis of the university, Bill Readings (1996) argued that the once central "idea of the university" (i.e., the construction of a national identity) has been eclipsed by the transnational corporations' need for consumers. The rapid embracing of "excellence" by universities is one example of this shift. Unlike past ideographs (such as "culture"), excellence has no content. Readings argues that excellence is empty. One can fill excellence with anything. On a university campus, it makes no difference whether one is a reactionary apologist, a Marxist revolutionary, or irrelevant dilettante. What matters is how "excellently" one apologies, revolutionizes, or dilettantes. And how is such excellence evaluated? By counting publications, reviews, and grant dollars. The university's turn toward *accountability* has become a matter of mere *accounting*. "Excellence" and "accountability" are elements of an amoral technical rationality that serve the interest of the transnational corporations more than that of the nation-states. As power shifts from *inside* the nation-state to *outside* it, the university has found that its purpose has also shifted from serving the needs of the nation-state to serving that of the transnational corporations.

Universities are not the only public institutions that have adopted the language of excellence and accountability. Public schools pursue excellence in the name of accountability as well. While, as Spring and numerous others have shown, public schools have been used to serve the interests of the corporation for more than a century, they have done so through the construction of a *national* identity. "Americanization" was not just a slogan; it served to justify a particular version of literature, history, and even science and mathematics. As long as our identity as citizens of the state formed the central mission of the public schools then the political struggle over the meaning of that identity made sense. Those of us who have argued against the privileging of high culture and against the use of the schools as vocational training institutions implicitly acknowledge the historic centrality of national identity to the public schools' mission. And when we argue that public schools form sites of democratic struggle, we implicitly project our own understanding of what that national identity ought to be. The twentieth century saw the consolidation of the nation-state with the corporate interest, but as corporations become transnational the desirability of strong national identity becomes counterproductive to their interests. To the extent that individuals maintain strong identity as a citizen of a nation-state, the power of transnational corporations is potentially challenged. As nation-state identities become replaced with ethnic identities and with lifestyle identities, consumership replaces citizenship in the construction of identity. As power moves outside of nation-states and into transnational corporations, state institutions think of themselves less as centers of democratic action and more as corporate entities providing services to individual and other corporate consumers.

While I share the hope that public schools may yet recover their democratic commitments, I fear that, despite the rhetoric of those of us who inhabit the academy, the voice of democracy in our public high schools speaks more softly than a whisper. While we might theoretically advance the idea that schools are arenas of democratic struggle, the day-to-day reality of the high schools that I visited found such discourse not only nonexistent, but meaningless. Like the Bush executive branch, American public schools have assumed the role of corporations to provide services for consumers. They have abandoned the idea that public institutions serve the *political* interests of its citizens. In other words, public schools have become virtual corporations.

New Puzzle, Same Rules

Tenth Grade Honors English
Greenwood High School
January, 2001

The students were in the third different grouping of the period. After their initial greeting and homework review, they had been shifted into groups to work on different aspects of a larger set of problems. One group had focused on characterization and another on plot and a third on values and a fourth on setting, and a fifth on theme. After working a while on their particular tasks, they had been reorganized so that new groups had at least one member of each of the prior groups to serve as an "expert." These worksheets had the students focusing on the intersection of the original literary categories of analysis (i.e., plot, theme, setting, character, values) around the broader unit theme, which was "ethics." They are finishing up their group worksheet when Ms. Warner interrupts. "Okay, let's move the desks back and I'll tell you what we're doing for homework." The students move their desks back to the original formation and returned to their original seats.

Ms. Warner asks, "What are the conflicts that a person might have?" She selects five volunteers who then give the five accepted types of conflict apparently presented to them in an earlier class. She then writes "moral dilemma" on the chalkboard and explains, "A moral dilemma is when there is no clear right or wrong action. It is opinion. Knowing what to do is difficult." They briefly discuss various group's conclusions from their small-group work particularly focusing on the "moral dilemmas" as revealed by the conflicts found in the text they were studying.

"For homework tonight you are to write a three-point-five essay that answers this." Ms. Warner then turns to the board and writes, "Heinz should…" Heinz is a character in a story that they have recently read. A "three-point-five" essay follows a particular formula favored by the Advanced Placement test that most of these students will be taking when they are seniors. Groans arise from the students. "You did a great job today," Ms. Warner states. "We're making great progress." She then moves to her desk and the students begin to chat for the few seconds remaining until the buzzer announces the end of class.

The Puzzlemasters

LH: From NPR News this is Weekend Edition, I'm Liane Hanson. And joining us is puzzlemaster, Will Shortz. Hi Will! [*Last comment spoken brightly, with enthusiasm*]

WS: Hi Liane.

LH: How have you survived the past week in the heat? [*Chuckle in her voice*]

WS: It was pretty brutal, pretty brutal.
    [*(yea) LH overlapping*]

LH: Pretty brutal (ah) here in Washington (uhhh) over the past week, but getting better, getting better. [Upturn in her voice at the end] Lot of people working on the challenge you gave last week. It was about a prominent news anchor. So why don't you repeat the challenge and where you found it.

WS: Well it came from listener and crossword constructor, Peter Gordon. And I said, "Take the first and last names of a prominent news anchor—nine letters total—re-arrange them to get the last name of a person who is prominently in the news recently. Who is it?
    —*Weekend Edition Sunday* (August 12, 2001)

So begins one of the most popular segments of National Public Radio's Sunday morning news program. The program quoted here introduces the typical puzzlemaster segment. In fact, nearly all of *Morning Edition Sunday*'s puzzle segments follow the same pattern from beginning to end. The segment quoted here might be called the "Greeting and Last Week's Puzzle." In it the *Morning Edition Sunday* host (in the quoted program regular *Sunday* host Liane Hanson) introduces puzzlemaster Will Shortz and greets him with a friendly exchange signaling warmth and human connection. Following the greeting, Mr. Shortz re-presents last week's puzzle. If you are familiar with this program, you will know what follows. After the restatement of last week's puzzle, the host announces how many entries and correct answers were sent in by listeners, announces a lucky winner, and invites the winner to solve a new puzzle on the air. After a brief greeting and exchange of "personal" information with the winner such as where the person lives, what they do for a living, and what NPR affiliate they listen to, Shortz introduces a new puzzle with a couple of samples ("The New Rules and Demonstration"). The guest (with the help of the NPR host) then attempts to solve the new puzzle by using the new puzzle rules just given by Shortz ("The On-Air Puzzle"). After solving the new puzzle, the host compliments the guest on his or her fine play (regardless of how well they played) and invites Shortz to present a new puzzle for listeners to solve for next week ("The New Puzzle, New Rules").

The Puzzlemaster Interaction Pattern

During the year that I visited high schools I found a similar pattern in the interaction of classroom players. In class after class, I found the period begin with *"The Exchange of Greetings"* in which the teacher and students exchanged a few pleasantries with each other and tried to establish friendly connections. This exchange of greetings was to be found both among the students with each other and between the teacher and the students. Immediately following this a second stage, which might be called *"Last Night's Puzzle,"* reviewed the assigned homework. In this stage, students and teacher interrogated each other: the teacher to make sure that the students had completed and understood their assignments and the students to both make sure that they understood and, more importantly, to perform for the teacher that they did understand their assigned work. After spending some time exploring last night's puzzle, the teacher then introduced new concepts or procedures with a series of demonstrations while the students performed primarily as audience (*"The New Rules and Demonstration"*). During this stage the teacher is the central actor but the students do have an important role to play for without an audience, an actor need not perform. Also during this stage, the students ask questions. Question-asking is a performance that not only helps to clarify the new rules, but reveals the extent to which the students are engaged in the performance. Questions eagerly asked show high engagement. Questions dragged out or slow in coming suggest low engagement. After "the new rules and demonstration," students worked individually or in groups on new problems while the teacher interacted with individuals or small groups of students (*"The In-Class Puzzle"*). "The in-class puzzle" required the students to perform in a manner that showed-off the new rules displayed during "the new rules and demonstration" stage. The interaction between teacher and students during this stage could occur at the teacher's desk or at the students' desks. The biggest difference between the classroom interaction pattern and *Sunday Edition*'s puzzlemaster segment occurred in the last stage. On the radio, the puzzlemaster introduces a new puzzle that uses new rules; in the classroom the teacher assigned new problems for homework that required the use of the same rules (*"New Puzzles, Same Rules"*). During this brief stage, the teacher announces orally or on the board (or overhead), the homework assignment. This assignment might be a set of problems in a textbook or worksheet or it might be something more elaborately developed in a handout. At this stage, the students' only contribution is to make sure that they have marked down in their planner what the assignment is. With only minor changes, this "puzzlemaster interaction pattern" is repeated again and again in every school, at every grade-level, and in nearly every single subject area. While a wide-range of teachers and students produce the puzzlemaster interaction pattern, let me reiterate that I found it more frequently with the better teachers and the better students in the more privileged schools.

In the 1950s, James Mursell (1954), an educational psychologist at Teachers College, identified "patterns of teaching and learning" in American classrooms. He asserted that the dominant pattern of teaching and learning in the 1950s was the "textbook-assignment-recitation" pattern. This pattern consisted of classes organized around small units presented in textbooks. Students would be assigned homework in the text and then "in class the main business is to ascertain whether this assigned study has in fact been done, and if so, how well" (pp. 28–29). This "textbook-assignment-recitation pattern of teaching and learning" is still alive in American high schools, but it is being challenged by a new pattern of teaching and learning. Stigler and Hiebert (1999) report that the typical American mathematics lesson consists of the following stages: warming up, checking homework, demonstrating procedures, and practicing the procedures. Stigler and Hiebert name this American lesson pattern "Learning terms and practicing procedures." More importantly, Stigler and Hiebert reveal how typical mathematics lessons in Japan and Germany are differently patterned in such ways that help explain why American students do not seem to learn mathematics as well as their counterparts in the other two countries. In many ways the "puzzlemaster interaction pattern" that I am suggesting is quite similar to the "American teaching method" that Stigler and Hiebert report, but there is also an important difference in what they are suggesting and what I am. Stigler and Hiebert (like Mursell before them) understand the patterns that they observed to be *teaching methods* and, therefore, they recommend that American teachers be taught different methods of teaching—ones that more closely match those methods used in Germany and Japan. Both Mursell in the 1950s and Stigler and Hiebert in the 1990s understand the pattern they observed in the classroom to be a teacher-imposed organization of teaching and learning. I, on the other hand, understand the pattern to arise out of an interaction among many players. For Mursell, Stigler, and Hiebert the pattern they observed in the classroom is the teacher's pattern. For me, the pattern that I observed is the result of interaction among all of those in the classroom, including students. Mursell talks about "patterns of teaching and learning," Stigler and Hiebert talk about "teaching methods," I am talking about "interaction patterns."

Interaction patterns should not be confused with teaching methods nor with patterns of teaching. My description of the puzzlemaster interaction pattern is not a description of what teachers do, but of what teachers and students do together. To understand fully what is happening in an interaction pattern, we must realize that the teacher is only one player. While it is true that the teacher typically has more power to influence and shape the interactions, every teacher knows that every class of students influences and engages the teacher's actions differently resulting in quite varied classroom experiences. The interaction patterns are formed by more than teacher performances; they are formed by student performances as well. This is particularly important in understanding the full implication of the success of the puzzlemaster interaction pattern in American high schools.

I suspect that many readers can identify with the puzzlemaster interaction pattern that I have presented. Certainly everyone with whom I have discussed it recognizes it immediately. Puzzles are games in which a set of specific rules are stipulated, a specific problem is presented, and a specific answer is expected (though sometimes unanticipated answers are found that meet the conditions of the stipulated rules and are, usually, accepted as correct). A few important aspects of puzzles should be noted. For one thing, puzzles are separate from the "real world." By this I mean that puzzles are created for the fun of solving them.[7] They are part of a game, not part of life itself. This may explain why "The In-Class Puzzle" part of the interaction pattern, when compared to the rest of the pattern, finds students the most engaged. After all, during this part, students are asked to do something. It may also explain why students tend to prefer the puzzlemaster interaction pattern to other interaction patterns. On the other hand, some people find puzzles fun, while others have little use for them. The latter group may seek activities more directly connected to their life. As you watch students engage in the activities of the classroom, some students engage the puzzles more actively than others. While a variety of students bring multiple reasons for their individual actions, certainly one variable includes the extent to which a student finds puzzles interesting.

Puzzles are not only separate from real life, they are entities in and of themselves. They are not connected to everyday life, nor must they be governed by the rules of the real world. They inhabit their own little world. The world of a particular puzzle is a stipulated world. All of the relevant conditions and rules are presented. The puzzle-solver is to accept this fictional world as the total world. Non-stipulated conditions or rules are considered "irrelevant."[8] Issues related to real-world ethics or morality are irrelevant. Above all else, the world of puzzles is a technical world—A world of givens with limited and known conditions and rules and with specific and particular answers.

We might see the technical nature of puzzles more clearly in mathematics and science, but the use of puzzles in literature and art turn these apparently nontechnical subjects into technical exercises. Take the tenth-grade honors English class at Greenwood high school presented earlier. In this example, we see the teacher, Ms. Warner, trying her best to hold on to the ethical and creative elements traditionally associated with teaching literature. She specifically and consciously requires them to write their own essay that engages basic issues of morality. But in this case, the "method" overrides the content. Excellence trumps "worthwhileness." For these "honors" students and their teacher, accountability (read "accounting") comes in the form of the advanced placement test. The advanced placement test expects students to know certain pieces of information and to follow specific formulas when writing essays. Both the students in this class and their teacher know that this class assignment is really preparation for taking the test. I suspect that nearly any moral response (short of the threat of violence against the school or its students) would be accepted. Certainly the teacher does not expect a reasoned, grounded, and informed moral argument. At best, she will find students reflecting on their feelings. Furthermore, few students would tolerate a teacher who moved them too far away from the technical knowledge necessary to score high on the advanced placement test or too far away from easily organized and mastered rules that lead to high grade-point averages. This assignment comes as a new puzzle that uses the same rules that organized the in-class puzzle. For the students, the real puzzle is not the moral one, but the technical one of organizing and completing an essay that uses the proper form and the expected terms.

Most teachers work hard to make their subject matter "relevant" to students. Many teachers feel comfortable within the puzzlemaster interaction pattern because they believe puzzles show the usefulness of their subject matter. Unlike traditional interaction patterns in which students are mere recipients of abstract knowledge unconnected to their lives, solving puzzles shows that the information can actually be *used* for something. It can be used to solve puzzles such as those given in class. Unfortunately, such created puzzles do not come out of the students' lives. They do not result from what Dewey called "indeterminate situations." They are not real-life problems but artificially created puzzles. To the extent that they connect to real-life issues at all, the connections are ones created by the teacher rather than the students. But my particular interest in the puzzlemaster interaction pattern follows less from the degree to which it is or is not interesting to students and more on the symbolic meaning that it ritually constructs.

THE PUZZLEMASTER INTERACTION PATTERN AS RITUAL

Much social action achieves instrumental goals. But many aspects of such action may also be ritualized performances with symbolic meaning beyond their instrumentality. Such social action will follow a recognizable form acted out in a manner that symbolically reinforces the rightness of certain ideas. The ritual aspects of social action work to create a belief in the rightness and goodness of the symbolic meaning of the rituals. They create a "sacred" attitude toward the symbols of the ritual (see Collins, 1975). The puzzlemaster interaction pattern presents a recognizable form that students and teachers act out. While this pattern achieves instrumental purposes (i.e., the learning of specific curricular objectives), it also performs a ritual honoring of particular symbolic constructions. While it may be an effective tool for achieving higher test scores, it also creates a sacred orientation toward a particular understanding as to what counts as knowledge and as learning. The puzzlemaster interaction pattern celebrates problem-solving as technical action.

To understand how the puzzlemaster interaction pattern symbolizes problem-solving as technical action requires some elaboration of problem-solving. There are at least three different ways to conceptualize problem-solving. Problem-solving might be understood to be conventional action, technical action, or meaningful action. I do not suggest these three categories exhaust the possibilities, but they do capture three distinct approaches that people might assume.

Problem-solving can be understood as conventional action. As such, when people solve problems, they utilize specific conventions or rules that have been developed for precisely the problems that are being faced. Conventional problem-solving is often said to utilize rule-based reasoning, because those who approach problem-solving in this manner often justify their actions by appealing to explicit rules. Such conventional problem-solving action is often associated with bureaucracies. Bureaucrats are often accused of applying rules without regard to their actual effects. The old military may be an iconic example of conventional problem-solving. Soldiers were expected to "follow the book." "To throw the book at them" is a phrase that suggests that every possible rule in the book will be used to discipline a miscreant. The textbook-assignment-recitation pattern described by Mursell might be seen as understanding problem-solving as conventional action. This traditional approach to organizing teaching and learning works hard to get students to learn specific information and then asks students to apply it. What teachers consider important in such conventional problem-solving is whether or not the students can give back to the teacher what the teacher or the text has given the student. In other words, do the students know the rules.

Problem-solving can also be understood as technical action. As such, when people solve problems, they select from a large collection of available rules one that will help them achieve a particular given end. Technical problem-solving is often said to utilize means-end reasoning because those who approach problem-solving in this way often appeal to the process as reasonable or rational to achieve the given ends. Engineers and other technical workers are often associated with technical problem-solving. Engineers are given particular ends to achieve such as building a bridge across the river and their job is to figure out how to do it. They are not asked whether it is a good idea to have such a bridge or if it is morally acceptable to build such a bridge, they are merely asked to design one that will work. We see a growing shift in bureaucratic organizations from understanding problem-solving as conventional action to understanding it to be technical action. In business, the oft-cited "bottom-line" is the ultimate end toward which the means must be directed. Capitalism, with its emphasis on efficiency, has pushed corporations to think more carefully about what means best achieve the desired ends (i.e., profit). Such bottom-line thinking has encouraged public policymakers to seek similar processes in other institutions. In education, this is seen in the government's shift away from state and local guidelines covering everything from the number of square-feet needed in a bathroom to the number of books needed in a library (conventional problem-solving) to the creation of "bottom-line ends" such as high-stakes testing for students and report cards for schools. In conventional problem-solving being able to state the rules is what is considered most important, whereas in technical problem-solving being able to apply the rules and achieve the given ends is what is considered most important. The puzzlemaster interaction pattern has developed around teachers and students who are committed to the idea that problem-solving is technical action. While students and teachers may agree that there are many different purposes to schooling, the primary purpose is to gain knowledge that can be applied when needed. As a result, the puzzlemaster interaction pattern serves as a ritual to celebrate technical action.

While the puzzlemaster interaction pattern does ritually celebrate technical action, puzzles are not exactly the same thing as real-life problems. As mentioned earlier, puzzles are bounded. They are discreet entities with all the relevant factors known including the desired end. In the ordinary lives of people, however, problems are unbounded. People do not know all the relevant knowledge necessary to solve their problems nor all the relevant rules to apply to such problems. They may not even understand what the basic problem is and they certainly do not know what the right end should be. In ordinary life, problem-solving is meaningful action because it requires the problem-solver to bring meaning to it or to create meaning out of it. In meaningful problem-solving, the problem-solver must define the problem, must conjecture the possible solutions, must surmise various ends. They must decide not only how to arrive at an end, but they must decide what end is desired. They even have to decide where the beginning point is. Meaningful problem-solving does require knowledge of techniques, but it also requires the ability to interpret and critique, to make moral choices and to commit to some action even when all the relevant information is not available. It requires the thinker to recognize and to construct larger patterns that can be used to make sense of particular instances. It requires creativity. It requires wisdom. In other words, it requires intellect. The recognition that intellect includes many different talents is as old as Socrates, and yet, recent history has equated "intellect" to "intelligence" and "achievement." The narrowing of intellect to IQ and achievement has encouraged schooling to ignore all the other aspects of the intellect from moral reasoning to creativity to abstract reasoning to pattern recognition. The narrowing of schooling to focus on problem-solving as technical action not only fails to develop intellect; it develops the opposite of intellect. It is anti-intellectual. As a result our high schools are not developing intellect at all. They are engaged in training, not education. While the puzzlemaster interaction pattern celebrates problem-solving as technical action, it does nothing to clarify problem-solving as meaningful action.

The anecdotes throughout this essay reconstructed from my field notes reveal the typicality of the puzzlemaster interaction pattern. Whether math or science or literature or art, I found this pattern celebrating technical means-ends reasoning. I must reiterate that the better the student, the better the teacher, the better the school, the *more* likely I was to find this pattern. At least the puzzlemaster interaction pattern requires some problem-solving even if only technical in nature. In the interaction patterns typically found in classrooms without the puzzlemaster interaction pattern, the ability to repeat knowledge and rules substitutes for the ability to use it to solve problems. Technical problem-solving as found in the puzzlemaster interaction pattern may be the best that we have. Such schooling may attain superior "training" but without any focus on meaningful problem-solving, it achieves an inadequate "education."

CONCLUSION

We should not mistake the pervasiveness of the puzzlemaster interaction pattern with a design perpetrated by American teachers or school administrators. The puzzlemaster interaction pattern is not a method. It is not an organization of teaching and learning imposed by teachers or their administrators on unwilling students. The puzzlemaster interaction pattern is a ritual created by all who participate. As Barbara Myerhoff (1978) pointed out, once ritual is recognized *as ritual*, it loses its effect. While many students actively resist the ritual aspects of schooling (see McLaren, 1999), other students do embrace them even if not enthusiastically. I have stated that the students in the top classes in the best schools frequently participate in classes marked by the puzzlemaster interaction pattern and successful students rarely resist. These students actively participate in the construction of the puzzle-master interaction pattern. Make no mistake about it. These students much prefer the puzzlemaster to more traditional classroom interaction patterns such as the textbook-assignment-recitation pattern described by Mursell. While teachers certainly must be the ones to initiate the classroom interaction pattern, they do not act it out alone. Nor can they easily substitute a more intellectual interaction pattern that favors meaningful problem-solving over technical problem-solving. During my year visiting high schools, I did see teachers occasionally try to move beyond mere technical thinking, but I also saw them quickly retreat when the students refused to follow. I also occasionally saw a student or two try to move beyond mere technical reasoning, only to also have to retreat either as a result of peer hostility or teacher resistance or both. The whole time that I visited classrooms, I only saw one classroom successfully engage the intellect for any sustained period (and that was in a creative writing class).[9] Far from being a pattern forced upon unwilling students, the puzzlemaster interaction pattern is welcomed by them.

In recent years, more scholars than ever have decried the infiltration of corporations into public schooling. These critics believe corporate thinking threatens democracy and they typically call for an insertion of democratic thinking into our schools. While I sympathize with their desires, I am more pessimistic in my analysis of such possibilities. While scholars of education may understand public schools as sites of democratic struggle, I failed to find any *performative* evidence of such understanding by anyone who inhabits one of the high schools that I visited. While I am certain that there are teachers and administrators within the schools that I visited who do believe that the democratic purposes of schools supersedes the economic, nonetheless such beliefs are not frequently performed in the daily actions of classrooms. While I agree completely with those who would like to see more democracy in evidence in our educational processes, I have come to the point where I would be satisfied just to see any kind of intellectual education at all.

"Intellectuals" and "intellect" are often confused. Intellectuals might be considered those people who, either through vocation or avocation, spend much of their time in pursuits of the mind. As Collins (2000) tells us, "Intellectuals are people who produce decontextualized ideas." "Intellect" might be understood as the *full use of the qualities of the mind to engage our world*. Intellect requires abstract thinking, moral reasoning, and meaningful problem-solving. But we should not confuse intellectuals with intellect. As Howley et al. (1995) wrote,

> On the one hand, intellectuals are often as foolish and full of mistaken ideas as other humans…After all, in our postindustrial society, the research and development departments of major corporations, the military, and government agencies and contractors—as well as the universities that these other entities dominate—are the places in which most intellectuals are likely to hold *jobs*. These institutions employ the mind to advance their particular concerns and secure their existence. The arrangement is not hospitable to care of the intellect. [P. 143; emphasis in the original]

Assuming that only intellectuals use intellect leads many Americans to reject their own use of intellect due to a cultural distrust of intellectuals (see Hofstadter, 1964). For example, during the 2000 presidential election, the media portrayed Al Gore as a reminder of the kid who sat in the front row in school, raised his hand all the time, and knew all the answers. And the 2008 campaign found Republican presidential candidate, John McCain, brag about his lack of academic success in college and the denigration of Democratic presidential candidate, Barack Obama, for his success at America's elite universities. Apparently many Americans distrust such people as Al Gore and Barack Obama, preferring the kid who sits in the back row knowing few of the answers and taking great pride in his ignorance of the things of school or the college student who finished fifth from the bottom of his class. Such anti-intellectualism should tell educators the degree to which Americans mistrust their enterprise.

While the confusion between intellect and intellectuals creates a problem for education from the right, the equating of intellect with high culture creates a problem for education from the left. Right-wing intellectuals have a long history of equating the intellect with Eurocentric high culture. Not only obvious conservatives such as Bloom and Bennett do so, but more "liberal" intellectuals such as Schlesinger (1998) and Hofstadter (1964) do so as well. But why have so many of us who are committed to progressive democratic life been so quick to accept the politically conservative understanding of intellect as limited to Eurocentric high culture? Why is it that when I try to talk with progressive *intellectuals* about the need for schools to do more to nurture *intellect*, I so frequently have to defend myself from accusations of reactionary, undemocratic principles? Antonio Gramsci

(1971) can hardly be accused of being a defender of high culture, when he argued strongly for the need for "organic intellectuals." W. E. B. Du Bois (1973), who helped create the pan-African movement, certainly did not equate European culture with intellectual endeavor when he argued for the need for African Americans to develop an educated "talented tenth." Giroux recognized the need for the nurture of intellect years ago. He wrote, "by arguing that the use of the mind is a general part of all human activity we dignify the human capacity for integrating thinking and practice..." (Giroux, 1988, p. 125). Like Gramsci, Du Bois, and Giroux, I encourage the development of organic, transformative, non-Eurocentric intellectuals. But I must admit that after spending a year visiting high schools, I would be pleased to see any kind of intellectual nurturing at all.

We should not equate the call for nurturing intellect in the public schools with the mistaken understanding of intellect promoted by such neo-conservatives as Bloom (1987), Hirsch et al. (1988), Bennett (1988), and Ravitch (1996). Educating the intellect is not only not antidemocratic, democracy depends on educated intellect. In this new postindustrial era in which the old enemy of progressive democracy (i.e., Western high culture) has become supplanted by a new enemy (i.e., transnational corporate culture), the nurturance of intellect has become essential. Nothing advances the interest of the transnational corporations better than anti-intellectualism. Since Hofstadter's book, the permeation of anti-intellectualism in American life is nearly complete. American culture, in general, and American public schools, in particular, are hostile to intellect. My fieldwork in high schools confirms that American schooling "purposively neglects care of the intellect" (Howley et al., 1995, p. 178). When the puzzlemaster interaction pattern with its ritual celebration of technical reasoning becomes American schooling at its best, then "education" (as opposed to "training") disappears.

For two decades Henry Giroux has been reminding us that we cannot engage merely in critique, that we must develop a language of possibility, a language of hope (e.g., see Giroux, 1988, 1997. While I remain committed to his point, I have changed my understanding of what that hope might be. In recent years, Giroux has shifted his attention from the public school arena to the educational arena of popular culture (see especially Giroux 1996, 1998, 1999b, 2000, 2001, 2005, 2006a, 2006b, 2008). Such a shift indicates that for Giroux the fundamental educational struggle for democracy is no longer within the public schools. I agree with him. The public high schools, as an institution of the state in a period in which the power of the transnational corporations have begun to eclipse that of the nation-state, under-stand themselves as virtual corporations and are organized almost exclusively to provide a consumer product for individual and corporate consumers. But while I believe that the primary education struggle lies in the world outside of schools, I am not quite ready to give up any hope whatsoever for continuing the struggle within our schools.

If schools are virtual corporations, then teachers and administrators and students are living within the belly of the corporation itself. At its most basic, a corporation is a being-in-itself. A corporation is "any group of people combined into or acting as one body" (*American Heritage Dictionary*). Schools being metaphorically corporate-beings suggests that, within the school, democratic forces can hide waiting for the right moment to retake control. Like dormant viruses within a human body waiting for the right conditions to arise to multiply and spread, intellect can exist in schools, waiting until that moment in which thinking, principled people can act in the interest of progressive democracy. While the present moment may not be right for control-ling the schools, the recent economic troubles may suggest that it is time for infecting the corporate body with the virus called intellect. Such "infection" requires administrators, teachers, and students to seek out those spaces where intellect has not been completely erased and to nurture it. Such "infections of intellect" might be the school equivalent to Bill Reynolds and David Gabbard's call for "exploration of spaces" or "lines of flight" in popular culture. Spaces where cultural resistance becomes political resistance (Reynolds & Gabbard, 2003). The transnational corporations rely on well-trained technical workers. Democracy requires well-educated meaningful problem-solvers. *The greatest irony in schooling today is that the most dangerous, revolution-ary act that any teacher and student can engage in is education itself.*

AN INTRODUCTION TO THE WORLD OF INTELLECT

Sophomore English
Abington High School
September 1962

Barely enough air moved through the small tilt-back windows in the acclaimed, modern building. The heat of summer had passed but the crisp coolness of fall had not yet arrived. Mr. G with his dark, wavy hair and black eyebrows stood in front of the room with our essays on Steinbeck's The Pearl *in his hand. He waited for silence and then began to pass back the papers. Like most of my friends I felt confident that this first essay of our high school careers would receive the high grade that it deserved and that I had been accustomed to receiving. But, as I began to hear gasps and groans as students received their papers, doubts rose in my mind. Then Mr. G began to talk. "First of all, the maxim is 'the love of money is the root of all evil.' You all deserve to fail on that basis alone." I slinked down into my seat fearing the return of my paper since I too had argued that the theme of The Pearl was "money is the root of all evil." Like my peers, I had mentioned nothing about the love of money. He paused and let that idea sink in as he passed out the rest of the "F" papers. He then went to the board, picked up a piece of chalk, turned to the class and said, "Besides, this book has nothing to do with that." Mr. G then turned his back to the class and wrote in very large letters the following two words on the board: "bourgeoisie," "proletariat." I remember wondering what in the world those "Communist" words had to do with* The Pearl *as he went on to explain about social class and privilege and class struggle. This was my introduction to the world of intellect. Mr. G was not a Marxist however (at least I don't remember him as such). He was an existentialist though. During that tenth grade year, besides the required texts such as* Cry, the Beloved Country, The Good Earth, *and* The Pearl, *we read other teacher-selected books by such authors as Kafka, Camus, Dostoevsky, and Gide. We were introduced to fundamental ideas of thought such as the meaning of existence and of death and of choice and responsibility and of self-creation. We carried our engagement with literature outside the classroom and began to see the same issues arising in movies and music. My friends and I traveled into the city to visit the only foreign language movie theater around so that we could watch movies by Trouffaut, Bergman, and Antonioni. We began to pay attention to the political struggles of the civil rights movement and the nascent movement to eliminate poverty soon to be called the "War on Poverty." As I remember it, with only a couple of exceptions, few of my teachers expected us to exercise the intellect. The primary exception was, of course, Mr. G. But once having been introduced to the world of the intellect, I could never really leave it fully behind. No matter what the pressures were to turn my back on that realm, ever since that warm, September day when I learned about "class struggle" and the ever important distinction between "money" and "the love of money," the world of the intellect has never been far away. I am certain that Mr. G had no idea where this seed would lead me or his other students. But I am also certain that he would be satisfied just to know that that seed had grown and matured with its roots dug deep in the hard, underdeveloped, yet potentially rich soil of the American experience.*

7

RITUAL CRITIQUE AND
THE NEW PEDAGOGY

If we understand ritual to be that aspect of action that is a formalized, symbolic performance, then we come to realize that nearly everything that happens in a school includes some ritual and every act has the potential for ritual effects. In other words, nearly everything that happens in a school is both effected by and affects the nonrational. And yet educators approach schooling as if it were a rational exercise. Examine any teacher's lesson plans, or any grade-level curriculum, or any statewide objective and the assumption is that schooling is about the rational. But I hope by now, this book has convinced you that not everything in a school can be reduced to the technical logic of rational self-interest. We must learn to consider the nontechnical reasoning of the nonrational if we are ever going to understand what is actually happening in schools. In fact, this book argues that the nonrational aspects of schooling are ultimately more important to most students and teachers than the rational and yet, the nonrational is seldom consciously considered by either. Rarely do students and their teachers actually focus on the cultural politics exemplified in the symbolic struggle embedded in ritual. And even more rarely are the material politics that support and form these symbolic struggles recognized.

THE NONRATIONAL ASPECTS OF SCHOOLING

The real work of schools takes place in the nonrational. I've stated this several times in this book. Let me examine this idea further.

The nonrational is central to our schooling because it is the nonrational that constructs "commonsense." It is in the nonrational that we find the "taken for granted," the "real world." Because the nonrational remains unexamined, its assumptions are attributed to nature. "It is only natural." "There will always be the poor." "Kids who do poorly in school don't value education and neither do their parents."

"If we don't test students, how are we going to know if they are learn-ing?" "If we don't have measurable objectives, how are we going to determine which methods actually work?" "The best way to construct a curriculum is to break down the desired outcomes into its building block bits of knowledge in a kind of pyramid and then teach the bits of knowledge and build the knowledge back up." "The only way to get students to invest in their learning is through punishing those who don't learn and testing those who do." "The purpose of school-ing is to get a good job and earn more money." "Smart kids are held back by dumb kids, so they need their own classes." "Anyone can be successful in American schools if they have the ability and good work habits." "What's wrong with American schools is that there is too much progressivism." "If we don't require teachers to raise test scores, they don't really try to teach." "Administrators need to hold teachers accountable." "School boards need to keep administrators account-able." "Sex education is something only parents have a right to teach." "Teaching about homosexuality encourages homosexual behavior, but teaching about drugs discourages drug use." "The market is the best adjudicator of good schools."

Which of that list of statements and questions is supported by empirical data? None. Yet, for all but a small minority of people, all of them are considered true. None of those assumptions derive from a technical rationality and yet all of them are taken as commonsense. How can that be? Because the nonrational aspects of our society's institutions including the media, churches, government, and schools utilize nonrational mechanisms such as ritual to lead us to accept them. As pointed out several times in this book, ritual works best when people do not realize they are participating in a ritual. When the ritual itself becomes "natural" or "ordinary" or "normal," its form recedes into the background and the narratives and meanings of its symbols become accepted as true and good, as natural, as com-monsense. Those who break the form or challenge the symbols do not merely question knowledge, they call for what nature will never permit. They have no commonsense. They undermine reality and morality and identity.

Reality

From Durkheim (1965/1915) we learn that ritual divides the world into the sacred and profane. The profane is open to ordinary questioning and debate. The sacred—because it is sacred or, perhaps, as the indicator of sacredness—is above question and debate. To challenge an idea such as the best way to decide whether students are learning is to test them with objective tests is not merely to challenge a profane belief; it is to challenge something that has become sacred to the education industry and educational decision-makers. That teachers overwhelmingly reject this assumption only proves their untrustworthiness. It is so much a part of commonsense that the only possible explanation for teachers' rejection of this sacred assumption is their desire to avoid being held accountable. Never mind that there is no evidence to support this commitment to testing because its acceptance has nothing to do with the evidence and everything to do with the nonrational commitment to this idea. But how else can we know if they can read if we don't test them? Nel Noddings answers that question by saying "Give them a book and ask them to read" (January 29, 2009, public lecture).

Making it sacred makes it so. It becomes the reality within which we live. By treating teaching as a technical enterprise where having the right toolbox of methods guided by the measurable objectives provided by the decision-makers becomes the reality. Students who score high on the tests are smart; those who score low are dumb. The students in the higher tracks deserve to go to college; those in the lower tracks should have no such expectations. The fact that social class is a better predictor of track placement than is intelligence seems to be irrelevant. The fact is written in the ritual aspects of class placement that puts such placement beyond question.

Morality

Ritual not only constructs our reality, but our morality as well. To act in congruence with that which ritual has constructed as sacred is to act as a member in good stead in our community. To challenge these "commonsense" assumptions is to put into doubt your worthiness of membership. The few parents who challenge their child's track placements are likely to be considered "troublemakers" who are "pushing" their child rather than parents who might actually know their child's capability. Of course, if the parents are themselves well-educated with advanced degrees and a good income, then we are much more likely to accept their objection, or, at least, to accommodate it. After all, when they challenge the school, they know the proper way to dress when they visit the principal and they use an elaborated code when they speak (Bernstein, 1977). They know how to perform the petitioner with just enough hint of deference backed by legitimate authority as to influence the teacher or the administrator in charge. These educated, middle-class parents are legitimate, moral beings. The unschooled, poor parents are simply less likely to perform as legitimate players. They act in ways that discredit their petition. In Bourdieu's terms, they lack cultural capital (Roscigno & Ainsworth-Darnell, 1999). Understand that this works at the nonrational level, not the rational. The administrators and teachers and parents are not working out the odds and calculating their self-interests and making decisions based on their calculations (or, at least, not exclusively so). Rather, they are performing in a game of sorts: One that requires that they accept their position and play it to the best of their ability. Bourdieu (1984) not only points out that cultural capital is knowledge-based, but it depends on the apparent "naturalness" of its performance, the ease with which it is played.

Ritual helps to declare which people are legitimate and which are not, but it also works to determine which values are legitimate and which are not. Educators who believe that teaching is as much about ethics as about efficacy and efficiency are warned that their classrooms must remain "objective" and "balanced." Ethics is not to be brought into it unless it is treated in a "neutral" way. The best way to accomplish this is through avoiding language of values altogether and focus, instead, on the language of efficacy and efficiency. This is, of course, precisely the problem that Habermas (1971/1968) pointed out decades ago. The "colonization" of the "practical realm" (i.e., the world of human interaction, communication, and meaning) by the "technical realm" (i.e., the world of technical logic) forces the replacement of the "practical interest" with the "technical interest." It erases an ethic built around human relationships with an ethic built around the rightful manipulation and exploitation of the external world. So, besides working to create commonsense reality, ritual works to create conventional morality.

Identity

To suggest that students may not be autonomous individuals whose test scores represent their unique individual abilities and achievement is to reject one of the fundamental American political assumptions. Kenneth Strike (1982) has suggested that autonomy is one of the three basic assumptions underpinning liberal democracy. That people have the ability and the moral responsibility to separate themselves from their culture and make decisions rationally may be the most sacred of American political assumptions. And yet the idea that people can reason outside of culture is clearly absurd. Try to reason without language; you will find it quite difficult. And, even for those who do reason through imagery instead of language, sooner or later, they must turn their images into language. And, of course, the moment they utilize language they are caught in the cultural logic of the language they use. Consider Navajo. As I understand it, the Navajo language has no static nouns. Everything in their world has a time marker associated with it so that no thing is static or stationary but always dynamic or in flux. Now compare that to English: a very noun oriented language. Not only is English noun oriented, but its preferred pattern is noun—transitive verb—noun. In other words, in English something does something to something. This is a great language for technical reasoning, for engineering, for science. But should we be surprised that in Navajo where the world is always in flux such technical reasoning is less obvious a solution to life's problems? Should we be surprised to find out that exclusively English-speaking Americans find themselves locked into a logic that privileges the performance of the rational? Anyone who knows more than one language well, knows that there are certain ideas in one language that just cannot be adequately expressed in another. Far from being autonomous beings capable of separating ourselves from our culture, we are linguistic beings trapped in the cultures of our languages.

And part of being trapped in language is being positioned through identity markers. Our language positions us in many ways. When I am in a classroom, I am an "instructor." When I am in conversation with the university's provost, I am a "professor." When I am at home, I am a "husband" and a "father." When I am with my siblings, I am a "brother." All of these terms have performative expectations associated with them. I must learn to perform to those conventional expectations or I bring into question my identity. Of course, these linguistic markers often have secondary traits associated with them so those of us who do not display the appropriate performative markers may find ourselves declared less legitimate. This is why many young female instructors of color are more likely to find themselves challenged than those of us whose physical attributes are congruent with the expected markers. Watch as the middle-school students learn to perform their social identity. Watch the boys learn to walk and move in a manner that is associated with masculinity. Failure for them to walk "right" or talk "right" or act "right" brings their gender and their sexuality into question. This was a major factor in Paul Willis's (1977) "lads" anti-school resistance that they interpreted as more masculine than a feminine pro-school compliance. Look at the way students of color begin to inscribe into their body their racial or ethnic identity. They have to learn to walk, move, talk, and groom in ways that present them as members of good stead to their identity and in opposition to those identities they must separate themselves from. Failure to do so is to bring into question their legitimacy as a member of their group. In this way, Signithia Fordham's (1996) kids at Capital High had their racial identity questioned.

Understood in this way, ritual works to construct reality, morality, and identity and yet in schools we ignore the nonrational and focus upon the rational. It makes invisible the forces that work to construct commonsense and conventionality and that position individuals into a classed, raced, and gendered society. It brings educators to focus upon whether or not scores on a multiple-choice math test are raised on average a question or two rather than on how to educate students to take their place in a democratic society. Surely we must ask who benefits from this distraction? By centering all of our attention on these measurable outcomes, rather than on the construction of reality, morality, and identity, some people gain, while others lose.

The Rational Aspects of Schooling

With No Child Left Behind (NCLB), and correlates such as research-based curriculum and object-based learning, and now Race to the Top, the rational has all but extinguished the nonrational aspects of schooling from consideration. This has not always been the case. There was a time in which teachers, administrators, and other poli-cymakers made decisions about schools because it was understood to be the right thing to do. The inclusion of the arts in the curriculum, the inclusion of recess, the intellectual engagement of a novel were all commonplace and are now rapidly retreating from our schools. If it isn't tested, why teach it?

Outcomes-Based Instruction

While there is much agreement among educators that high-stakes test-ing is being overused as a solution to our schools' problems, there is much less understanding that outcomes-based reasoning results in sim-ilar problems as testing. To paraphrase a former American president's well-known attitude to something else: Outcomes-based education is not the solution to the problem; it is the problem. Once we predeter-mine the specific outcomes of a curriculum, we turn the process of edu-cation into one of engineering. Once I know the end and the starting point, my job as a teacher is simply to manipulate the learning process to achieve that end. Teaching is reduced to a means-ends rationality—a technical exercise to which the solutions must also be ones of technique, or method. If we just have the right instructional method "proven" to be the best through "research," then all teachers need do is implement it. Of course, even if we accept a means-ends rationality, there are many reasons to reject such simplistic reasoning. The point being made here is not that all technical rationality leads to such overly simplistic practices, but that the very process of identifying specific outcomes to learning inherently turns teaching into a technical exercise.

The state of Texas has recently announced its new standards for social studies (Knowles, 2010). The extreme conservative ideology of these standards has erased Thomas Jefferson from having any influence in world history replacing him with St. Augustine and Thomas Aquinas. These new standards have also determined that the United States is no longer to be considered a democracy but as a constitutional republic instead. Set aside for a moment, the political extremism of such moves; consider instead the absurdity of having a committee decide what is and is not to be included in textbooks on history. Consider how any committee anywhere should be expected to name the specific learning outcomes of a course that is to cover the history of the whole world or of a nation. Surely anyone can recognize that the important events in history are infinite. To leave to a committee of fifteen to decide which of those pieces of knowledge to include and which to exclude seems little more than folly.

But, my critics are likely to argue, how are we to ensure that students receive a good education in world history if we don't identify the learning outcomes? That such a question is so regularly asked shows just how far the technical rationality has penetrated the world's commonsense. Before I answer that question, let me ask a different one: Why do we want students to study world history in the first place? What is our purpose? Or, perhaps I should ask, "what are our purposes," since there are obviously many reasons why we wish to educate people about the history of the world. Only E. D. Hirsch and his supporters are likely to answer that the purpose is to come to share in a common set of knowledge and only that answer provides justification for identifying the precise learning-outcomes of a course in world history. Let me suggest some alternative possible purposes. How about we study world history in order to better understand our connections to the world? Of course, to better understand "our" connections to the world will change depending on the antecedent to the pronoun our that makes it impossible for any committee to decide ahead of time what those connections would be. Or how about we study world history in order to learn how to see the world through others' eyes? Or to gain a complex understanding of our world? Or to become enthused about learning history? Or to learn to read the world? None of these purposes requires preset learning outcomes; in fact, preset learning outcomes can only interfere with such purposes.

What advocates of outcomes-based education often do not understand is that focusing on the rational ends of schooling distracts us from the nonrational reality of learning. By centering our attention on the means-ends of schooling, we pay little attention to the equally important learning that occurs both cognitively and affectively in education. Let me clarify once again what I refer to when I speak of "rationality" and "nonrationality." Rationality is a term that has special meaning in social theory. It refers specifically to the kind of reasoning that assumes people are in a zero-sum game in which to act "rationally" means to act to win the game in their own individual interest. Anyone not trying to "win" the game is acting, by definition, nonrationally. When we turn schooling into a technical-rational process, we assume that students act in their own individual interest to achieve the highest learning possible because it is in their individual interest to do so. If we assume that to be the case, a teacher's job is to utilize the techniques that will make that achievement possible for the greatest number and this increases the competition amongst the students pushing them to even further achievement. This way of thinking is at the heart of the classical liberalism that has come to dominate the American hegemony since the so-called Reagan Revolution. But such thinking is absurd on its surface. To believe that everyone acts selfishly all the time or even that they understand that they are in a zero-sum game or any game at all is obviously so incongruous that one has to wonder how so many people have come to accept this as commonsense. The thought that we are all in competition with each other so that the best and smartest win and make the world better for the rest of us clearly advances a Eurocentric, white supremacist worldview, promotes a patriarchal ideology, and, above all, works to complete a hegemonic corporate culture.

For over thirty years schooling has become more and more rational in its practice that may improve training, but diminishes education. Let me clarify another point, when I argue against outcomes-based learning, I am not arguing against having broad goals or purposes for education. I am also not arguing against some basis upon which to decide whether or not education is happening in a classroom or a school. I am simply arguing against the assumption that what is important about a course can be reduced to specific measurable outcomes. I liken this thinking to trying to determine the quality of a song one might be listening to on a radio while driving down the highway by using the mile markers outside the window. Surely, the markers are objective, neutral, and standardized. Certainly they tell us something about the song, but not very much. When I hear people say, "the data may not be perfect, but it is the only data we have," I point to those mile markers and suggest that such data are useless.

My point is that the focus on learning-outcomes, on standardized tests, on research-based instruction is a part of the politics of distraction. Spending all our effort on trying to do research to support specific methods in order to raise test scores distracts us from what is actually happening in our schools. Is there anyone who doubts that American schools work better for some groups of children than for others? While the great school legend (Greer, 1972) may lead many to think that American public schools play a foundational role in the strength of our democracy, countless studies reveal the way in which schools work to advantage the few over the many. The fundamental distracting idea of the technical rationality embedded in the present so-called educational reforms is the idea that the problems can be solved through technical means. But methods can only solve technical problems. To the extent that the reason that many children do poorly in school is the result of poor techniques, then such means-ends, technical rationality will address the problem. But, to the extent that the reason many students fail in school has to do with something other than technique, no change in instructional methods or research-based curriculum or outcomes-based instruction is likely to improve anything.

John Ogbu's Question

Let's face it: We do not expect much of students in American public schools. For so many students to fail to learn the little that is expected of them requires these students to actively resist learning. This actively working against learning was what John Ogbu (1974, 1978, 2003, 2008) spent his career trying to understand. While I do not agree fully with Ogbu's basic explanation for this resistance, I do agree with his belief that there needs to be some reason behind why so many African American students refuse to learn what they are being taught in school. Ogbu, a Nigerian American, knew that there was nothing inherent about African culture to explain such a thing, since African students tend to work hard in school. Obviously, it must have something to do with the American situation that created this resistance. Of course, we have plenty of studies to show the way in which many groups of students have adopted anti-school behavior including Latinos/as (Cordeiro & Carspecken, 1993), and working-class whites (Willis, 1977). In fact, it may not just be working-class boys who perform dismally in American schools. In all but the upper-middle-class communities, boys' school performance continues to suggest a lack of investment in their own schooling.

PAULO FREIRE'S QUESTION

Paulo Freire's work has been central to the development of critical education theory. Those influenced by Freire frequently point to the need to engage in dialogic education, to form culture circles, to focus on the political aspects of their situation; but many pay little attention to some other of his basic assumptions of teaching and learning. Freire (1973) began his educational career in adult literacy where he developed a technique based on a deep philosophical understanding of the conditions of illiteracy. Freire's work leads us to understand that learning to read and write is as natural for human beings as learning to speak and to understand the spoken word. This is a startling assertion, but one readily acceptable when we think of it. The intellectual task of reading and writing is quite similar to the intellectual task of speaking and understanding the spoken word except that one requires reading and producing aural signs and the other reading and producing visual signs. So how many of us had to go to school to learn to speak? I suspect, no one, and, yet, we seem to have to go to school to learn to read and write. Why might this be? One important difference between learning to speak and learning to read is maturation. We learn to speak beginning around eighteen months, but only begin to be able to manipulate the visual signs of reading around five or six years of age. In other words, we learn to speak when we are closely integrated into the primary family unit, but begin to learn to read as we enter into the larger social world outside the family unit. It is this different context that leads to the failure of some children to learn to read for in the isolated family unit, the learner is fully integrated with their social world; but in the school, many learners are alienated from and separate from the social world.

Freire's work forces us to reverse the fundamental question we ask about literacy. Most literacy experts ask what it is *that we need to do to make it possible* for students to learn to read and write. Freire's ideas lead us to ask what is it *that we do that prevents* students from learning what is otherwise a natural thing for them to learn. Freire's answer to this question is found in his recognition that the children of the oppressed learn to read at an age and in a context in which their and their family's control over their material world is absent. The six-year-old leaves the family unit and enters a public world of schools in which they have no control over their situation and that fails to recognize their world as legitimate embedding many of these student in a culture of silence where they have no legitimate voice. Freire helps us see that the solution is to create a process in which children learn to read through the process of recognizing that their culture is valuable and worth "speaking." Freire's adult literacy campaigns were so successful that he could teach a whole rural Brazilian village to read and write sophisticated material in less than a year by understanding the problem of literacy as primarily a political problem rather than a technical one. Of course, uncovering the political oppression through the process of becoming literate was seen as threatening to those who benefited from the political oppression and led to Freire's exile from Brazil.

We do not have to accept Freire's specific answer to his question to recognize the question as central. G. H. Mead (1967/1934) argued that there is a major shift in children's social interaction when they associate only with "significant others" compared to when they begin to enter a world of "generalized others." The world of two- and three-year-olds is a world in which everyone is a concrete other whose significance is specific and unique. During this time children engage in what Mead called "play" in which they took on the role of the specific others in their lives. When they play "mommy and daddy," they play their own mother and their own father. When they play doctor, they play their own doctor. But at age six or seven, children move into a broader arena in which they must learn to play a kind of game in which they are assigned a position with certain expectations placed upon them. They are no longer a specific individual nor do they interact with specific and concrete others. Rather they are representations of an abstract category. Rather than being Bryant or Jenny, they are "a student." They must learn to act "as a student" and learn to leave that unique part of Bryant and Jenny at the schoolroom door. Brian McCadden (1997) shows precisely this process at work in his study of ritual in a kindergarten. Before one can learn to read and write in school, one must learn how to act as "a student." And Jette Kofoed (2008) shows the same process at work on the school playing fields. The more readily one accepts their student roles and the better one is able to perform such roles, the more successful one is likely to be in the game of school both in and out of the classrooms.

Pierre Bourdieu (1974; Bourdieu & Passeron, 1977) argued that schools don't actually teach much, but rather they confirm which students already know. Students who learn how to read and write at home perform well on the reading and writing tasks of school, while those who do not learn to read and write at home do not do well on these tasks. Schools mistake the success of their middle-class students as evidence of the school's effectiveness while explaining the failure of the poor students as evidence of poor family values. Bourdieu suggests that it is the other way around. The success of middle-class students in school is evidence of the success of middle-class, educated parents teaching their children, while the low performance of poor children is evidence of the poor performance of the schools.

Regardless of whether we prefer Freire's answer or Mead's or Bourdieu's, Freire's question needs to become central to our pedagogical task. What are we doing that prevents students from learning? And whether or not we accept Ogbu's specific answer to his question, Ogbu's question also needs to be addressed. What are we doing that leads students to refuse to learn?

THE POLITICS OF SCHOOLING
Cultural Politics

The present "reform" movement in education focuses on setting objective, measurable goals and leaving the methods for achieving those goals to the schools. The schools' approach to accomplishing these objectives is to devise an ever narrowing curriculum and the intensification of present method. Rather than opening up the curriculum, schools have opted to eliminate anything not measured on the tests. This is not only true for the lower achieving students, but also for the Advanced Placement courses aimed at the higher achieving students. The only difference is which test the students are being prepared for and the knowledge and skills required to score well. The higher classes focus on covering as much material as possible in the hope that students will remember enough to score well. Little discussion or critical thinking is asked of students in most AP courses.

On the other hand, for everyone else, the emphasis is on the intensification of methods that have already been shown to not work. For many school decision-makers, the reasoning appears to be that if the students have not learned sufficiently in the past, then the solution is to ask them to do more of the same. If reading and filling out the questions at the end of a chapter is not sufficient, then add worksheets. If adding worksheets is not sufficient, add more worksheets. If that is not sufficient, eliminate recess and have students complete more worksheets. If that is not sufficient, require more homework and develop tutoring programs and Saturday classes so students can do more worksheets. The answer seems to be, in the words of a Fox News personality from Alaska, "Drill, Baby, Drill!"

Meanwhile, educational scholars, scrambling for those research grants and tenure, pursue some kind of "data" to "drive" educational reform. But since the only kind of data that counts is that which can be "objectively measured" and "predicted," it only leads to the refinement of techniques for the increased efficiency of uncritical training. These approaches assume that students fail because we are failing to do something. If we could only do something else such as design interactive computer programs with exciting visuals or publish textbooks with colorful and interesting pictures and graphs or develop better objectives or design better computer programs for tracking individual student learning objectives; if only we were to develop a better engineered teaching program, we would get those test scores up. The search is on for that magical technique.

As I have already mentioned, what we ask students to learn in American schools is not very demanding. There are only a very few students who are intellectually incapable of learning the watered-down curriculum in our schools. If students aren't learning, it is unlikely to be because we have yet to figure out the right technique. Many students in the world learn the very same material with little or no innovative instructional methods. If our students are not learning the little we demand of them, perhaps it is because they refuse to learn it.

So, what if the problem is not one of technique; what if the problem is that many students are just refusing to learn? Maybe we have to understand that the students who score low on these tests just don't see their importance or the importance of the technical education they receive in schools? Maybe what we have to do is provide the right incentive? Maybe we can give them a party if they score well on the test or we can partner with a corporation such as McDonald's and provide coupons to students with perfect attendance every month or reward good students with a field trip or give their school an "A" on a report card or a flag for their flagpole proclaiming their "excellence" (see Anna S. Kuhl Elementary School, Port Jervis, NY, 2010)? Maybe we could have more teacher-parent meetings or school outreach programs? Maybe we could create a parent education program to teach the parents what they should know about how to "properly" raise their child? All of those strategies are being tried today in a desperate attempt at getting students and their parents to buy into their schools. But such approaches make a big mistake by confusing students' (and their parents') lack of support of schools as lack of support for education. Just because students are anti-school does not mean that they are anti-education. Perhaps, we need to begin to respect our students and their parents and rethink what it means when they develop anti-school attitudes and behaviors. Perhaps, there may be good reasons for their doing so.

We might better understand what those reasons are if we shift our attention away from the rational aspects of schooling and focus more on the nonrational. Remember that this book has shown that the ritual aspects of school action may be just as important as the rational. Chapter six pointed out an emphasis on the puzzlemasters interaction pattern in many high schools and while one might point out that the puzzlemasters pattern is not drill and fill, it is also not critical thinking. The puzzlemasters pattern may be more intrinsically interesting to students, since it requires them to be active, but it is also a pattern that promotes technical means-ends problem-solving. What is it that led Paul Willis's (1977) "lads" to consider that schooling was emasculating them? Or what led Signithia Fordham's (1996) students at Capital High to consider schooling to be de-racializing them or Cordeiro and Carspecken's (1993) Latinos/as to believe school to be Anglicizing them (Cordeiro & Carspecken, 1993)? While undoubtedly the formal history and literature curriculum could lead to such interpretations from the students, it really is hard to believe that students refuse to learn algebra because the knowledge of algebra in itself is understood to be feminine or white or Anglo. By addressing the nonrational aspects of schools such as its ritual aspects we can begin to understand what students are really being taught and why they may be resisting.

To understand the specific content of these lessons, we must first return to some of the basics of ritual. Ritual is a public performance of meaning-making. Through ritual we perform for those around us our commitments, our values, our beliefs. Through participating in rituals with others, we confirm our acceptance of a common understanding of the world, of reality. And because our body treats as sacred the symbols of our actions, when we stand up and proclaim with our body that which is of value to us, we define our morality, too. And finally, by learning and performing these rituals we proclaim our membership in an identity group. By embracing the performances of one group we publicly create our self as, at one and the same time, belonging to one group while distancing ourselves from other groups. To succeed in our present schools requires many students to abandon their home identity, their home reality, their home morality, and their people and take a chance that their gamble of abandonment will pay off. Learning to read and do mathematics and science and understand our history are critical to every person's success and well-being. It is in their interest to learn, but it may not be in their interest to succeed in school. Not if it means surrendering to a status quo that systematically dominates them and people like them. To succeed in America's schools requires many students to abandon their self, family, and people and become an "autonomous individual" at the mercy of the whims of a system stacked against them. We should not be surprised that many students refuse to participate in such rituals. Instead, we should be surprised that so many students seem so willing to try despite the costs and despite the odds against success.

We should also be surprised that so many well-meaning people could continue to mess this up so badly. Thirty years ago, one of our most underappreciated sociologists of education Ray McDermott, along with his coauthor Kenneth Gospodinoff (1979), suggested, "Our problem is neither racist teachers nor dumb kids. Our problem is that our school systems are set up to have conscientious teachers function as racists and bright little children function as dopes even when they are all trying to do otherwise" (p. 189). In this groundbreaking article, McDermott and Gospodinoff pointed to the way in which "ethnic differences" became "ethnic borders" through the construction of solidarity. The mistake that educational decision-makers continue to make is their assumption that such effects are by-products of education rather than the inevitable effects of policies designed to shift our attention away from the ritual effects of schooling to focus on the rational.

Material Politics

So far this chapter has pointed to the contribution that ritual makes to the creation of reality, morality, and identity. It has focused on the way in which the nonrational works to construct meaning, to create commonsense; and, as a result, the part that schooling plays in cultural politics and that cultural politics works to undercut schooling. But culture is not merely about identity politics. And identity politics is not merely about culture. To separate schooling, culture, meaning, morality, and identity from material politics is to misunderstand the fundamental process at play. Ultimately, schooling is about material power. It works to legitimate an illegitimate distribution of power, to justify an unjust distribution of wealth, to validate the invalid treatment of the expendable, to make invisible the subaltern, and to authenticate authoritarian rule over the disempowered.

In the same way that the idea of the autonomous individual is a myth, so too the idea that society is made of independent cultural groups is also a myth. Culture is not merely a matter of heritage passed down from generation to generation. Rather, culture is constantly under construction by members of groups working to maintain solidarity against forces functioning to dissipate their power. It should come as no surprise that schools work in the interests of those who control them. How is it that so many still accept the idea that schools work for the general interest of society when it is clear that the mechanisms of education are controlled by the special interests of the transnational corporations? It takes a giant refusal to see what is right before our eyes and to continue to believe in the benevolence of our schools. Like all other social institutions—such as the media, governments, corporations, courts, and the military—schools are being turned to serve the interests of the most powerful. This is not just an American problem. As an example, look at the so-called Bologna Accords in which a few European education ministers successfully pushed through a plan to standardize higher education in Europe. By centralizing and standardizing, the Bologna Accords turn the purpose of higher education to serve the interests of the transnational corporations (Paraskeva, 2010).

Chapter six of this book reveals the way in which ritual helps to construct schooling to serve the interest of transnational corporations. It also reveals the way in which this new focus creates an imbalance among the traditional American commitments to piety, democracy, and economy. While I do not wish to return to the days in which American schools overtly taught Protestantism, I am in favor of public schools developing a commitment to the teaching of public ethics and democracy. The abandonment of these twin goals leaves the schools as little other than corporate training grounds at the public's expense. One does not have to be a Marxist or a socialist or even a progressive to believe there is something wrong with a public school system that has abandoned its responsibility to the polity. One only has to be committed to a belief in democracy and the values necessary for a democracy to thrive. As things stand now and if things do not change, the crushing inequality and injustice of the American economic system will continue to be made invisible and the dispensable will find themselves the victims of what Appadurai (2006) has referred to as econocide, the "worldwide tendency to arrange the disappearance of the losers in the great drama of globalization" (p. 40). Make no mistake about it; schools work in the cultural realm, but their effects have real consequences for the distribution of material power.

A NEW PEDAGOGY

Many teachers in my classes become frustrated for the lack of methods taught. "All of this may be interesting, but what are we to do?" they ask. They wish for me to give them techniques that will solve the problems in their classes, but as mentioned many times already, the problems in the classroom result not from lack of good methods, but from problems located in politics. Since the problems are not a matter of technique, neither are the solutions. What follows is a discussion of some principles that can guide teachers and administrators as they attempt to revise their pedagogy to transform their classrooms. Nothing discussed here is a technique. None of the principles are to be taken and mechanically applied. Unfortunately for some, to improve classrooms requires teachers who are permitted and willing to think. Which leads me to the first principle.

Teaching as Critical Problem-Solving

Teaching requires critical problem-solving more than good technique. This is not to be confused with puzzle-solving as discussed in chapter six. Solving puzzles requires only the application of specific rules to new data; solving problems requires figuring out what rules to apply or even to realize when there are no rules that apply. Problem-solving requires teachers to observe and to reflect and to think. That American teachers are not given the time to do any of those things does not make it less true, only more difficult to achieve.

Teachers must stop looking to others to solve their classroom problems. Only the teachers with their students and their parents can figure out the best way to an education. Certainly educational policymakers are not likely to do so and neither are college professors or think-tank flunkies. Bureaucrats of all types will never make a bad teacher into a good one; but time and time again, they turn good teachers into bad ones. The only policies that will work to improve education are those that encourage and reward teachers who take responsibility for their own pedagogy by studying their students and their communities and work with each other to create the right educational experiences for their students.

While there is no one correct way to address their situations, we can borrow some ideas from Paulo Freire as a place to start. Perhaps we can ask, "What is it that the students don't know?" I do not mean by this question what the specific learning objectives of a subject should be. I do not mean, for example, that a proper answer might be that they don't know how to multiply or to identify figures of speech or the contents of the Gettysburg Address. Instead I mean to ask what it is about their world that leads them to misread their world leading them to either resist their schooling or embrace its hegemonic mythologies.

For example, undergraduate students at my university are smart people who score high on standardized tests and maintain high grade point averages, but most of them are completely ignorant of the fact that 5 percent of the population controls 60 percent its wealth (Kennickell, 2009) or that American health care cost twice as much as that in countries such as France or Sweden and three times as much as that in Portugal and Spain and four times as much as that in the Czech Republic and Hungary (Reinhardt et al., 2004) but ranks thirty-seventh in health according to a World Health Organization report (World Health Organization, 2000) or that since the 1890s the United States has toppled at least fourteen foreign governments (Kinzer, 2006). My point here is not that I think that any one of those things is wrong (I do, of course, but that is not my point here): My point is that in a democracy shouldn't the citizens at least know these things, if they are being asked to make decisions on taxation and health care and the secret operations of their government? As teachers, shouldn't they at least know that there are certain political movements whose goal is to eliminate public schools due to the belief that the market is always the best solution and government always the worst? Shouldn't they at least know that the research on the policies of the last thirty years of educational reform is ambiguous at best and refuted by most? Shouldn't they know that advocates of the culture of poverty, such as Ruby Payne (2005), have some very powerful counterarguments (Bomer et al., 2008)? But who amongst us is so confident of our knowledge that we feel that we can construct a list of all of the knowledge that students need to learn? Who even knows one subject so well that we feel we can leave it to them to decide what is important knowledge and what is not? Isn't the importance of a piece of knowledge contextual? Doesn't it depend on what the problem is that we are trying to address? And when we are considering it? So when I ask the question of what the students don't know, I'm echoing Freire's (Freire & Macedo, 1987) well-known idea that to read the word, you must read the world. Understanding what it is about the world that the students don't know is a good place to begin.

I begin my undergraduate course with discussions about the differences among the terms "education," "training," and "schooling." I also have them explore the idea of the public and the private and of the difference between the mechanisms of democracy and the idea of democracy. I begin my master's courses by exploring the concept of the autonomous individual, which, when looked at objectively, makes little sense. I know a high school English teacher who starts the year by helping students learn the relationship between income and school attainment. It may be hard to believe, but this relationship is something that most of them just don't know.

Of course, the answer to the question of what the students don't know requires that the teachers learn about their students and their students' communities. It also requires they learn about their students' identities and cultural heritage. It means that what the students in Scarsdale don't know will likely be different than the students in Bushwick and, therefore, requires that the teachers develop different strategies for their classes.

It also requires that the answer to what the students don't know must be age appropriate. It makes little sense for a third grade teacher to teach about American foreign policy, but it can start with helping students learn that they are part of a community or that they must learn to move back and forth between the private world of their family and the public world of their schools. And this is one place where ritual in the classroom becomes central. For it is through ritual that these kinds of things are taught. Turning these into lessons with measurable objectives to be put down on a test is irrelevant to the real problem. What these students need to learn is what it means *in practice* rather than in the abstract and that is best accomplished through ritual. As it is now, what they learn is to perform as isolated individuals in competition with each other for the scarce rewards of the classroom. They also quickly learn that those rewards go to certain kinds of students and not to others.

In other words, what the teacher must do is understand what the political conditions are that lead to the students' ignorance and how those political conditions are replicated in the nonrational aspects of the classroom. Chapter five of this book explores the way in which the American concept of the individual works against seminar-style classes at the undergraduate level. If instructors of undergraduate seminar-style classes wish for them to work as hoped, they must first invest in the construction of rituals that work to deconstruct and dismantle the idea of the autonomous individual. After eighteen years of living in our American culture, however, the idea of the autonomous individuals remains a stubborn commonsense to most college students. What amazes me is not the degree to which that idea remains in my classes, but the extent to which it is readily given up by so many. In just a fifteen-week semester many students begin to rethink their own individualism (though few move far enough to overcome the fear of public performance).

Chapter 6 of this book shows the way that many American secondary classes for the best and brightest students utilize the puzzlemaster interaction pattern leading to the reduction of education to training and serving the transnational corporate interest. Why are college professors surprised that their students are unwilling to become fully involved in their education when they have rarely experienced education at all? The ritual patterns of classrooms are powerful constructors of commonsense and when the commonsense is filled with ignorance, it is best addressed by changing the ritual patterns.

Education, Not Training

Henry Giroux (1988) has called for teachers to become transformative intellectuals and reject a role as reproductive intellectuals. I agree. Teachers must become transformative intellectuals, but before they are willing to take up this role, most will have to be convinced to embrace the role of intellectual of any sorts. When I ask practicing teachers in my graduate classes how many consider themselves intellectuals, only a few will readily identify as such. Teachers must begin to reject the anti-intellectualism that this suggests and embrace the idea that if teachers in our schools are not to be intellectuals, we should not be surprised to find little intellectual activity in the classroom. Yet, intellectualism is precisely what is needed. The act of educating can only be accomplished when students find themselves in an intellectual culture guided by intellectuals. As chapter six has shown, while the anti-intellectualism of American culture is a longtime trait, its present form clearly works in the interest of transnational corporations and against the interests of democracy.

While obviously schools must perform some training (how to use a pencil, how to spell, the grammatical rules of the language of higher education), that schooling has all but abandoned the wider purposes of education should be seen as the abandonment of the children's futures. We should be shamed. Instead, we adopt policies that erode education in favor of training even more than the present ones do. The new pedagogy must return to education—transformative and critical education, for sure—but education of any sorts as a start.

At the end of chapter six I state that education just might be the most radical thing that schools can do. Whose interests are served by schools that provide well-trained young adults able to read and follow directions and apply techniques but unable to read and critique the world and apply moral and political reasoning? Surely not the general public. The public interest can only be served by a well-educated citizenry able to see through the fallacies and absurdities that passes for news today. The general interest can only be served by a critical education that allows citizens to demystify the mythical world of commonsense.

The new pedagogy must step back and look at the whole picture of the classroom and the school. It must examine the interaction patterns and reflect on whose interests the ritual aspects serve. Consider, for example, the critically compassionate intellectualism for Latina/o students suggested by Julio Cammarota and Augustine Romero (2006), which combines critical pedagogy, compassionate student/teacher relationships, and social justice content to counter "the institutional silencing that prevents their [Latina/o students] full and active participation in shaping their futures" (p. 18). Like Cammarota and Romero, the wise teacher, as opposed to the well-trained teacher, must work to construct interaction patterns that work to counter the anti-intellectualism that the broader American culture perpetuates. This is not an easy task. Remember that during the Bush-Gore presidential campaign, one of the candidates was belittled in a whispering campaign, which became much louder and more public than whispers, as reminiscent of the kid who sat in the front row, raised his hand all the time, and knew all the answers. The nation apparently preferred the kid who sat in the back row with his cap on backward and bragged about having read only one book until after graduating from college. Apparently being a good student is a disqualification in the eyes of the majority of voting Americans. That should tell you of the difficulty of the teacher's task of transforming their classroom from a training ground to an educational experience. But such transformation is necessary. A new pedagogy will exchange education for training as the fundamental purpose of schooling.

Value-Based, Not Outcomes-Based

Today's pedagogies (as taught in most educational methods courses and as demanded of most policymakers) are organized, developed, and judged on the twin values of efficiency and efficacy, in that order. We must get the "biggest bang for the buck," as is frequently said. We want the highest test scores for the least amount of money. We may want high test scores, but, even more, we want to spend less money. For example, we could easily raise the test scores of high school students by letting them sleep a couple of more hours and not start schools until 9:00, but that would require purchasing and running twice the number of buses at much more cost. We could also increase the test scores by having students engage in physical fitness regimens every day, but that would require investing in the equipment and training teachers to run such fitness programs (Reynolds, 2010). Try to get a levy passed to spend money on exercise bikes and stairmasters. We could raise test scores by reducing the size of the schools, but states and districts are enamored with the false promise of economies of scale and insist on building large schools. We do want efficacy, but only if it is efficient.

But when efficient, efficacy is all that seems to matter. Right now educational decisions are supposed to be supported by research. Unfortunately such research only seems to matter when the research supports what policymakers want. Dozens of studies have shown that charter schools are either no better or significantly worse than regular public schools, but charter schools are central to Arni Duncan's "Race to the Top." Most district-wide decisions are based on getting those test scores up so that school boards, superintendents, principals, and teachers are desperately looking for that magical curriculum or enchanted pedagogy to effectively raise those test scores. Sometimes I think that if I were able to show that torturing students with electrodes attached to their chairs could raise test scores, I'd be able to convince some school boards to adopt torture as a pedagogy—after all, isn't the elimination of recess for elementary students coming pretty close to that?

Let me reiterate what I stated earlier in this chapter: I am not arguing against having broad goals, but I am arguing against specific learning outcomes as a basis for organizing curriculum. So, if we are not to base our instruction on measurable objectives, upon what should we base our teaching? Rather than basing our teaching on the students' outcomes, I am suggesting that we organize around the values with which we start. We build a course not from the end backward, but from the beginning outward. We do so by adopting a set of values with which to organize our decisions. If we keep true to our values, then the results of the teaching process, whatever they might be, will be positive and desirable. This shifts the basis for decision-making and assessment from efficacy and efficiency to ethics.

Such a shift is scary to many. There seems to have developed a belief in the United States that if we make decisions based on the technical rationality of efficacy and efficiency we need not consider ethics. Such a cultural attitude is convenient to our corporate leaders. Milton Friedman (1970) once famously wrote that the only social responsibility of corporations is to increase profit.

> The political principle that underlies the market mechanism is unanimity. In an ideal free market resting on private property, no individual can coerce any other, all cooperation is voluntary, all parties to such cooperation benefit or they need not participate. There are not "social" values, no "social" responsibilities in any sense other than the shared values and responsibilities of individuals. Society is a collection of individuals and of the various groups they voluntarily form.

To the extent that we can develop a cultural "commonsense" that reduces ethical decisions to technical questions of "the bottom line" we remove the need for the inefficiency and the inconvenience of democracy.

This reductionism is supported by a culture that suggests that ethics and morality are based in religion and since, in the United States, we separate government from religion; any discussion of ethics/morality must be located in the personal and private religious lives of individuals.

Such reasoning removes the possibility of discussions of ethics/morality from public spaces. But there are many problems with this logic. First of all, there is no reason to think all questions of ethics or morality must be based on religion. Surely this is obvious. Not all of the more than thirty-four million Americans who self-identify as nonbelievers are totally without moral bearings (U.S. Census, 2010)? And yet we have reached the point where Americans are afraid to commit to particular moral values in public spaces; we prefer to hide those values beneath a veneer of objectivity and neutrality and balance. Somehow it has become reasonable for schools to eliminate recess and art and critical thinking in order to raise test scores, but it has become unreasonable for schools to encourage creativity and critical thought based on a commitment to their value as a part of an educated citizenry.

So, a place to begin is to replace our emphasis on outcomes-based education with an emphasis on values-based education. We must shift away from the technical rationality that inherently guides education decisions to be based on efficacy and efficiency to one that also considers ethics. We must move away from the false assumption that people act "rationally" (i.e., as individuals in a competition with others for their own interest) and replace it with the recognition that people are guided at least as much by nonrationality (i.e., as members of communities that organize life through processes of signification and ritual in which one's own unique self-interest is frequently rejected for different kinds of interests).

Why not start relying on wisdom and ethics to make many of our educational decisions? If we can develop a set of values that we can agree upon, then teachers can make their curricular and pedagogy decisions based on those values. And as long as they keep those values in the front of their minds, the result of the learning will be appropriate.

Of course, public schools require values that are in the public's interest. It requires people to come together and develop a set of values that they can agree upon. Such values must be of the sort that one's private values (whether religious or not) are neither required nor disallowed. In other words, they must be values that both the very religious and the atheist can embrace. Each set of values must be decided locally by the students, their parents, the teachers and administrators, and the community at large. Let me discuss some of the kinds of values that might be arrived at.

Democracy

One place the right and the left seem to agree is that if we evoke values as a basis for educational decisions, we must necessarily court the imposition of one group's private morality onto another group.

But this is only true when we equate ethics and morality with private beliefs. Are there no public values that Americans can agree upon regardless of their private moral beliefs? For example, can we not all commit to democracy as a fundamental value? It makes no difference if one is a right-wing religious fundamentalist or a left-wing secular humanist, can't we use democracy as a moral principle for decision-making. Is any group of Americans ready to stand up and declare their opposition to democracy as a basis for educational decisions?

I think the number would be few and their public declaration of being antidemocratic would be helpful in our public conversation. Of course, just because most of us might commit to the value of democracy does not mean that we agree on what that means. But isn't that the point? Isn't democracy, at the very least, an engagement in public space about how we are to live together? Shouldn't the first basis of that engagement be around what democracy means to us? Shouldn't our schools teach in a manner that is both congruent with this ethical principle and in a manner that educates our young to participate in a democratic society? Shouldn't they learn how to reason through problems, gather evidence, consider consequences, explore values, listen to others, and advocate for positions? Shouldn't we be asking our math and reading and history and science teachers to start their classroom practices and curriculum with this basic ethical commitment?

Let us agree that public schools must provide an education congruent with democracy. In what ways do the ritual aspects of American public schools work to teach the value of public engagement of ideas to live and work together? Most of my undergraduates enter our course without having even thought about public space. In today's rhetoric, the public has been reduced to the private. Everything is private, even public schools. Vouchers and charter schools are essential practices of turning public money over to private interests. It is time for public schools to entertain public purpose. A new pedagogy will find ways to build public space into the nonrational practices of their classrooms. It will seek out age-appropriate and locally relevant interaction patterns that lead students to take as commonsense the practices of democracy. We often hear extreme right-wing television personalities ask progressive guests why they hate America. Let these hosts argue against democracy in schools and let us respond by asking why they hate democracy.

Diversity

Diversity is not merely nice. Having a diverse student body and teaching force is not merely a matter of fairness. Diversity is an essential part of education in a democracy. Historically, American schools overtly taught homogeneity. The public schools were tasked with the Americanization of early-twentieth-century immigrants. Until 1963, most American schools were overtly Protestant in their practices beginning the day with a recital of the Protestant Lord's Prayer and a reading from the Protestant Bible. Many schools were legally segregated by race until the 1950s. But in recent years, schools have adopted a rhetoric of commitment to diversity. Many policymakers and administrators probably actually think that they are taking real concrete steps toward increasing diversity. Most teachers consider their meager attempts to incorporate a famous figure or two to represent people of color sufficient to achieve diversity in their curriculum. But consider how present-day schools address diversity in the nonrational realm. Look at the form and symbols of the ritual aspects of schooling and you will find that they nearly all celebrate uniformity and a singular truth that just happens to be congruent with the culture of the privileged.

A new pedagogy will work to create a set of nonrational practices that challenge the commonsense of today's schools. It will create a set of rituals that make diversity of persons, of cultures, of ideas, and of values central to the educational process. Students and teachers will perform in such a way as to honor engagement of ideas through critical thought in order for all to grow and learn. This is the essential character of democracy that permits a society to grow and transform itself for the new challenges of the new historical moment. This is why we value democracy. It, and it alone, organizes a community around the value of diversity for its future. Only when schools develop interaction patterns whose ritual aspects also value honest and true diversity in a way that requires students to engage each other and each other's ideas will we be able to achieve a true democracy. Without a commitment to diversity, democracy withers and so does an education for democracy.

Respect

If we are skeptical that we can organize our schools and curriculum around ethical principles such a democracy and diversity, then how about building them around a relational ethics such a respect. Certainly this is an ethical value that we should be able to agree upon regardless of our personal, private moral values; and yet, there are few places where less respect exists than in American public high schools. Too many students fail to respect teachers and too many teachers fail to respect students and too many administrators fail to respect teachers or students who, in turn, fail to respect administrators and neither administrators, teachers, nor students are likely to respect the school staff of secretaries, cafeteria workers, and custodians. High schools just may be the place where people show each other the least respect of any institution in America. Teachers reading this right now may doubt my claim that, as a rule, teachers fail to show respect to students, but when my undergraduates speak to the few teachers whom they respect, it becomes clear that they are also the few teachers who respected the students. Perhaps it is time that we try to reform education by demanding more respect rather than higher test scores.

Yes, I am aware that we don't all agree on what respect requires. But once again, isn't that the point? If high schools are not able to work as communities toward understanding the demands of respect, then can we ever expect to find respect in the larger society? Today's schools often do attempt to demand respect of students for each other and for their teachers, but how many of them actively work to demand respect of teachers to their students or of principals to their teachers?

Ray McDermott (1977) has argued that teaching methods are less important than the construction of trusting relations. Trusting relations are, for McDermott, the result of people working together to address problems. They are to be achieved. Trusting relations are not a psychological attitude (though certainly an attitude of trusting others is undoubtedly helpful in the construction of trusting relations), but a way to describe a social community's way of working together. Among other things, communities that have achieved trusting relations will show respect toward others.

Respect is a ritual performance. It is a way in which we honor another's being as sacred, as belonging, as important. The interaction patterns we typically use in American classrooms and in the hallways and playgrounds and sporting fields show little ritual respect. In fact, just the opposite. Watch the typical classroom and watch all of the ways that students are reminded that they have little status, that their ideas are irrelevant, that who they are doesn't count for much (unless they are the child of a prominent citizen). Why are we surprised when students begin to disrespect schooling when they have experienced little but disrespect from their schools. Teachers and others then tend to attribute that anti-school attitude to something intrinsic to the students or their parents or their neighborhood or their culture instead of recognizing it for what it is—a response to the disrespect they have endured through the years and the loss of hope that enduring such disrespect has nurtured.

A new pedagogy will construct classrooms in which students are respected by their teachers and by their peers because the interaction patterns will require public performance of honest respect. However, don't confuse respect with deference or simply being nice. Sometimes respect is shown by arguing against a person's position or action. We show respect when we take a person seriously; when we listen to that person; when we acknowledge that we might be wrong. We show respect when we honor a person's experience instead of dismissing it; when we admire a person's culture, instead of ignoring it.

Take, for example, the disrespect many schools show indigenous people by adopting Native American images and symbols as mascots. Mascots are themselves symbols of identity for a school and its athletic teams. They are designed to help create solidarity, to bring students together. Why choose as a mascot something that divides the students? Why bring a majority of students together, but push a minority away by telling them that they do not belong? Or look at the similar example of the pledge of allegiance to the American flag still spoken every morning by hundreds of thousands of students. This pledge is designed to create solidarity among the American people, to pledge to each other our brother and sisterhood. So why include the words "under God" in the pledge and tell 30 percent of the students that they don't belong in America, that they and their atheist friends do not deserve our allegiance? Why show so much disrespect to so many people?

Do we really need another study to tell us that many black and Latina/o students believe that schools are not in their own interests; or that gays, lesbian, and other queer identified students really are harassed in schools; or that science and femininity are defined as mutually exclusive; or that success in school of any sorts can bring into question a high school boy's masculinity? To disregard the complaints of these students and their parents and the spokespersons for them in their community shows little more than disrespect. After such disrespect, why do we wonder that so many resist what school has to teach them?

From my perspective, it is time for high-school and middle-school teachers and administrators to start to respect students other than those with the highest grade point averages and touchdowns scored. It is time to respect working-class children and their parents enough to really listen to them and to believe that they may actually have something to contribute to the success of the school. It is time to respect ethnically and racially marginalized students sufficiently to take their complaints seriously. It is time to hear the pleas of gay and lesbian students and teachers to be free from harassment at school. It is time to realize that when people complain about the school practices that they may actually have something important to say and are not merely "troublemakers."

Social Justice

I recognize that Glenn Beck (2010), the Fox news entertainer who poses as a news commentator, has convinced a group of followers that a commitment to social justice is evil incarnate, but that is not a reason to avoid a commitment to social justice in education, rather it is a reason to raise that value to the top of our educational processes and goals. Only an uneducated populace could confuse the very American commitment to social justice with some kind of anti-American value. Are Mr. Beck and his followers really ready to argue for the moral superiority of a school system designed to achieve injustice? Let the riled tea partiers storm the school board with cries of liberty and injustice for all! We have nothing to fear in that debate. No value could be more central to the American experience than social justice and its commitment to freedom and equity. Why would anyone try to argue against the desire to live in a just society? Or to argue against the need to teach our young the values and skills necessary for maintaining justice?

For example, there is great confusion about freedom. In today's America freedom has been reduced to mere liberty. It has been reduced to what has been called "negative freedom" or "freedom from." The "negative" in "negative freedom" does not refer to a judgment of goodness, but to the direction the freedom takes. It refers to the kind of freedom that individuals have *from* being imposed upon by others. In the United States we are free to send our students to any school that we can afford. If we can afford to live in the community, our children can attend those schools. If we can afford the tuition of a private school, we may send our children to that private school. No government is going to tell us that we may not do so. We have the *freedom from* government interference in our decision.

Positive freedom refers to the kind of freedom we have when we are able to take advantage of situations and make things happen for ourselves. We have the *freedom to* do things. While Americans have the liberty to send their children to any school they can afford, they do not have the *freedom to* send their children to any school they may wish to because most poor parents cannot afford the rent to live in a district with excellent schools or the tuition to send their children to America's best private schools and certainly a $7,000 voucher is not going to help much.

A new pedagogy should adopt a value of social justice committed to positive freedom and not be willing to settle for merely negative freedom. It must examine the nonrational aspects of its schooling practices and see to what extent it is organized to help all students accomplish their rightful goals rather than merely allow them to if they can get their act together and achieve it on their own.

I'm thinking of nonrational approaches such as Helane Adams Androne's "ritual pedagogy" for reading texts by African American and Chicana women that creates the possibility of racial and ethnic healing. Androne's "ritual pedagogy" builds upon Tey Diana Rebolledo's (1995) idea of salpicón analysis to piece together from various sources her own approach, "salpicón pedagogy." Androne's (2005) pedagogy provides a possibility of cultural renewal through a four-moment ritual process leading to "re-connection with their communal, ancestral and spiritual selves" in order to better understand "their relationship to and possession of power." While not to be taken as a linear process, Androne's ritual pedagogy suggests four "moments" that include recognition of their alienation from power leading to revolt, recovery of a sense of wholeness through collectivity, a struggle between self-assertion and communalism (or inward and outward control over sociopolitical realities), and the reconnection of the fragmented self and collective in healing. The key to Androne's pedagogy is the recognition that in the analysis of resistance texts written by African American and Chicana women, students can themselves repeat again and again the four moments of the ritual helping to lead to their own self and collective healing. In Androne's ritual pedagogy we see how thinking of the nonrational aspects of the classroom can lead to students who typically are invisible in classroom rituals to recover and reconstruct those identities leading toward positive freedom.

A new pedagogy will set up interaction patterns that ritually affirm the desirability of a community designed to support the common good of education for all rather than having it reduced to a private consumer good. It will not ritually reward students whose primary quality is being the son or daughter of the already educated while ritually punishing the students whose primary fault is being the son or daughter of the invisible and undesired poor.

Courage

Virtue has received a bad rap in progressive writing. The religious right has adopted "character education" as a central educational goal. Built upon the traditional Christian virtues, this conservative curriculum has rightfully been rejected by others as a stealth attempt to interject private religious values into public classrooms. But just because virtue ethics has been claimed as uniquely Christian does not mean that virtue itself, as an ethical code, is not appropriate for public spaces. After all, no one is more closely associated with virtue than the pre-Christian, ancient Greek philosophers, Socrates, Plato, and Aristotle. Are there no virtues that could be embraced and engaged as a public, rather than private, virtue?

Isn't there also a place in our public space to value and promote courage to stand up for one's beliefs or the courage to resist just following the crowd or the courage to speak to injustice when it arises? Is that too considered controversial? If so, why? What is so controversial about teaching our young people that they have a responsibility as a citizen in a democracy to stand up if they think certain practices are undemocratic such as the secret CIA assassination of the American Muslim cleric Anwar al-Awlaki (Leonard, 2010); or the legal, but immoral, practices of America's largest financial institutions. Once again, isn't that what democracy is? The public engagement of how we are to live together? Do we expect our adult citizens to suddenly develop the skills, knowledge, and dispositions to be active citizens when they leave schools without having had an education that teaches the kind of courage it requires to speak and act democratically?

Henry Giroux has frequently written of the need for progressives to nurture courage in their struggle against oppression (e.g., see Aronowitz & Giroux, 1985). Isn't courage something that many local communities could adopt as a fundamental value? Of course, like all values, courage does not have a set and agreed upon meaning. But once again, isn't that the point of democracy? To engage each other and develop a way for us to live together? The traditional Christian virtues are constructed as dualisms with each virtue paired with a vice. In Christian virtue, courage is paired with the vice cowardice. But Aristotle argued that each virtue is a median point between two weaknesses. In the case of courage, one can be under-courageous, or cowardly, or one can be over-courageous, or foolhardy. Clearly democracy requires individual and community courage to struggle for social justice and for equity and for education.

Chapter five explored the way in which undergraduates in seminar-style classes remain unwilling to engage each other in the ways that faculty understand to be seminar patterns. Instead they adopt a pattern I called the wagon-wheel in which they direct their comments directly to the instructor. I tried to show that students, due to a deep-seated commitment to individualism, may be leery of engaging each other, which requires them to leave each other unchallenged. It takes courage for the undergraduate to break this pattern and stand up and direct comments to fellow students. In fact, a democracy requires all citizens to have the courage to step forward and speak their mind and the courage to listen to others even when they disagree. A democracy requires its citizens to have the courage to speak the unpopular and risk social isolation.

In what ways do the nonrational aspects of our schools work to support or undermine courage? A new pedagogy should consider the development of nonrational practices that support those who question commonsense and who challenge established practices that show disrespect toward minority populations. Students and teachers should be encouraged to advance unpopular views in a climate that promotes counterviews and ritually speaks to the desire of community engagement of ideas. Recently a national right-wing movement has accused professors of not being balanced in their instruction. There is a call for instructors at all levels to be "neutral." But such calls are illusionary. What is understood as "neutral" is just that which is congruent with commonsense and, therefore, works in the interest of the status quo. So, the call for neutrality is duplicitous. Nor is the call for "balance" any better. The point is not for "all sides" to be included, such a thing would be impossible—there are just too many sides. And if we are committed to the values of democracy and respect, we should not give "equal time" to antidemocratic positions that exclude certain categories of people from the public conversation or belittle their being whether intended or not. Do we really want to give equal time to the Holocaust deniers or the Turkish genocide deniers or the Serbian ethnic cleanser apologists? Given the commonsense assumption that the United States is the "most peace loving nation on earth," shouldn't we at least allow some teachers to point out that the United States has fought more wars in the twentieth century than any other nation? And reward students who are willing to stand up and suggest that American institutions, in the name of being colorblind, merely make whiteness invisible? The point is not to engage in propaganda, as Stanley Fish (2008) fears, but to create a safe and viable place for the engagement of ideas, which is the very heart of democracy and surely requires people nurtured to develop the courage necessary for its success.

So, a place to begin is to replace our emphasis on outcomes-based education with an emphasis on values-based education. We must shift away from the technical rationality that inherently guides education decisions to be based on efficacy and efficiency to one that also considers ethics. We must move away from the false assumption that people act "rationally" (i.e., as individuals in a competition with others for their own interest) and replace it with the recognition that people are guided at least as much by nonrationality (i.e., as members of communities that organize life through processes of signification and ritual in which one's own unique self-interest is frequently rejected for different kinds of interests).

RITUAL CRITIQUE FOR A NEW PEDAGOGY

The critical tradition aims to trouble commonsense, to demystify the mythologies of conventional thought, to align the narratives we tell of our world with the way that is congruent with material power. This is what Habermas (1971/1968) called critical knowledge: The clarification, through a process of honest engagement across differences, of the distortions that our meaning making creates. Ritual critique provides a way to proceed in this task by turning our attention away from the rational aspects of schools and place it on the nonrational. When we stand back and observe what is happening in front of our eyes separate from the stated learning objectives in a class, we learn to see what the lasting lessons of schooling are. We become able to see how commonsense is constructed in a manner that is undemocratic, inequitable, and immoral. We come to understand that when marginalized youth become anti-school, they may have good reason for doing so. We understand the way that schools distort the world with a lens that works against the interests of some students and for those of other students. Since ritual works in the nonrational, we should not be surprised that the students of the upper-middle-class seem to have good values that include the desirability of education, while all the rest simply feel like they don't belong. As Bourdieu (1974) has shown, it isn't that the children of the poor can't learn the cultural capital that leads to success in schools, but that they don't already posses that capital when they enter school and their success requires that they gain it in a school that does not overtly teach it, but only covertly expects it through the practice of ritual.

Ritual critique helps make visible the invisible hand of the nonrational, and, as it does so, it softens its impact. As stated several times in this book, ritual works best when participants do not realize they are participating in a ritual, illuminate it and its power is reduced. Ritual critique has the power to do precisely that. My hope is that scholars and practitioners alike will begin to look at the nonrational parts of their classrooms as much as they do the rational. I firmly believe and have full confidence that when commonsense and nature are understood to be mere ideological constructions that work in the interest of powerful elites that their power will be revealed and real transformative action can occur. I have no illusion that the problems of material inequality found in a rigged economic system can be remedied by merely telling new stories, but I also am firmly convinced that the restructuring of our economic lives can only begin with a populace educated to take their places in a viable and participatory democracy. Based on critique of present school practices, educators will adopt a new pedagogy: One that implements ritual practices that work in the interest of democracy and justice and begins to restore the promise that our nation once had of a people bound together in an endless process of engagement and growth as we live and work together in public space.

NOTES

2 SCHOOL RITUAL AS PERFORMANCE

An earlier version of this essay was published as Quantz, R. A. (1999). School ritual as performance: A reconstruction of Durkheim's and Turner's uses of ritual, *Educational Theory, 49*(4), 493–513.

1. The idea that one might "perform" for oneself may seem strange, but imagine the nineteenth-century English colonialist of literary, if not historical, reality insisting on keeping the ritual of teatime even when all alone in the jungles of India or the single person who maintains the practice of saying grace before eating a meal even though eating at home all alone.

3 FROM ETHNOGRAPHY TO RITUAL CRITIQUE

This chapter is substantially rewritten from two earlier essays published as Quantz, R. A. & O'Connor, T. W. (1988). Writing critical ethnography. *Educational Theory, 38*(1), 95–109 and as a postscript in Quantz, R. A. (2003). The puzzlemasters: Performing the mundane, searching for intellect, and living in the belly of the corporation, *The Review of Education, Pedagogy, and Cultural Studies, 25*, 95–137.

1. Other terms used to refer to this same concept are "polyglot," "multivocality," and the one we prefer, "multivoicedness." We will develop the concept of multivoicedness more fully in this chapter.
2. The fixing of these concepts to the terms "performance" and "account" is my own attempt to capture these ideas in two readily understood American English terms.

4 NONRATIONAL CLASSROOM PERFORMANCE

An earlier version of this chapter was published as Quantz, R. A., & Magolda, P. M. (1997). Nonrational classroom performance: Ritual as aspect of action, *The Urban Review, 29*(4), 221–238, with kind permission of Springer Science and Business Media. The authors would also like to thank those who participated in this class, especially the instructor.

1. Pseudonyms are used throughout this manuscript including that of Mrs. Freeman and the Harmon School to protect the identities of faculty members, students, and schools. The description of the morning ceremony at Harmon School was

provided by a member of the staff of that school in a personal communication. It is presented here anonymously to protect confidentiality.

5   ON SEMINARS, RITUAL, AND COWBOYS

A earlier version of this chapter was published as Quantz, R. A. (2001). On seminars, ritual, and cowboys, *Teachers College Record, 103*(5), 896–922. I would also like to thank my colleagues and their students who graciously permitted me to observe their classes.

6   THE PUZZLEMASTERS

A earlier version of this chapter was published as Quantz, R. A. (2003). The puzzlemasters: Performing the mundane, searching for intellect, and living in the belly of the corporation," *The Review of Education/Pedagogy/Cultural Studies, 25*, 115–157. The author would also like to thank the administrators, teachers, staff, and students in all five of the high schools who openly and graciously shared their lives with me.

1. All but the last anecdote in this essay are my reconstructions of actual rooms and events that I observed at one of five high schools during the school year 2000–2001.
2. My failure to observe the puzzlemaster pattern in orchestra and band may be a consequence of the small number of observations I actually made of orchestra classes though I suspect that I might never observe it in orchestra or band given the nature of these classes. My failure to observe the pattern in social studies classes is much more interesting. I'm sure that somewhere, the puzzlemaster interaction pattern manifests itself in social studies classes, but none of the social studies classes that I happen to visit revealed it. The reasons for this and its implications may be the subject of a future essay. Those who may be interested in this finding might wish to read Wegwert (2008).
3. Cremin (1980) writes, "When it came time to design a seal for the new nation, it is said that Franklin wanted it to portray Moses bringing down the waters upon the Pharoah [*sic*], while Jefferson would have preferred a rendering of the children of Israel in the wilderness, with a cloud leading them by day and a pillar of fire by night" (p. 17).
4. Masao Miyoshi (1993) explains the differences between multinational corporations and transnational corporations this way: "The distinction between the two corporate categories is certainly problematic: the terms are frequently used interchangeably. If there are differences, they are more or less in the degrees of alienation from the countries of origin...Thus, a multinational corporation (MNC) is one that is headquartered in a nation, operating in a number of countries. Its high-echelon personnel largely consists of the nationals of the country of origin, and the corporate loyalty is, though increasingly autonomous, finally tied to the home nation. A truly transnational corporation, on the other hand, might no longer be tied to its nation of origin but is adrift and mobile, ready to settle anywhere and exploit any state including its own, as long as the affiliation severs its own interest (p. 736). Similarly Leslie Sklair (2001) writes "*transnational* refers to forces, processes, and institutions that cross borders but do not derive their power and authority from the state" (p. 2; emphasis in the original).

5. Woodrow Wilson received a doctorate from Johns Hopkins in 1885 but had studied law at the University of Virginia five years earlier and had been a practicing attorney before entering Johns Hopkins. After receiving his doctorate he first taught history at Bryn Mawr and then became a professor of jurisprudence and political economics at Princeton (Morris, 1961).

6. The fact that Josiah Bartlet, the fictional Democratic president of the television series *West Wing*, holds a PhD in economics rather than political science suggests just how deep into the American culture the desirability of an economic, rather than political, background for a president has permeated.

7. While people will occasionally refer to a real world problem as a "puzzle," when they do so, they really use the term metaphorically, which suggests that the real life problem is *like* a puzzle in that the answer is evasive.

8. Cooper and Dunne show how such non-stipulated conditions can affect students' success on tests that use questions attempting to construct "real life" problems to solve (Cooper, B. & M. Dunne, 1998).

9. Perhaps there is irony (or perhaps not) in the realization that the most "intellectual" class I found was a class in the "arts" rather than in a more traditionally academic area such as literature or science or history. The arts classes in general surprised me for I not only found instances of the puzzlemaster interaction pattern in arts classes but I also found that the visual art was the one subject area that had built into its pedagogy a space for intellectual activity. Almost all art classes have a period of critique following a project. Art projects are typically displayed and the students publicly critique their own and others' work. In this critique students are expected to draw on the concepts of art to organize their critiques. Some teachers and some students appear to be better able to develop the intellectual potential of this process but nearly all of them try.

REFERENCES

Anderson, V. D. (1991). *New England's generation: The great migration and the formation of society and culture in the seventeenth century.* New York: Cambridge University Press.

Androne, H. A. (2005). Untamed tongues: Reading ritual intersections between fiction by African-American and Chicana women. *Phoebe: An Interdisciplinary Journal of Feminist Scholarship, Theory, and Aesthetics, 17*(1), 35–57.

Anna S. Kuhl Elementary School, Port Jervis, NY. (2010, June 7). Retrieved from http://www.portjerviscsd.k12.ny.us/ASK/PerfectAttend/ask_Perfect Attendance.htm.

Appadurai, A. (2006). *Fear of small numbers: An essay on the geography of anger.* Durham: Duke University.

Aronowitz, S., & Giroux, H. A. (1985). *Education under siege: The conservative, liberal, and radical debate over schooling.* South Hadley, MA: Bergin & Garvey.

Bakhtin, M. M. (1973). *Problems of Dostoevsky's poetics.* Ann Arbor, MI: Ardis.

———. (1984). *Rabelais and his world* (H. Iswolsky, trans.). Bloomington: Indiana University Press.

———. (1993). *Toward a philosophy of the act* (V. Liapunov & M. Holquist, trans.). Austin: University of Texas Press.

Beck, G. (2010, March 23). Retrieved from http://www.foxnews.com/story/0,2933,589832,00.html.

Bennett, W. J. (1988). *Our children and our country: Improving America's schools and affirming the common culture.* New York: Simon and Schuster.

Bergen, P. L. (2001). *Holy war, inc.: Inside the secret world of Osama bin Laden.* New York: Free Press.

Berke, R. L. (2001, March 11). Bush is providing corporate model for white house. *New York Times.* Available: http://www.nytimes.com/.

Bernstein, B. (1977). *Class, codes and control: Volume 3, Towards a theory of educational transmissions* (2nd ed). London: Routledge & Kegan Paul.

Bloom, A. D. (1987). *The closing of the American mind: How higher education has failed democracy and impoverished the souls of today's students.* New York: Simon and Schuster.

Bocock, R. (1974). *Ritual in industrial society: A sociological analysis of ritualism in modern England.* London: George Allen & Unwin.

Bomer, R. J. E. D., Laura May & Peggy Semingson. (2008). Miseducating teachers about the poor: A critical analysis of Ruby Payne's claims about poverty. *Teachers College Record,* http://www.tcrccord.org/content.asp?contentid=14591.

Bourdieu, P. (1974). The school as a conservative force: Scholastic and cultural inequalities. In J. Eggleston (ed.), *Contemporary research in the sociology of education* (pp. 32–46). London: Methuen.

Bourdieu, P. (1984). *Distinction: A social critique of the judgment of taste.* Cambridge, MA: Harvard University Press.

Bourdieu, P., & Passeron, J. C. (1977). *Reproduction in education, society and culture.* London; Beverly Hills: Sage Publications.

Bowles, S., & H. Gintis. (1976). *Schooling in capitalist America: Educational reform and the contradictions of economic life.* New York: Basic Books.

Boyles, D. (1998). *American education and corporations: The free market goes to school.* New York: Garland Pub.

Buber, M. (1955). *I and Thou* (R. G. Smith, trans.). New York: Scribner (original publication 1937).

Burnett, J. H. (1976). Ceremony, rites, and economy in the student system of an American high school. In J. I. Roberts & S. K. Akinsaya (eds.), *Educational patterns and cultural configurations: The anthropology of education* (pp. 313–323). New York: McKay.

Bushnell, M. (1997). Small school ritual and parent involvement. *The Urban Review, 29*(4), 283–295.

Callahan, R. E. (1962). *Education and the cult of efficiency: A study of the social forces that have shaped the administration of the public schools.* Chicago: University of Chicago Press.

Cammarota, J., & Romero, A. (2006). A critically compassionate intellectualism for Latina/o students: Raising voices above the silencing in our schools. *Multicultural Education, 14*(2), 16–23.

Clifford, J. (1983). On ethnographic authority. *Representations, 1*(2), 118–146.

Clifford, J., & Marcus, G. E. (1986). *Writing culture: The poetics and politics of ethnography.* Berkeley: University of California Press.

Collins, R. (1975). *Conflict sociology: Toward an explanatory science.* New York: Academic Press.

———. (1979). *The credential society: An historical sociology of education and stratification.* New York: Academic Press.

———. (2000). *The sociology of philosophies: A global theory of intellectual change.* Cambridge, MA: Belknap Press of Harvard University Press.

Connell, R. (1982). *Making the difference: Schools, families, and social division.* Sydney; Boston: Allen & Unwin.

Cooper, B., & Dunne. M. (1998). Anyone for tennis? Social class differences in children's responses to national curriculum mathematics testing. *The Sociological Review, 46*(1), 115–148.

Cordeiro, P., & Carspecken, P. (1993). How a minority of a minority succeed: A case study of 20 Hispanic achievers. *International Journal of Qualitative Studies in Education, 6*(4), 277–290.

Crapanzano, V. (1985). *Waiting: The whites of South Africa.* New York: Random House.

Cremin, L. A. (1980). *American education, the national experience, 1783–1876.* New York: Harper and Row.

Cusick, P. (1973). *Inside high school: The student's world.* New York: Holt, Rinehart, & Winston.

Derrida, J. (1973). *Speech and phenomena, and other essays on Husserl's theory of signs* (D. B. Allison, trans.). Evanston: Northwestern University Press.

Dostoevsky, F. (1981). *The idiot.* Toronto: Bantam Books.

Du Bois, W. E. B. (1973). *The education of black people: Ten critiques, 1906–1960.* New York: Monthly Review Press.

Durkheim, E. (1964). *The division of labor in society* (G. Simpson, trans.). New York: Free Press of Glencoe.

———. (1965). *The elementary forms of the religious life* (J. W. Swain, trans.). New York: The Free Press.

———. (1973). *Moral education: A study in the theory and application of the sociology of education* (E. K. Wilson & H. Schnurer, trans.). New York: Free Press.

Ensign, J. (1997). Ritualizing sacredness in math: Profaneness in language arts and social studies. *The Urban Review*, 29(4), 253–261.

Firth, R. (1973). *Symbols: Public and private*. Symbol, myth, and ritual series. Ithaca: Cornell University.

Fish, S. E. (2008). *Save the world on your own time*. New York: Oxford University Press.

Foley, D. E. (1990). *Learning capitalist culture: Deep in the heart of Tejas*. Philadelphia: University of Pennsylvania.

Ford, P. L. (Ed.). (1904). *The writings of Thomas Jefferson 1816–1826* (Vol. 10). New York: G. P. Putnam's sons.

Fordham, S. (1996). *Blacked out: Dilemmas of race, identity, and success at Capital High*. Chicago: University of Chicago Press.

Freire, P. (1968). *Pedagogy of the oppressed* (M. B. Ramos, trans.). New York: Seabury.

———. (1973). *Education for critical consciousness*. New York: Seabury Press.

Freire, P., & Macedo, D. P. (1987). *Literacy: Reading the word & the world*. South Hadley, MA: Bergin & Garvey Publishers.

Friedman, M. (1970). *A Friedman doctrine: The social responsibility of business is to increase its profits*. Retrieved May 31, 2010, from http://proquest.umi.com. proxy.lib.muohio.edu/pqdweb?index=0&did=223535702&SrchMode=2&sid=1 &Fmt=10&VInst=PROD&VType=PQD&RQT=309&VName=HNP&TS=127 5318980&clientId=26867.

Geertz, C. (1972). Deep Play: Notes on the Balinese Cockfight. *Daedalus*, 1–37.

Gennep, A. V. (1960). *The rites of passage* (M. B. Vizedom & G. L. Caffee, trans.). Chicago: University of Chicago Press.

Gilmore, D. (1975). Carnival in Fuenmayor: Class conflict and social cohesion in an Andalusian town. *Journal of Anthropological Research*, 31(4), 331–349.

Giroux, H. A. (1983). *Theory and resistance in education: A pedagogy for the opposition*. South Hadley, MA: Bergin & Garvey.

———. (1988). *Teachers as intellectuals: Toward a critical pedagogy of learning*. Granby, MA: Bergin & Garvey.

———. (1996). *Fugitive cultures: Race, violence, and youth*. New York: Routledge.

———. (1997). *Pedagogy and the politics of hope: Theory, culture, and schooling: A critical reader*. Boulder, CO: Westview Press.

———. (1998). *Channel surfing: Racism, the media and the destruction of today's youth*. New York: St. Martin's Griffin.

———. (1999a). *Corporate culture and the attack on higher education and public schooling*. Bloomington, Ind.: Phi Delta Kappa Educational Foundation.

———. (1999b). *The mouse that roared: Disney and the end of innocence*. Lanham, Md.: Rowman & Littlefield.

———. (2000). *Impure acts: The practical politics of cultural studies*. New York: Routledge.

———. (2001). *Stealing innocence: Youth, corporate power, and the politics of culture*. New York: Palgrave.

Giroux, H. A. (2005) *Against the new authoritarianism*: Politics after Abu Ghraib. Arbeiter Ring Publishing.

———. (2006a) *Beyond the spectacle of terrorism: Global uncertainty and the challenge of the new media*. Paradigm Publishers.

———. (2006b) *Stormy weather: Katrina and the politics of disposability*. Paradigm Publishers.

———. (2008) *Against the Terror of neoliberalism: Politics beyond the age of gree*. Paradigm Publishers.

Glassie, H. (1982). *Passing the time in Ballymenone: Culture and history of an Ulster community*. Philadelphia: University of Pennsylvania.

Gluckman, M. (1962). Les Rites de Passage. In M. Gluckman (ed.), *Essays on the ritual of social relations*, (1975 ed., pp. 1–52). Manchester: University Press.

Goffman, E. (1959). *The presentation of self in everyday life*. 1973 ed. Woodstock, NY: Overlook Press.

———. (1967). *Interaction ritual: Essays on face-to-face behavior*. Garden City, NY: Anchor Books.

Goody, J. Religion and ritual: The definitional problem. *British Journal of Sociology* 12 (1961): 142–164.

Gramsci, A. (1971). *Selections from the prison notebooks of Antonio Gramsci* (Q. Hoare & Nowell-Smith, eds. & trans.). New York: International Publishers.

Green, A. (1990). *Education and state formation*. New York: St. Martin's Press.

Greer, C. (1972). *The great school legend: A revisionist interpretation of American public education*. New York: Basic Books.

Grimes, R. L. (1982). *Beginnings in ritual studies*. Lanham: University Press of America.

———. (1990). *Ritual criticism: Case studies in its practice, essays on its theory*. Columbia, SC: University of South Carolina.

Habermas, J. (1971). *Knowledge and human interests* (J. J. Shapiro, trans.). Boston: Beacon Press.

Hall, S., and Jefferson, T. (eds.) (1976). *Resistance through rituals: Youth subcultures in post-war Britain*. London: Hutchinson.

Hansen, D. T. (1989). Getting down to business: The moral significance of classroom beginnings. *Anthropology and Education Quarterly*, 20(4), 259-274.

Hays, K. (1994). *Practicing virtues: Moral traditions at Quaker and military boarding schools*. Berkeley: University of California.

Hebdige, D. (1991/1979). *Subculture: the meaning of style*. London ; New York: Routledge.

———. (1988). *Hiding in the light*. London: Routledge.

Henry, M. E. (1993). *School cultures; Universes of meaning in private schools*. Norwood, NJ: Ablex Pub. Corp.

Hirsch, E. D. (1987). *Cultural literacy: What every American needs to know*. Boston: Houghton-Mifflin.

Hirsch, E. D., Kett, J. F., & Trefil, J. S. (1988). *Cultural literacy: What every American needs to know*. New York: Vintage Books.

Hofstadter, R. (1964). *Anti-intellectualism in American life*. New York: Knopf.

Howley, C. B., Howley, A., & Pendarvis, E. D. (1995). *Out of our minds: Anti-intellectualism and talent development in American schooling*. New York: Teachers College Press.

Kaestle, C. F. (1983). *Pillars of the republic: Common schools and American society, 1780–1860*. American Century Series. New York: Hill and Wang.

Katz, M. B. (1970). *The irony of early school reform: Educational innovation in mid-nineteenth century Massachusetts*. Boston: Beacon Press.

Kertzer, D. I. (1988). *Ritual, politics, and power*. New Haven, CT: Yale University.

Kiesewetter, S. (2001, March 29). Head of Fairfield schools vows to do better. *Cincinnati Enquirer*, pp. B3.

Kinnickell, A. B. (2009). Ponds and streams: Wealth and income in the U.S., 1989 to 2007. Finance and Economics Discussion Series. Washington, D.C.: Federal Reserve Board. Retrieved April 23, 2010, from http://www.federalreserve.gov/pubs/feds/2009/200913/200913pap.pdf.

Kinzer, S. (2006). *Overthrow: America's century of regime change from Hawaii to Iraq*. New York, NY: Times Books.

Knowles, D. (2010, March 12). Texas Yanks Thomas Jefferson from Teaching Standard. Retrieved May 31, 2010, from http://www.aolnews.com/nation/article/texas-removes-thomas-jefferson-from-teaching-standard/19397481.

Kofoed, J. (2008). Appropriate pupilness: Social categories intersecting in school. *Childhood*, 15(3), 415–430.

Laboree, D. (1997). *How to succeed in school without really learning: The credentials race in American education*. New Haven, CT: Yale University Press.

Leonard, T. (2010). Barack Obama orders killing of US cleric Anwar al-Awlaki. Telegraph.co.uk. Retrieved April 7, 2010, from http://www.telegraph.co.uk/news/worldnews/northamerica/usa/barackobama/7564581/Barack-Obama-orders-killing-of-US-cleric-Anwar-al-Awlaki.html.

Lesko, N. (1988). *Symbolizing society: Stories, rites, and structure in a Catholic high school*. New York: Falmer.

Levine, A., and J. S. Cureton (1987). *When hope and fear collide: A portrait of today's college student*. San Francisco: Jossey-Bass.

MacCannell, D., & MacCannell, J. F. (1982). *The time of the sign: A semiotic interpretation of modern culture*. Bloomington: Indiana University.

Magolda, P. M., & Gross, K. E. (2009). *It's all about Jesus!: Faith as an oppositional collegiate subculture*. Sterling, Va.: Stylus.

Maloney, C. (2000). The role of ritual in preschool settings. *Early Childhood Education Journal*, 27(3), 143–150.

Marx, K. (2007). *Economic and philosophic manuscripts of 1844* (M. Milligan, trans. Dover ed.). Mineola, NY: Dover Publications.

Marx, K., & Engels, F. (1984). *Capital: A critique of political economy* (S. Moore & E. Aveling, trans.). New York: International Publishers.

Mauss, M. (1954). *The gift: Forms and functions of exchange in archaic societies*. Glencoe, IL: Free Press.

McCadden, B. M. (1997). Let's get our houses in order: The role of transitional rituals in constructing moral kindergartners. *The Urban Review*, 29(4), 239–252.

McDermott, R. P. (1977). Social relations as contexts for learning in school. *Harvard Educational Review*, 47(2), 198–213.

McDermott, R. P., & Gospodinoff, K. (1979). Social contexts for ethnic borders and school failure. In Wolfgang, A. (ed.), *Nonverbal behavior: Applications and cross-cultural implication* (pp. 175–195).

McLaren, P. (1999). *Schooling as a ritual performance: Toward a political economy of educational symbols and gestures* (3rd ed.). Lanham, MD: Rowman & Littlefield.

McLellan, M. (1991). *Bread and glue: Ritual and celebration in the lives of four American families*. Unpublished doctoral dissertation, University of Minnesota.

Mead, G. H., & Morris, C. W. (1967). *Mind, self, and society: From the standpoint of a social behaviorist.* Chicago, IL: University of Chicago Press.

Middleton, J. (1977). Ritual and ambiguity in Lugbara society. In S. F. Moore & B. Myerhoff (eds.), *Secular ritual* (pp. 73–90). Amsterdam: Van Gorcum.

Miyoshi, M. (1993). A borderless world? From colonialism to transnationalism and the decline of the nation-state. *Critical Inquiry, 19,* 726–751.

Molnar, A. (1996). *Giving kids the business: The commercialization of America's schools.* Boulder, CO: Westview Press.

Moore, S. F., & B. G. Myerhoff (Eds.). (1975). *Symbol and politics in communal ideology: Cases and questions.* Ithaca: Cornell University.

———. (1977). *Secular ritual.* Amsterdam: Van Gorcum.

Morris, R. B. (1961). *Encyclopedia of American history* (Rev. and enl. ed.). New York: Harper.

Morrow, R. A., & Torres, C. A. (1995). *Social theory and education: A critique of theories of social and cultural reproduction.* Albany: State University of New York Press.

Mursell, J. L. (1954). *Successful teaching: Its psychological principles* (2d ed.). New York: McGraw-Hill.

Myerhoff, B. (1978). *Number our days.* New York: E. P. Dutton.

———. (1992). *Remembered lives: The work of ritual, storytelling, and growing older.* Ann Arbor: University of Michigan.

Noblit, G. W., Flores, S. Y., & Murillo, E. G. (2004). *Postcritical ethnography: Reinscribing critique.* Cresskill, NJ: Hampton Press.

Ogbu, J. U. (1974). *The next generation: An ethnography of education in an urban neighborhood.* New York: Academic Press.

———. (1978). *Minority education and caste: The American system in cross-cultural perspective.* New York: Academic Press.

———. (2003). *Black American students in an affluent suburb: A study of academic disengagement.* Mahwah, NJ: L. Erlbaum Associates.

———. (2008). *Minority status, oppositional culture, and schooling.* New York: Routledge.

Ohmae, K. (1995). *The end of the nation state: The rise of regional economies.* London: HarperCollins.

Paraskeva, J. (Ed.). (2010). *Unaccomplished utopia: Neoconservative dismantling of public higher education in the European Union.* Rotterdam: Sense.

Parsons, T. (1951). *The social system.* Glencoe, IL: The Free Press.

Payne, R. K. (2005). *A framework for understanding poverty* (4th ed.). Highlands, TX: aha! Process.

Perkinson, H. J. (1968). *The imperfect panacea: American faith in education, 1865–1965.* New York: Random House.

Quantz, R. (1985). The complex visions of female teachers and the failure of unionization in the 1930s: An oral history. *History of Education Quarterly, 25*(4), 439–458.

Radcliffe-Brown, A. R. (1952). *Structure and function in primitive society.* Glencoe, IL: The Free Press.

Rappaport, R. A. (1978). Adaptation and the structure of ritual. In N. B. Jones & V. Reynolds (eds.), *Human behaviour and adaptation* (Vol. XVIII, pp. 77–102). London: Taylor & Francis.

Ravitch, D. (1996). *National standards in American education: A citizen's guide.* Washington, D.C.: Brookings.

Readings, B. (1996). *The university in ruins.* Cambridge, Mass.: Harvard University Press.

Rebolledo, T. D. (1995). *Women singing in the snow: A cultural analysis of Chicana literature.* Arizona: University of Arizona.

Reinhardt, U. E., Hussey, P. S., & Anderson, Gerard F. (2004). U.S. health care spending in an international context. *Health Affairs, 23*(4), 10–25.

Reynolds, G. (2010, September 15). Phys ed: Can exercise make kids smarter?. *The New York Times.* Retrieved September 16, 2010, from http://well. blogs.nytimes.com/2010/09/15/phys-ed-can-exercise-make-kids-smarter/?src=me&ref=general.

Reynolds, W., & Gabbard, D. (2003). We were soldiers: The rewriting of memory and the corporate order. In K. Saltman & D. Gabbard (eds.), *Education and enforcement: The militarization and corporatization of schools.* New York: Routledge, Farmer, 2003.

Rodrik, D. (1997). *Has globalization gone too far?* Washington, D.C.: Institute of International Economics.

Roscigno, V., & Ainsworth-Darnell, J. (1999). Race, cultural capital, and educational resources: Persistent inequalities and achievement returns. *Sociology of Education, 72*(3), pp. 158–178.

Rousmaniere, K. (1997). *City teachers: Teaching and school reform in historical perspective.* New York: Teachers College Press.

Said, E. (1973). *Orientalism.* New York: Pantheon Books.

Schechner, R., & Appel, W. (1990). *By means of performance: intercultural studies of theatre and ritual.* Cambridge; New York: Cambridge University Press.

Schechner, R. (2006). *Performance studies: an introduction* (2nd ed.). New York: Routledge.

Schlesinger, A. M. (1998). *The disuniting of America: Reflections on a multicultural society* (rev. and enlarged ed.). New York: W.W. Norton.

Scully, P., & Howell, J. (2008). Using rituals and traditions to create classroom community for children, teachers, and parents. *Early Childhood Education Journal, 36,* 61–66.

Siddle Walker, V. (1996). *Their highest potential: An African American school community in the segregated South.* Chapel Hill: University of North Carolina Press.

Sklair, L. (1991). *Sociology of the global system.* Baltimore: Johns Hopkins University Press.

———. (2001). *The transnational capitalist class.* Oxford; Malden, Mass.: Blackwell.

Smith, A. (2003). *The wealth of nations* (Bantam classic ed.). New York, NY: Bantam Classic.

Spradley, J. P., & McCurdy, D. W. (1972). *The cultural experience: Ethnography in complex society.* Chicago: Science Research Associates.

Spring, J. H. (1972). *Education and the rise of the corporate state.* Boston: Beacon Press.

Stigler, J. W., & Hiebert, J. (1999). *The teaching gap: Best ideas from the world's teachers for improving education in the classroom.* New York: Free Press.

Strange, S. (1996). *The retreat of the state: The diffusion of power in the world economy.* New York: Cambridge University Press.

Strike, K. A. (1982). *Educational policy and the just society.* Urbana, IL: University of Illinois Press.

Tocqueville, A. (1863). *Democracy in America* (Henry Reeve, trans.). Cambridge, MA: Sever & Francis.

Trow, M. (1977). The second transformation of American secondary education. In J. Karabel & A. H. Halsey (eds.), *Power and ideology in education* (pp. 105–118). New York: Oxford University.

Turner, V. (1964a). Betwixt and between: The liminal period in *Rites de Passage*. In M. Gluckman (ed.), *Closed systems and open minds: The limits of naëivety in social anthropology* (pp. 93–111). Edinburgh: Oliver & Boyd (original publication 1957).

———. (1964b). Symbols in Ndembu ritual. In Gluckman (ed.), *Closed systems and open minds*, pp. 20–51.

———. (1967) *The forest of symbols: Aspects of Ndembu ritual*. Ithaca, NY: Cornell University.

———. (1974). *Dramas, fields, and metaphors: Symbolic action in human society*. Ithaca, NY: Cornell University Press.

———. (1977) *The ritual process: Structure and anti-structure*. Ithaca, NY: Cornell University.

———. (1988). *The anthropology of performance*. New York: PAJ Publications.

———. (1996). *Schism and continuity in an African society: A study of Ndembu village life*. Washington, D.C.: Berg.

Tyack, D. B. (1974). *The one best system: A history of American urban education*. Cambridge, Mass.: Harvard University Press.

U. S. Census. (2010). Retrieved from http://www.census.gov/compendia/statab/2010/tables/10s0075.pdf.

Varenne, H. (1978). *Americans together: Structured diversity in a Midwestern town*. NY: Teachers College.

Volosinov, V. N. (1976). *Freudianism: A Marxist critique* (I. R. Titunik, trans.). New York: Academic Press.

———. (1986). *Marxism and the philosophy of language* (L. Matejka & I. R. Titunik, trans.). Cambridge, MA: Harvard University Press.

Vygotsky, L. S. (1978). *Mind in society: The development of higher psychological processes*. Cambridge: Harvard University Press.

Warner, W. L. (1941). *The social life of a modern community*. New Haven, CT: Yale University.

———. (1959). *The living and the dead*. New Haven, CT: Yale University.

Weber, M. (1978). *Economy and society: An outline of interpretive sociology* (G. Roth & C. Wittich, trans.). Berkeley: University of California.

Wegwert, J. C. (2008). Democracy without dialogue: A civic curriculum of "the middle class promise" for citizens of the corporation. Unpublished doctoral dissertation, Miami University, Oxford, OH.

Weiler, K. (1998). *Country schoolwomen: Teaching in rural California, 1850–1950*. Stanford, Calif.: Stanford University Press.

Weis, T. (1985). *Between two worlds: Black students in an urban community college*. Boston: Routledge & Kegan Paul.

Willis, P. E. (1977). *Learning to labour: How working class kids get working class jobs*. Farnborough, Eng.: Saxon House.

———. (1981). *Learning to labor: How working class kids get working class jobs*. (Morningside ed.). New York: Columbia University Press.

World Health Organization. (2000). Retrieved from http://www.who.int/whr/2000/media_centre/press_release/en/index.html.

Wright, C. E., & Viens, K. P. (1997). *Entrepreneurs: The Boston business community, 1700–1850*. Boston: Massachusetts Historical Society: Distributed by Northeastern University Press.

INDEX

account *see* signification, performance/account
agency 49, 50
Androne, Helane Adams 175
anti-intellectualism 93, 107–110, 141, 143, 144, 166, 167
Appadurai, Arjun 162
autonomy 6, 150–151, 160, 161, 164, 165

Bakhtin, Mikhail 46, 51–71
Bakhtin Circle 47–71, 117
Bergen, Peter 130
Bernstein, Basil 27, 28, 38, 117, 149
Birmingham Centre for Contemporary Cultural Studies (CCCS) 87
Bocock, Robert 78
Bourdieu, Pierre 150, 157–158, 178
Boyles, Deron 128–129
Burnett, Jacquetta Hill 12
Bushnell, Mary 12

Cammarota, Julio (and Augustine Romero) 166–167
carnival 52–59, 65
  carnivalesque 52–53, 58–59
Carspecken, Phil *see* Cordeiro, Paula
ceremony 2–3, 11–14, 33, 35, 73–75
Clifford, James 46–47
Collins, Randall 27–28, 121–122, 138, 142–143
commonsense 19, 147–152, 154, 165, 166, 168, 170, 171, 177, 178
communitas 29–30, 32, 33
Cordeiro, Paula 155, 160
costume *see* ritual, types of ritual, display
courage 175–177
cultural politics *see* politics, cultural

Cureton, Jeanette *see* Levine, Arthur
Cusick, Philip 88

diversity (as value) 170–171
Durkheim, Emile 6–7, 10, 21, 24–28, 30, 43, 148
  Durkheimians 24–28, 117

Ebben Gross, Kelsey 15–16
econocide 162
embodiment *see* ritual, and body
enfleshment *see* ritual, and body
Ensign, Jacque 15

Firth, Raymond 27
Foley, Douglas 40–41
Fordham, Signithia 123, 152, 160
Freire, Paulo 96–97, 156–158, 163

Geertz, Clifford 67–68
Giroux, Henry 48, 115, 128–129, 144–145, 166, 176
Goffman, Erving 11, 25, 34, 35, 37, 74
Great Panacea 118–119
Great School Legend 121, 155
Greer, Colin 121, 122, 155
Grimes, Ronald 22, 34

Habermas, Jürgen 150, 178
Hansen, David 27
Hebdige, Dick 87, 103, 104
Henry, Mary 13
heteroglossia *see* multivoicedness
Hiebert, James 135–136
history *see* signification, and ideology
Holquist, Michael 69
Howell, Jacqueline 12
Howley, Craig 143

and symbol 2–3, 8, 17, 21, 22, 23,
  25, 26, 27, 31, 33, 36, 37,
  38–39, 41, 42, 93, 94
types of ritual 4–5, 12
  ceremony 2–3, 11–14, 33, 35,
    73–75, 78, 79
  decorum *see* types of ritual,
    interaction
  displays 4, 37, 38, 39, 86, 87, 93,
    102, 109
  of everyday life *see* types of ritual,
    interaction
  of identity 4, 13, 14, 16, 26, 38,
    44, 87, 103–104
  interaction 35, 44, 74, 77, 79
  resistance (opposition) 39, 59, 79,
    104, 109
  rites of passage 29–30, 31, 32, 33
  social drama 31, 32, 33, 44
  of solidarity 4, 12–14, 31, 37, 39–40,
    41, 99–100, 102, 107, 109
  staging 86, 93–94
  style *see* types of ritual, displays
  transitional 88
  see also types of ritual, rites of
    passage
ritual critique 16, 18, 19, 66–71,
  177–178
Rodrik, Dani 125, 129
Romero, Augustine *see* Cammarota,
  Julio
Rousmaniere, Kate 123

sacred/profane 4, 11, 15, 22, 24–26,
  41, 75, 138–139, 148, 149,
  160, 172
Saussure, Ferdinand de 32
Schechner, Richard 34, 36
Scully, Patricia 12
signification (semiotics) 23, 38, 66 71,
  169
  and behavioral ideology 49
  dialogue 48–50, 51, 62, 67, 69, 71
  event/retelling *see* signification,
    performance/account
  and history 49, 67–71
  and ideology 49, 63–64
  langue 35, 67
  multivoicedness 31, 32, 34, 46, 48,
    50–52, 62–64, 71, 79

parole 35, 67
performance/account 68–71
sign 67–71
speech
  inner 51, 62
  inward/outward 49, 50, 63, 64
  reported 68–70
  text 16, 22, 36, 47, 48, 52, 57, 59,
    67–71
  utterance 48, 67–71
  voice 50, 51, 52
Sklair, Leslie 124, 129, 130, 180–181
social justice 174–175
Spring, Joel 128, 131
Stigler, James 135–136
Strange, Susan 124, 130
Strike, Kenneth 150
structure 7, 14, 18, 27, 28, 29, 30, 35,
  52
  anti-structure 30, 35
  poststructuralism 6, 66, 67, 68
  structural-functionalism 27, 30, 32,
    33, 35, 121
  structuralism 22, 32, 33, 43,
    44, 117
subjunctive 35, 44
symbolic *see* ritual, and symbol
text *see* signification, text
transnational corporations
  (TNC) 124–132, 145, 162,
    165, 166, 180–181
transnational capitalism 130–131
transnational capitalist class 129, 130
transnational culture 130
transnational system 129, 130

Turner, Victor 10, 21, 28–44
  Turnerians 28–32

Value-based 167–169
Van Gennep, Arnold 30–31
Varenne, Herve 104, 105
Volosinov, V. N. 47, 48, 49, 63–64, 65,
  67, 68
Vygotsky, L. S. 50–51

Warner, W. Lloyd 28
Weber, Max 7–8, 78
Wegwert, Joseph 13–14, 180
Willis, Paul 48, 123, 151, 155, 160